THE SHAKER SPIRITUAL NARRATIVE

"Shakers at New Lebanon," in *La Illustracion Española y Americana*, December 1, 1873.

THE *Shaker*
Spiritual
Narrative

BY DIANE SASSON

THE UNIVERSITY OF
TENNESSEE PRESS
KNOXVILLE

Library of Congress Cataloging in Publication Data

Sasson, Diane, 1946–
  The Shaker spiritual narrative.
  Bibliography: p.
  Includes index.
  1. Shakers—United States—History—19th century.
  2. Shakers—United States—Biography. 3. Autobiography.
  I. Title.
  BX9766.S27 1983   289'.8   83-3666
  ISBN 0-87049-392-2

TO MY PARENTS
Dorothy and Arnold Hyde

CONTENTS

ILLUSTRATIONS

PREFACE

Personal narratives, shaped and nourished by the experiences of life in the New World, have characterized American literature from its earliest moments. Reports and chronicles of early explorers, descriptions by travelers, journals and diaries of early settlers, and captivity and slave narratives were abundantly produced and found a ready audience. But the most frequently written of all first-person narratives were accounts of spiritual life.

In England, those authors who felt impelled to record the workings of the divine upon their souls were usually members of dissenting religious groups, and the most prolific writers of spiritual autobiography were the Quakers. A similar pattern held true in the New World. In the early years Puritans recorded their life histories seeking signs of their election. Quakers frequently wrote autobiographical narratives detailing the manifestations of the "inner light." And after the formation of the Republic, members of less established religious groups, particularly those who believed in the direct experience of divine revelation, composed large numbers of spiritual narratives. While the earliest spiritual autobiographies written by Puritans and Quakers have been well studied, few scholars have explored religious narratives written in America after the Revolution.

In this study I begin to explore this relatively uncharted corpus of American literature by examining in detail the narratives of a well-defined, nonélite American religious group which produced a sizeable body of nineteenth-century personal narrative. Although usually regarded as a religious folk society, the Shakers left an abundance of written documents, many of which preserve personal experiences. Not only did the Shakers record their religious experiences in writing, but they continued to reinterpret them throughout the nineteenth century. Thus, it is possible to analyze not only the development of Shaker narrative tradition but to delineate the Shaker authors' modifications and innovations in response to the changing concerns of the community of Believers.

Members of the United Society composed many types of first-person narratives, including numerous diaries, journals, and "daybooks" which preserved records of the day-to-day events in the community. This study focuses on two types of Shaker first-person narrative, the testimony and the autobiography, both of which preserve a unified account of a significant portion of the author's life. Shaker authors composed written testimonies as early as the second decade of the nineteenth century. The earliest Shaker autobiography, "A Sketch of the Life and Experience of Issachar Bates," was written in 1833, and the latest example of the genre, the narrative of Elder Abraham Perkins, was published in 1901; but by far the largest number of Shaker autobiographies were composed between 1850 and 1880.

For this inquiry I have examined approximately forty Shaker autobiographies. I have also drawn upon all published Shaker testimonies, as well as numerous unpublished testimonies and accounts of "spiritual gifts." A vast body of similar material is as yet unexplored, and frequently uncatalogued, in Shaker collections.

Only seven Shaker autobiographies were published during the nineteenth century. Two others, the autobiographies of Issachar Bates and Richard Pelham, have appeared in *The Shaker Quarterly*. Additionally, in *Gifts of Power* Jean Humez has recently established a composite autobiography of Mother Rebecca Jackson. The remaining narratives survive in manuscript. Shakers copied and circulated the texts deemed most exemplary by the leadership. For this reason, the autobiographies of prominent Believers such as Issachar Bates and Calvin Green exist in several copies, transcribed by two or more different scribes. The effort to analyze Shaker autobiographies therefore presents numerous textual difficulties. As much as possible, I have used the author's holograph rather than manuscript copies made by other Shakers. Since the manuscripts of Shaker narratives are not readily available to most readers, I have quoted liberally from the texts and have transcribed quotations as they appear without any attempt to regularize or correct spelling and punctuation. Any word that was unclear in the manuscript has been enclosed in brackets. Manuscripts from the Western Reserve Historical Society Shaker Collection are designated by the symbol OClWHi, and their numbers refer to those used by Kermit Pike in *A Guide to Shaker MS in the Library of the Western Reserve Historical Society*. Manuscripts from the Library of Congress Shaker Collection are referred to as MS DLC. Biblical passages are cited according to the King James Version, the scripture that was used by the Shakers themselves.

The study is divided into two parts. The first part explores the sources for the vocabulary and conventions of Shaker first-person narratives and traces the emergence of Shaker autobiography from the specific experiences offered by Shaker culture. Part I emphasizes the similarities among a large number of Shaker narratives and explores the relationships between testimony and autobiography and the problems of the redaction of the narratives by scribes. In Part II five examples of Shaker autobiography composed between 1850 and 1880 are analyzed to illustrate the variety within the corpus of Shaker autobiography. All of these narratives were written after the waning of Mother's Work, when Shakers composed testimonies less frequently. Therefore, my discussion focuses on how the authors selected events out of their past experience to include in the narrative, adapted materials drawn from personal experience to the genre of spiritual autobiography, and utilized the conventions and vocabulary of earlier Shaker first-person narratives. Since Part II examines closely specific autobiographical texts, I have arranged the chapters to illustrate different strategies Shakers used to create images of themselves.

These narratives suggest the variety of ways Shakers portrayed their past and the diverse backgrounds of the men and women who became Believers. The narratives written by women, which make up less than a fourth of the surviving texts, tend to be more lyrical and more introspective than those written by their male counterparts. The two women autobiographers chosen for detailed study, Jane Blanchard and Rebecca Jackson, are both more interested in charting internal spiritual development than recording the events in the external world. The autobiography of Rebecca Jackson is also significant as the only extant narrative by a black Shaker. The autobiographies selected represent both leaders of the community and ordinary Believers. Men and women prominent in the leadership of their societies composed over a third of the surviving narratives. William Leonard, Rebecca Jackson, and Calvin Green are all in this category. Jane Blanchard and John Brown present the perspectives of ordinary Believers.

Not only do the examples in Part II represent the variety of the authors' experiences before becoming Believers, but they also recall the ways of life in different Shaker communities of the nineteenth century. Members of the Lebanon Society, the home of the Shaker Ministry, wrote about half of the surviving autobiographies. Two authors who resided at Lebanon for most of their lives are considered, and one each from New Enfield, New Hampshire; Harvard, Massachusetts; and Watervliet, New York. Unfortunately, few narratives by members of the Western Shaker societies have survived. There are several possible reasons for the scarcity of texts from outside New England: Shaker narrative tradition may have been less vital in the West; the leaders of the Western societies may have offered less encouragement for their members to record their experiences; or literacy may not have been as high in the West as in the East. It is also possible that Western Shakers did compose autobiographical narratives but that these texts have not survived into our day. Consequently, Shaker autobiography as discussed here depends heavily on narratives written by New England Shakers and, in effect, traces an Eastern literary tradition.

My examination of Shaker narrative pays particular attention to how Believers structured their narratives, how they selected events deemed worthy of inclusion, and how they ordered these events into a narrative sequence. Therefore, I have not hesitated to apply the tools of literary criticism to unlock the meanings coded in a narrative's form and structure, or to use the insights of recent scholarship that regards autobiography as a form of imaginative literature. At the same time, however, it has been useful to retain generic categories and to establish lines of demarcation not only between autobiography and its related forms but between specific types and subgenres of autobiographical narrative.

Because the Shakers established unusually close-knit communities which isolated members from the influences of "the world," and because they were exceptionally homogeneous in belief and practice, the relationship between the Shaker authors' religious and cultural identity and the structure of their narratives is especially strong. Having little access to literary productions of "the world," Shaker authors looked within their own culture for narrative precedents. Worship and song, as well as testimony, suggested vocabulary and metaphors from which the Believers fashioned their autobiographies.

By concentrating on the literature of a single nineteenth-century religious community, this work will contribute to the study of American autobiography; it will also, I hope, initiate a more rigorous approach to the study of spiritual narrative. An implicit assumption of this study is the value of closely examining autobiographies written by ordinary men and women rather than confining either literary or cultural analysis to a few well-known personal narratives. This approach will, I hope, help those who wish to subject the vocabulary, conventions, and structure of narratives written by other American religious groups to a more focused and intensive analysis. After such studies are completed, future scholars may undertake comparative and phenomenological studies of American spiritual autobiography. It will then be possible to compare the narratives of contemporaneous religious groups and explore the diversity and continuity of specific strands of spiritual narrative which may exist despite temporal or sectarian barriers. Such studies, I believe, will lead to a reassessment of many current assumptions about spiritual autobiography in America.

25 November 1982
Jerusalem, Israel

ACKNOWLEDGMENTS

Daniel W. Patterson has shared generously his unmatched knowledge of Shaker sources and has often directed me to material which has never been indexed. He has given both his time and his counsel freely. I am grateful for his help, his encouragement, and above all for his friendship. Joy S. Kasson and Charles G. Zug, III, have read earlier versions of this study and have offered me perceptive advice. I am happy to thank them for their interest in my work. Winthrop Hudson was kind enough to comment on individual chapters of the manuscript. Jean M. Humez graciously responded to bibliographical queries.

The United Society of Shakers at Sabbathday Lake, Maine, allowed me access to its rich manuscript library. The members were warm in their welcome and generous with their encouragement. I am also grateful to James B. Casey, Western Reserve Historical Society, Cleveland, Ohio; Denis J. LeSieur, Berkshire Athenaeum, Pittsfield, Massachusetts; James Corsaro, New York State Library at Albany, and the staff of Wilson Library, University of North Carolina, Chapel Hill.

Carol Orr of the University of Tennessee Press welcomed the submission of my study and shepherded it through many steps before its publication in the present form. I think myself fortunate not only for her care and attention, but also for her choice of reviewers. Albert E. Stone and Stephen A. Marini read my MS critically and offered suggestions for improvement. I am grateful to Katherine Holloway for supervising the production of this book. I appreciate the support of Dean George R. Holcomb and the University of North Carolina Office of Research Administration in providing financial aid to purchase copies of Shaker manuscripts.

Mrs. Jacob Kaplan typed the final version of this study. She not only faithfully rendered quotations from manuscripts, idiosyncratic in their spelling and punctuation, but she also saved me from many infractions against the English language. I deeply appreciate all that she did in my behalf.

Finally, I want to thank my husband, Jack. Without his support and understanding, I could never have completed this work.

PART ONE

THE SHAPE OF
THE SHAKER
SPIRITUAL
NARRATIVE

"Shakers Dancing," in Henry Howe, *Historical Collections of Ohio*, vol. 2.
(Cincinnati: C. J. Krehbiel, 1904.)

CHAPTER I

And when we find ourselves in the place just right,
'Twill be in the valley of love and delight.

THE SHAKERS
IN AMERICA

"Simple Gifts"

Ann Lee and a small band of English followers set foot on American soil in August 1774, convinced that God's Providence had led them to the New World in order to establish His Kingdom on earth. Known to her followers as Mother Ann, this charismatic leader was the daughter of a Manchester blacksmith, John Lee. She was born into a working-class family on 29 February 1736. With no opportunity for formal education, the child labored in the cotton mills of Manchester. Many years after her death in 1784, Shakers remembered that Ann Lee had been precociously filled with "religious impressions" and that even before her marriage in 1762 to Abraham Sanderin, a blacksmith, she felt an aversion to sexual relations. The marriage proved calamitous; Ann Lee bore four children in a few years, losing them all in infancy or early childhood. During these years, she endured great mental struggles, feeling "overwhelmed with sorrow." According to later Shakers, Mother Ann recalled suffering so intensely that the "flesh-consumed upon my bones, bloody sweat pressed through the pores of my skin and I became as helpless as an infant."[1]

Four years before her marriage, Ann Lee had joined a group of religious enthusiasts that had separated from the Society of Friends.[2]

---

1. Anna White and Leila S. Taylor, *Shakerism: Its Meaning and Message* (Columbus, Ohio: Press of Fred. J. Heer, 1904; rpt. New York: AMS Press, 1971), 17.

2. Although later Shaker writers attempted to trace these radical Quakers to the French Prophets, there is no evidence of any direct contact. More likely, the early Shakers were influenced by the evangelical revival led by the Wesleys and George Whitefield that swept England in the mid-eighteenth century. Mother Ann herself claimed to have been one of

Led by Jane and James Wardley, these "Shaking Quakers," as they were labeled by their detractors, welcomed charismatic "gifts of the spirit," visions, prophecies, speaking in tongues, and bodily "exercises." The Wardleys, like many sectarian Protestants of their day, believed that pentecostal "gifts" were evidence that the millennium would soon begin and that "the second appearing of Christ was at hand."[3] Ann Lee confessed her sins to the Wardleys, as was customary among the followers, but she continued to experience great spiritual anguish. She confided feeling polluted by her marriage bed, and Jane Wardley advised her to do as she and James did: to live together but not to "touch each other any more than two babes."[4] Ann Lee became increasingly vehement about the need for sexual renunciation, and in 1770 she saw in vision that sexual intercourse was man's original sin. Eventually becoming the leader of a small group which declared the necessity of celibacy, Mother Ann attracted opposition as well as converts.

It is impossible to gauge how much of later Shaker doctrine originated with the teachings of Mother Ann. Only two basic requirements, celibacy and confession, can be attributed to her with some certainty. While the Wardleys and their followers had practiced confession of sins, the conviction that "the lustful gratification of the flesh" is the root of all evil seems distinctive to Mother Ann. It was this revelation which Mother Ann believed God intended her to proclaim in the New World. Early Shakers believed that Mother's gospel could never take hold in the Old World, where "the stolid, conservative minds of the common people did not open readily to the new, strange doctrine." They insisted that God intended for it to flourish in the New World, "a land where speech was free, religion untrammeled and where men, unshackled by the independence of pioneer life, quickened by its emergencies, freed from

---

Whitefield's "hearers." The relationship between the Shakers and the French Camisards seems to be one of spiritual affinity, not historical development.

3. [Benjamin Seth Youngs], *The Testimony of Christ's Second Appearing*, 2nd ed. (Albany, N.Y.: Printed by E. and E. Hosford, 1810), xxiii.

4. [Seth Y. Wells, ed.], *Testimonies of the Life, Character, Revelations and Doctrines of Our Ever Blessed Mother Ann Lee, and the Elders with Her* (Hancock, Mass.: n.p., 1816), 49. In subsequent chapters, unless indicated otherwise, page numbers following the words of Mother Ann and the early Shaker leaders, or excerpts of recollections about them, refer to this work.

precedent and customs, could think and act for themselves."[5] While still in England, Mother and her followers received signs that God willed they should sail for America and establish a new religious order there. Mother told an early Believer, Abigail Babbit, that she saw in vision "that I must come over to New England." When she communicated this vision to her followers, they received so many "gifts in confirmation of our coming (such as prophecies, revelations, visions and dreams)" that they "had a joyful meeting and danced till morning."[6] James Whittaker, then a young man, whom Mother had raised from childhood, reported visions of the Church of Christ established in America and of his own soul uniting with Mother in the New World.[7] John Hocknell, a well-to-do textile manufacturer, arranged passage for the small band of Believers, who set sail from Liverpool in May 1774. On her journey to the promised land, Mother Ann was accompanied by her husband, Abraham; her brother, William Lee; James Whittaker; John Hocknell; Richard Hocknell, son of John; James Shepherd; Mary Partington; and Nancy Lee, Mother Ann's niece.

Providential signs during the journey confirmed to Believers that they were following the will of God. While sailing on a leaky, "condemned" vessel, Mother testified against the wickedness of the seamen and led her followers in song and dance. The captain, outraged by such behavior, threatened to throw them overboard, but at that moment the boat sprang a leak. The captain feared disaster, whereupon Mother Ann comforted him: "Captain be of good cheer; there shall not a hair of our heads perish. We shall all arrive safe at America. I just now saw two bright angels of God standing by the mast, through whom I received this promise." At these words, a large wave swept over the boat and slapped a loose plank back into place, sealing the leak. The captain and his crew were thus among the first to witness the wonders of Divine Providence working through Ann Lee and her followers.[8]

5. White and Taylor, 28.

6. Testimonies (1816), 14.

7. Ibid., 13.

8. [Benjamin Seth Youngs], *The Testimony of Christ's Second Appearing,* 4th ed. (Albany, N.Y.: The United Society Called Shakers, 1856), 621–22. The earliest preserved version of this story appears in the 1816 *Testimonies,* 67–68.

According to Shaker writings, Mother believed God had led her to the New World where He had already prepared a "chosen people" to accept her message.[9] On 6 August 1774 when they arrived, however, the new land must have seemed inhospitable to the small band of Believers. Times were hard, and in order to gain a livelihood the Shakers broke up into smaller units. In New York Mother Ann nursed her husband through a long illness, supporting the two of them by taking in washing. According to Shaker literature, "Abraham at length recovered, so as to be able to walk the streets; and by associating with the wicked, he soon lost all sense of the gospel, and began, in a very ungodly manner, to oppose Mother's faith; and finally refused to do any thing for her, unless she would live in the flesh with him, and bear children. This proposition Mother utterly and positively rejected, which caused a final separation between her and Abraham Stanley."[10] Mother Ann lived in abject poverty until the spring of 1776 when she joined other Believers in Albany. Not only were the physical and economic realities of New England harsh, but the political climate of the mid-1770s also seemed to hinder the fulfillment of Mother's visions. The impending Revolution divided the country, and many colonists looked upon recent British immigrants with suspicion. Yet Mother never succumbed to doubts, firmly maintaining that God would establish His true church through her.

By September 1776 Believers had assembled on land purchased by John Hocknell in Niskeyuna, seven miles from Albany. For more than two years, while the Revolutionary War swept through the country, Mother and her followers cleared the wilderness and toiled to sustain themselves. When a few complained of the hardships and doubted that God would fulfill His promise to them, Mother rebuked them and pointed to "gifts of the spirit" as evidence of God's favor. According to Believers, the "visions, revelations and gifts of God" which had prepared the way for Ann Lee when in England continued to increase in America until the Church became firmly established.[11] During these early years, Mother's gifts

9. *Testimonies* (1816), 64.

10. Ibid., 10–11. Mother Ann's husband is referred to as Abraham Stanley in early Shaker literature.

11. [Youngs], *Testimony*, 2nd., xxviii.

gave strength and encouragement to the small band of English Believers, and once she proclaimed, "God is about to raise up a people here in America, who will serve him and honor the gospel."[12] In the fall of 1779, when a Believer voiced doubt that God would ever "open the gospel" in the American wilderness, Mother led her followers into the forest for a joyful meeting. She announced that, in vision, she had seen "great numbers coming" to receive her revelation and that Believers must begin storing provisions; she said, "We shall have company enough before another year comes about, to consume it all." In visions Mother continued to receive confirmation of God's promise, seeing "great men come and bow down their heads and confess their sins." Thus, she convinced her followers that they must wait for "God's appointed time" when "great numbers of people" would accept her gospel.[13]

Later Shakers believed that the years at Niskeyuna before the "opening of the gospel" paralleled the time Moses and the Israelites spent wandering in the wilderness before reaching the promised land. Just as God had tested the faith of the Israelites, so He tested Mother Ann and the early Believers. Finding them worthy, He prepared the way for the spread of the gospel in the new land.

Thus in the spring of 1780, after a powerful revival swept through the area around Albany, New York, men and women with sharpened religious expectations flocked to Niskeyuna to visit the "Elect Lady." Many of these first visitors, believing that the day of judgment was imminent, eagerly sought signs that they were living in the last days. When they arrived at Niskeyuna and saw Mother and the Elders "shaking, trembling, speaking in unknown tongues, prophesying and singing melodious songs," many were convinced that the Shakers were the true successors to the apostolic church.[14] Providential signs, including the Revolutionary War, indicated to other early converts that a new age was beginning. Issachar Bates, an early convert who fought in the Revolutionary War, records omens of judgment: northern lights flashed until "the whole heavens appeared . . . like a flaming Brusheap," comets streaked through the skies, and "appiritions" appeared. These signs of impending

12. *Testimonies* (1816), 12–13.
13. Ibid., 14–15.
14. Ibid., 16.

revelation culminated in a dramatic natural occurrence on 19 May 1780, when New England turned dark from a solar eclipse. To Mother Ann this Dark Day was God's sign that the time had come to proclaim the gospel in the New World. To the many who, like Bates, had been caught up in the restless search for religion, the coming of the Shakers was a further sign that the millennium was at hand: "And what next! — Right on the back of this — On came the Shakers! and that made it darker yet — for they came forth to fulfill the VII chapt of Ezekiel that was read in the open air—Yea! and I am a witness that they did fulfill it . . . for they testified, that an end was come on them; and proved it, by their life of seperation from the course of this world; and by the wicked persecutions they endured, from this adulterous generation." [15]

In May 1781 Mother Ann and the Elders began a series of missionary journeys, traveling through Massachusetts and Connecticut "opening the gospel" to potential converts. Believers record many tales of the sufferings and persecutions which these early Shakers endured in their efforts to establish the new faith in America. Exhausted from their arduous expedition, the leadership returned in August 1783 to Niskeyuna, later known as Watervliet. The following July Mother's closest companion, her brother William Lee, died. After Father William's death, her own health declined precipitously, and Ann Lee died 8 September 1784 at the age of forty-eight. At the time of her death, more than 1,000 converts to Shakerism were scattered throughout New England. Yet at this stage of development Shakerism was a vaguely defined cluster of beliefs which focused on the need for a New Birth through commitment to sexual purity and for constant renewal through the experience of "gifts of the spirit." The Society had little formal organization and its future appeared uncertain.

On the day of Mother's funeral, James Whittaker delivered an impassioned exhortation to Believers to continue in the faith. The grief-stricken followers of Mother Ann agreed that "the gift of God" rested upon Father James, that "Mother's mantle had fallen upon him, and that God had anointed him to lead and protect the peo-

---

15. Issachar Bates, "A Sketch of the Life and Experience of Issachar Bates," *Shaker Quarterly* 1 (Fall 1961):113–14.

ple. "[16] Believers recognized Whittaker as their "Elder" and the successor to Mother Ann in the leadership of the Society. Father James
appears to have been a highly spiritual man who forcefully expressed his deep convictions against the "lusts of the flesh" and
repeatedly emphasized that Believers must continue to receive spiritual gifts in order to overcome sexual desire. In 1785 Father James
"withdrew" the Shaker testimony from the world and ceased proselytizing efforts. Traveling throughout New England, Whittaker focused his energies on exhorting the loosely associated converts to
continue to be faithful to the principles enunciated by Mother Ann.
Father James's talents, however, did not include organization, and
at his death on 20 July 1787 Shakerism was yet to be structured.

It remained to the organizational genius of Joseph Meacham,
formerly a Baptist preacher and one of the earliest of Mother's
American converts, to consolidate the Society and to draw its members "into order." Believers recalled that Mother had seen in vision
the role which Meacham would assume. Said Mother: "Joseph is
my first Bishop; he will have the keys of the Kingdom; he is my
Apostle in the Ministry, my first Bishop; what he does, I do."[17]
Under Meacham's leadership the distinctive organization of the
Shaker community emerged. He gathered the scattered Believers
and organized them into "families," each of which established a
community on land owned by members. In the early years, Believers had of necessity shared all worldly goods, but during Meacham's
tenure communal ownership of property became a basic tenet of
Shaker belief and practice. Meacham also appointed Lucy Wright
as First Eldress of the community, thus instituting one of the most
innovative characteristics of Shaker organization, a dual governing
order with leadership shared equally by both genders. When Father
Joseph died in 1796, he left behind a Shakerism transformed from
a union of eccentric visionaries and their followers into a millennial community whose organization, Shakers believed, reflected
a divine archetype.

In 1797 Mother Lucy Wright once again "opened" the Shaker
testimony to the world. Shakers began to recruit converts actively

16. *Testimonies* (1816), 355–56.
17. Ibid., 220.

and, as in the "first opening of the gospel," the timing was auspicious. On the American frontier signs of the Second Great Awakening were multiplying. Upon reading reports in Eastern newspapers about the great revivals in Kentucky, Ohio, and Tennessee, Mother Lucy felt a "gift" to send missionaries from the Lebanon Society to spread the gospel of Shakerism in the West. In February 1805 Benjamin Seth Youngs, John Meacham (son of Joseph), and Issachar Bates arrived in Tennessee and proceeded into Kentucky and Ohio, where they found many who were responsive to the Shaker pronouncements that the millennium had begun and that the confession of sin and taking up the cross of sexual abstinence would allow participation in "the resurrection life." By 1826 the Shakers had established nineteen societies, including communities in Kentucky, Ohio, and Indiana, as well as Maine, New Hampshire, Massachusetts, Connecticut, and New York. At its peak Shaker membership totaled around 5,000 souls.

During the formative period of Shakerism, the Shaker gospel paralleled the teachings of the evangelical "New Light" preachers. These religious leaders rejected Calvinistic notions of predestination and election, preached against secularism, believed that the millennium was imminent, and taught that man can directly and individually experience the Holy Spirit. Many of these "New Light" preachers also dwelled on the need for "gathering" the righteous into communities consisting solely of unblemished saints. The Shakers, however, did not merely proclaim such beliefs; they insisted that Mother Ann's followers put these creeds into practice. Thus, Shakers actually gathered their adherents into separate communities. One could not become a Shaker Saint simply by declaring the experience of God's power. Shaker converts had to give up "the life of the flesh," confess their sins, agree to live within a hierarchically organized community, and, upon accepting full covenant, surrender all worldly property to the Society and devote all labor and spiritual "gifts" to the furtherance of a millennial kingdom.

The perfectionism inherent in Shakerism reflected beliefs that were widespread in the late eighteenth and early nineteenth centuries, but the Shakers' contention that perfection was unattainable by individuals outside the order and protection of the holy community set them apart. Thus, although Shakers shared many of the assumptions of their religious and cultural milieu, they nevertheless rejected values cherished by mainstream society. Most obviously, the Shakers rejected sexuality and the biological family as organizing principles of society, but they also, implicitly, shunned individualism and self-reliance. Again and again Shaker converts testified that their attempts to live a righteous life as individuals had failed, and that only within the context of the community did they progress morally and spiritually. Likewise, the Shakers asserted that only through mutual cooperation, through the sacrifice of selfish interests and desires, could men and women create a just and righteous society.

The first step toward spiritual progress was the confession of sins. For the novitiate Shaker, confession to an Elder or Eldress of the Society was an opportunity to evaluate past experiences through a newly acquired spiritual perspective. Confession was oral, but in their personal narratives many Shakers wrote about their first confession, when they "opened" their "whole life" to the Shaker leadership. From such descriptions it is clear that confession was more than a formality; it was a serious and often lengthy process. Some Shakers relate that they continued to unburden themselves in confession for days and even weeks before they lightened their "load of sin." Thus, the period of confession served as an initiation of the new Believer into both Shaker theology and the distinctive vocabulary Believers used to interpret their experiences.

Like the Puritans, who looked to both natural phenomena and external events for signs of God's intentions and judgments, Shakers probed their past for evidence of providential direction. Like the Quakers, who searched their souls for evidence of the "inner light," Shakers detailed the spiritual manifestations they received. Thus in the second decade of the nineteenth century, when Shakers began to compose their autobiographical narratives, they employed a religious vocabulary shaped by confession and reinforced in worship and song. Although it is impossible to trace the development of early Shaker rhetoric with great precision, Believers drew upon the vocabulary of late eighteenth- and early nineteenth-century evangelism when they first began to produce theological statements and personal literature. The Shakers shared with other American sectarians of this period — Freewill Baptists, Universalists, and even radical Quakers—assumptions about the nature of religious experience and a common vocabulary through which they interpreted it.

In his autobiography the "New Light" preacher David Ferris, for example, uses language and metaphors strikingly similar to those found in Shaker narratives. In many ways Ferris's life resembled that of many early converts to Shakerism. He began preaching under the influence of the Methodist itinerant George Whitefield; later he converted to Quakerism and participated in the revival and expansion of Quakerism in New England in the latter 1770s.[18] Ferris not only shared the experience of evangelical preaching, but he also held some of the religious assumptions common to both Quakers and Shakers: the belief that mankind could progress toward perfection and that the "inner light" of spiritual revelation was accessible to all. Many of the recurring phrases in Ferris's *Memoirs* are identical to those that appear in Shaker literature. He writes of "taking up a cross," of "being called out of the world," of receiving the revelation that he should become God's "instrument," and of experiencing "inward manifestations."[19] To be sure, Shaker writers modified the meaning of such phrases to show their different understanding of the nature of sin and the Second Appearing of Christ in Mother Ann. In Shaker usage the more generalized meaning of the Quaker terminology became more specific. For example, to the Quaker writer the "cross" referred to the burden of religious commitment; to the Shaker it meant a life of sexual abstinence and self-denial. To the Quaker "being called out of the world" referred to the attempt to lead a life of purity and simplicity; to the Shaker it signified uniting with a community of Believers. The similarity in vocabulary is important because for both the Quaker and Shaker narrator the perception of experience was to a great extent determined by the words with which it was comprehended. Implicit in the language itself was a way of structuring and ordering experience.[20]

18. Stephen A. Marini, *Radical Sects of Revolutionary New England* (Cambridge, Mass.: Harvard Univ. Press, 1982), 43–44.

19. David Ferris, *Memoirs of the Life of David Ferris, an Approved Minister of the Society of Friends* (Philadelphia: Merrihew & Thompson's Press, 1855).

20. In his influential article "Language," *Encyclopaedia of the Social Sciences* (New York: Macmillan, 1933), vol. 9, 155–169, the linguist Edward Sapir suggests that the language hab-

FIGURE 1: Spiritual drawing by Miranda Barber: "Peace on Earth and Good Will to Mankind." (Courtesy of the Western Reserve Historical Society.) A spiritual drawing by Miranda Barber of Lebanon, New York, depicting the millennium that Shakers believed began with the second appearance of the Christ Spirit in Ann Lee.

The broad outlines of Shaker personal narratives often resemble those of other spiritual autobiographies: the narrators recollect past errors, remember warnings which prevented them from falling into sin, and recall guideposts which, when properly interpreted, allowed them to progress on a path leading to the community of Believers. Like many other nineteenth-century spiritual autobiographers, Shaker writers often describe confrontations with false religions, trials that tested their faith, and their successes in overcoming the devil's temptations. The structure of Shaker autobiographical literature is most similar to that found in Quaker narratives: "For the edification of other Friends and in conformity with the aims of the Society, he [the writer] might hope . . . to isolate the essential phases of Quaker thought and experience from his life—the influence of pious parents, decisive or extraordinary spiritual experiences, adoption of Quaker beliefs, and the evangelizing activities, frequently involving extensive travel, which followed his new conviction."[21] With the exception of the final period of evangelical activity, the stages of the Shaker life history correspond closely to this outline.

The life stories written by Shakers *after* they joined the Society, however, differ in several respects from the religious lives recorded by Quakers and other American spiritual autobiographers. For the Shaker writer the period after uniting with Believers was usually one of adaptation to the demands of the communal religious life. Only a few of the leaders of the Society, men like Issachar Bates, Calvin Green, and Richard Pelham, were able to travel extensively after becoming Believers. Since the order of the community regulated the external events and circumstances of their lives, Shaker writers focused on their inner, spiritual lives when describing their experiences after conversion. The arena of the struggle had changed, as had the goal they struggled toward. No longer did Believers examine natural occurrences or events in the world for providential direction; instead, they searched their memories during confession and sought to purify their lives of "the world, the flesh, and the devil."

---

its of a group largely predetermine the interpretation of experience which consequently affects behavior.

21. Daniel B. Shea, Jr., *Spiritual Autobiography in Early America* (Princeton, N.J.: Princeton Univ. Press, 1968), 5.

After conversion, Believers looked primarily to "gifts of the spirit" including dreams and visions, for evidence of spiritual progress.

While Puritan spiritual autobiographers did record events that they viewed as providential signs, most were reluctant to attribute significance to dreams and visions. This distrust was widespread, since such manifestations might be sent by the devil to tempt men and women and to lead them astray.[22] Even evangelical Protestants such as the Methodists, who believed in individual access to the divine, "felt uneasy in assuming the divine origin of dreams."[23] Still, the Shakers were not unique in according value to dreams and visions. The Quakers also believed that the "inner light" might be manifest through such experiences. Those who, like the Shakers and the Quakers, believed in a continuum between the world of men and the world of the spirit, accepted dreams and visions as one way God might communicate with His chosen people. Members of other radical millenarian groups, such as the Mormons, who sought to reinstitute the apostolic church, viewed spiritual gifts, especially those enumerated by Paul in I Corinthians 12, as evidence that they were the true successors to the primitive church.[24] Such men and women found the words of the prophet Joel, repeated by Peter at the first Pentecost, fulfilled in their own experiences: "And it shall come to pass in the last days, saith God, I will pour out of my Spirit upon all flesh: and your sons and your daughters shall prophesy, and your young men shall see visions, and your old men shall dream dreams" (Acts 2:17). Early Shakers believed that they, like Christ's apostles after his death, were ushering in a new era that had begun with Mother Ann's revelation. Thus they interpreted prophecies, dreams, and visions not merely as evidence of an individual's religious convictions but as confirmation of Shakerism's divine ordination.

22. Evelyn Underhill, *Mysticism: A Study in the Nature and Development of Man's Spiritual Consciousness* (New York: World, 1955), 280–81, notes the warning by St. John of the Cross of the dangers of encouraging those who see "forms and figures of those of another life, saints or angels, good or evil, or certain extraordinary lights and brightness."

23. Donald Edward Byrne, Jr., *No Foot of Land: Folklore of American Methodist Itinerants* (Metuchen, N.J.: Scarecrow Press, 1975), 55.

24. Klaus J. Hansen, *Mormonism and the American Experience* (Chicago: Univ. of Chicago Press, 1981), 21–37, discusses the visions of Joseph Smith and the importance of belief in visionary experience among the Mormons.

The personal vision, the most distinguishing characteristic of Shaker autobiographical literature, is also commonly encountered in the spiritual narratives of Quakers. The following comment on the dreams of Quaker writers applies equally to those of the Shakers:

> Reporting of supra-rational experiences such as dreams and visions was fairly common among Quakers, whose belief in an intuitive access to divine Truth allowed for the possibility that God might choose such a medium for revelation. The Quaker's narration of a dream thus establishes a meeting ground of the personal and impersonal. Dreams came unbidden, and their enigmatic qualities frequently puzzled the writer himself; yet in fairly obvious ways they tended to allegorize his preoccupations. A deeply personal concern might in this way be presented as the least personal of testimonies, an authoritative confirmation of Truth which had no dependence on Self.[25]

Like many Shaker writers, the Quaker journalists often asserted that they did not know whether they were asleep or awake when the dream or "vision of the night" occurred. Quaker writers, like their Shaker counterparts, also experienced significant dreams at times of personal crisis or conflict. And many of the motifs and symbols of the Quaker visions in both their pictorial form and their meaning resemble those encountered in Shaker literature. The dream of Quaker Jacob Ritter, who "tried in vain to climb a high tower by first entering an upper story with a ladder," is similar to the vision of Shaker autobiographer James Wilson, who resisted the temptation to climb over a wall with the aid of an unsteady ladder. Both men understood through their visions that one must begin the climb to perfection from the bottom in humility and mortification before attempting to scale the heights. Other Quaker journalists dream of trying to climb high hills to enter a "spacious house," a common motif of Shaker narrative. One Thomas Shillitoe dreamt, as did the Shaker John Lyon, of traversing a narrow path on the edge of a precipice. And the Quaker Benjamin Seebohm saw women washing linen until it was beautifully white. He understood from this dream that he must also go through "the

25. Shea, 15.

washing of regeneration."[26] Reports of similar dreams appear in the autobiographies of Calvin Green and Rebecca Jackson, both Shakers.

In spite of these similarities, Shakers were not directly familiar with Quaker literary tradition. Both Quakers and Shakers, however, did draw upon a common stock of religious language and a common understanding of religious experience. Writers from both groups were convinced that the divine might be presented to the human mind through symbolic forms.

In American literature one of the best-known religious narratives is the journal of the Quaker John Woolman. The intensity of Woolman's feelings, his opposition to slavery, and his belief that it degrades both the enslaved and the enslaver are most clearly and memorably revealed in his dreams.[27] Woolman, like many Shakers, expresses the depth of his convictions most convincingly through the symbolic vision. Likewise in Shaker narratives the highest artistic moments often occur when the writer records, and perhaps interprets, visionary experiences. Shaker writers recorded significant dreams that reveal the individual imagination shaping waking experience into symbolic forms. Dreams and visions were part of a long and complex religious and literary tradition. Shakers valued them as avenues of communication with the spiritual world, and they had been exposed to the dream interpretations of other Shakers, especially during the Era of Spiritual Manifestations (1837–1850) when visionaries frequently reported their experiences to the community.

Shaker theology, especially its emphasis on the reception of spiritual gifts, seems to have had a greater impact on the development of the Shaker narrative than did literary traditions of spiritual autobiography. Although the writings of John Bunyan reached the height

26. Howard Brinton, "Dreams of the Quaker Journalists," in *By-ways in Quaker History,* ed. Howard Brinton (Wallingford, Pa.: Pendle Hill, 1944), 214–16. Surprisingly, in their personal narratives few Shakers even show familiarity with the life and writings of George Fox, the seventeenth-century English preacher who founded the Society of Friends.

27. Shea, 69, writes of Woolman: "Perhaps it is meaningless to praise a man very highly for his dreams. . . . Still it is obvious that the material from which dreams are fashioned is waking experience, and that the recording of a dream involves certain acts no different in their nature from those of the poet or novelist giving shape to his experience, real or imagined."

of their popularity in America in the mid-nineteenth century, few Shakers were familiar with them.[28] Even in the rare case where a Shaker author alludes to Bunyan, the influence of Bunyan is much less significant than Shakerism itself. After joining other Believers, the Shaker had little opportunity to read the spiritual narratives of non-Shaker writers. Of far greater importance to the development of Shaker autobiography was the desire to illustrate Shaker theological concepts, to shape narratives in imitation of testimonies, and to use imagery and symbols familiar to Shaker culture.

The symbols and metaphors which inform Shaker narrative developed over the early decades of the nineteenth century. Metaphors of nourishment and travel, images of jewels and precious metals, the depiction of the stripping away of dirty attire and assuming the garments of righteousness, the portrayal of the New Zion as a clean, spacious house or a fruitful garden—all are ultimately biblical in origin and are occasionally found in the religious language of other Christians.[29] These metaphors and images, however, gained particular prominence among the Shakers, who modified meaning and intent to accord with Shaker belief. The symbols were also common in other forms of Shaker imaginative expression, and communal experience provided accepted interpretations. When the Shakers worshipped, their songs were filled with these same images; when they listened to testimonies and stories of personal experience, they recognized their symbolic import. During the 1840s members of each Society made a pilgrimage twice yearly to a sacred spot within each community, usually located on a hill or mountain top. There Believers participated in an elaborate spiritual pageant in which mediums delivered messages and gifts from the spirit world, many of which incorporated these familiar symbols. Shakers viewed the travel to the mount as an emblem of the difficulties and rewards of spiritual travel; the symbolic feast

28. David E. Smith, *John Bunyan in America* (Bloomington: Indiana Univ. Press, 1966).

29. The Shaker religious imagination was grounded in the scriptural tradition. Many passages in Shaker literature and even song that at first appear to be incoherent often prove to be paraphrases of biblical texts. For example, Daniel W. Patterson, *The Shaker Spiritual* (Princeton, N.J.: Princeton Univ. Press, 1979), 60–61, refers to an early song attributed to Father William Lee as "inchoate." The text, however, "O will I love, O my love? Come my love, my dove, O pretty love, my joy," alludes to the *Song of Songs* and points up the belief of early Shakers that they were the lovers of Christ.

18

on the mountain top represented not the taking of the body and blood of Christ but a Shaker eucharist consisting of food from the tree of life, water from the living fountain, and spiritually intoxicating wine. At such times, as well as on many other occasions during this period, Believers received many symbolic gifts, including verbal messages, drawings, jewels, choice fruit and food, and golden balls. Such experiences, shared by the community, were a rich source of religious vocabulary which Shaker authors might then employ to portray their own personal experiences.

Not only did Shaker authors draw upon the images and metaphors current in their cultural milieu, but they also turned to incidents from the lives of Mother Ann and the early Believers as a source for the paradigmatic patterns established by the founders of Shakerism. Just as Mother Ann and her band of followers crossed the Atlantic to found the United Society in America, many of those who later joined portray their movement to Believers as a journey, a pilgrimage through the wilderness. Father James's vision of the tree of life as an image of the growth and development of the Society greatly influenced subsequent interpretations of both the history of the community and the history of the individual life. Shaker authors also drew upon incidents in the life of Christ or other major biblical figures, particularly Paul, in depicting events in their personal past. In this way, Shaker autobiographers firmly placed their lives within a providential plan, one that had begun with God's first revelation to mankind but could attain full realization only during their own lifetimes.

Shaker authors did not arbitrarily select incidents, symbols, and metaphors common in Shaker culture and superimpose them upon the raw materials of their lives. Like other autobiographers, religious or secular, Shaker writers were limited by the details of their lives, by the temporal and geographical boundaries of their past. Therefore, they selected from the repertory of Shaker religious symbols those that helped them to best present their past within a religious perspective. The interpretation of incidents and experiences these symbols and metaphors made possible was based on the perspective of the Believer at the time the narrative was composed, not at the time the experiences actually occurred. Shaker images were thus a crucial device in shaping the autobiographical narrative, helping to unify past and present experience, aiding authors in presenting a coherent perspective when viewing their entire lives. Through the use of symbol and metaphor, skillful Shaker authors were able to write a history of their personal past and at the same time relate the history of their spiritual development.

CHAPTER II

Now there are diversities of gifts, but the same Spirit.

I CORINTHIANS 12:4

METAPHORS
OF THE
SPIRIT

The first Believers who migrated to America, as well as their early converts, accorded great importance to the reception of pentecostal gifts. Those who had known Mother Ann and the first Elders treasured memories of the founders of Shakerism, and they passed down, at first orally, then in writing, stories about the extraordinary spiritual bounties which the first Believers possessed. The metaphors that later Shaker authors employ when describing their own religious experiences frequently originate in the sayings and visions of the early Shakers, particularly in recollections about Mother Ann Lee and Father James Whittaker.

Mother, herself illiterate, left no written accounts of her experiences. The first edition of the *Testimonies* (1816) preserves some of the earliest stories about her life. Believers recalled that Mother Ann received many visions: visions that revealed the way to a sinless life; visions that portrayed a mystical union with Christ; visions that permitted communication with the dead; and visions that predicted future events. The distinctive tenet of Shaker doctrine, the need for sexual purity, was first revealed to Mother Ann in a vision wherein "she received a full revelation of the root and foundation of human depravity; and of the very transgression of the first man and woman, in the garden of Eden. Then she clearly saw whence, and wherein all mankind were lost and separated from God, and the only possible way of recovery" (6). In Mother's interpretation of the Genesis story, Adam and Eve succumbed to sexual temptation, and their fall brought suffering and death. The only possible way to salvation, the only way to overcome the separation from God which occurred in Eden, was to renounce sexual relations and to lead pure "virgin" lives. Thus Mother Ann preached that through chastity men and women might establish a New Creation.[1]

In her visions Mother also employed metaphors of love and marriage, similar to those used by other religious mystics, to describe states of union with Christ.[2] Believers remembered Mother saying, "When I first gained the victory over a carnal nature, I was brought into great clearness of sight. I saw the Lord Jesus, and met with him as a lover, and walked with him, side by side" (208). Mother describes Jesus not only as her lover but also as her husband. In a striking passage, she describes her experience both in paraphrases of Psalm 23 and in terms of a spiritual marriage: "The Lord, who brought me over the great waters, has redeemed my soul. I hear the angels sing! — I see the glory of God, as bright as the sun! — I see multitudes of the dead, that were slain in battle arise and come into the first resurrection! — I see Christ put crowns on their heads, of bright, glorious, and changeable colours! — I converse with Christ! — I feel him present with me, as sensible as I feel my hands together! — My soul is married to him! — He is my Husband! — It is not I that speak; it is Christ who dwells in me" (206–7).

Later editions of the *Testimonies* were careful to eliminate references "which could foster any misunderstanding of Shaker belief or character, particularly when it could be misrepresented that they believed Mother Ann had a 'love affair' with Jesus."[3] Metaphors of marriage to Christ occur most frequently in very early Shaker literature. Father James said, "The marriage of the flesh is a covenant with death, and an agreement with hell. If you want to marry, you may marry the Lord Jesus Christ."[4] And Mother Lucy Wright often enjoined Believers to put on the clean, white bridal garment.

---

1. Marini, 12–13, 46, shows how rhetoric about the New Birth and the need to separate the saints from the world and gather them together were common features of radical evangelism at the end of the 18th century.

2. Underhill, 70–94.

3. Thomas Swain, "The Evolving Expressions of the Religious and Theological Experiences of a Community . . . ," *Shaker Quarterly* 12 (Spring 1972):3–31; (Summer 1972):61.

4. Edward Deming Andrews, *The People Called Shakers* (New York: Dover, 1963), 48.

When later Believers use such metaphors, however, they most often extend them to suggest the procreation of offspring, as well as a holy marriage. From the early days members of the Society addressed their leaders as "Mother" and "Father," and Mother Ann often referred to her followers as her children. Thus an early Shaker could write that "the seed of the Gospel sown by the Bride . . . took deepest root in the living earth — in man; sons and daughters of God have sprung up; by their united labor have built up the beginning of the Holy City, wherein no man's labor shall be able to stand."[5]

Belief in the duality of the godhead, in a Father and a Mother in the deity, fostered Shaker understanding of Christ and Mother Ann as spiritual rather than biological progenitors. When Joseph Meacham, whom Mother called her "first born son in America," assembled converts at Lebanon, New York, in 1787, he organized the most spiritually advanced into a "Church Family." The Shakers at Lebanon subsequently established six other "families." As the Shakers expanded and organized other societies, they followed the kinship pattern instituted at Lebanon. "Meacham's genius was to transfer the basic social categories and metaphors of the biological family that Believers had abandoned to the Shaker community itself. As members made the transition from carnal sexuality to spiritual celibacy they gave up the biological family for the holy family of 'spiritual relation.'"[6]

The "parents" of each family were the two elders and eldresses who headed it. Other members considered themselves brothers and sisters and addressed each other as such. While all Shakers were equal siblings, offspring of the same Heavenly Parents, they were also children in relation to the leaders of the Society. The analogy of Shaker life to an extended biological family helped converts understand the role they must assume within the hierarchically organized community. In the years following Meacham's death, Shaker writers frequently testify that all Believers must become like innocent little children willing to obey the Society's leaders who are anointed by the power of God to be parents and shepherds in Is-

5. White and Taylor, 81.
6. Marini, 129.

rael. The metaphor of the family reflects both theology and the actual organization of the Society of Believers. It is no wonder, then, that Shaker writers, past and present, love to contrast life in "the world," in the natural family, to life in the community of Believers, the spiritual family.

Occasionally, this twofold metaphor of mystical marriage to Christ and procreating spiritual children appears in a single narrative. Annie S. Colley, of Canterbury, New Hampshire, reported the following vision:

> As I sat in a dark corner, feeling as I have described, lost from God, a bright vision appeared before me, — two persons came into the room, bringing a cradle, in which lay a beautiful babe. They placed it before me, and I saw its sweet face, all smiling and beautiful. This was soon taken away and while I was wondering what this could mean, there stood before me a person, with majestic air, with manly form and height. As he advanced toward me, the room became as light as day. A crown of glory was upon his head, he came to me with outstretched hands, and all my sorrow fled away. This was the first time in my life I had ever known the love of God. Every band was sundered, my pride was gone and my soul was released.[7]

At the time of this vision Colley was twenty years old. A year after her conversion, in which she loosened her ties to the natural world and spiritually united with God, Colley joined the Shakers at Canterbury. There she found her vision confirmed, for Colley was eventually placed in charge of the children. In the context of her later experience, Colley understands that her vision foretold her destiny. Rather than achieving sexual union with an earthly man, she would live in a "spiritual relation" with Christ, one in which she could experience the releasing power of God's love. Instead of bearing children of her own, she would become the nurturing mother of Shaker spiritual children. Colley, like most Shaker writers, portrays the spiritual family not merely as a substitute for the biological family but as the divine archetype that all should seek to emulate. Because of their belief in a divine Mother and Father, Shaker writers freely combine metaphors of spiritual marriage with those

---

7. Eldress Harriett Coolbroth, Alfred, Me., "Sketch of the Life of Annie S. Colley," Canterbury, N.H., 1845, MS, Sabbathday Lake, Me.

of the family, finding both metaphors, consistent with their theological perspective.

Mother taught Believers that Pentecostal experiences were evidence of living in the New Creation. In the 1816 *Testimonies* she reports having seen angels, once telling those with her, "The room
over your heads, is full of the angels of God. I see them and you
could see them too, if you were redeemed from the nature of the
flesh" (230). Mother Ann believed that God granted mystical visions of heavenly beings, lights, and bright colors to those who
live a pure life, undefiled by the flesh; and she once told Zeruah
Clark, "When you see little bright lights, like stars, be thankful to
God: for they are specks of angels' wings." Zeruah then understood
that such lights are the "notice of God" given to "those that feared
the Lord" (331).

Believers remembered Mother reporting visions in which she
communicated with the spirits of the dead. She once told Samuel
Fitch, "I saw by revelation, the loss of all mankind, not only the
present generation, but the generations of past ages; and I saw
them as it were, clothed with blackness and darkness many of whom
I knew. I saw my own natural mother in the same condition, and
when I saw her, I cried to God; for I had thought that my mother
was a good woman, if there were any good upon earth." Mother
also said, "I have seen souls in the world of spirits, who had wan-
dered in regions of darkness, in such agony and distress, that, in
appearance, they had mourned and wept, till they had worn gut-
ters in their cheeks, with their tears; and when the gospel was offered to them, they were so hungry for it, that they would come,
with their mouths wide open, to receive it. I have seen vast numbers of the dead rise, and come to judgment, and receive the gospel, and begin their travel in the regeneration" (42–43).

Mother sees the damned "clothed with blackness and darkness,"
and she discovers that even her own mother, a good woman but
one who never gave up the sexual life, resides in hell. In Mother's
visions, as in most Christian literature, "blackness and darkness"
represent sinfulness, while white suggests salvation. In Shaker usage,
however, such common symbolism attains more specific meaning:
those in black have lived carnal lives, while those in white have renounced sexual relations and have consequently been saved. In this

vision, Mother also employs the metaphors of nourishment and travel, which are characteristic of later Shaker literature. The gospel of sexual abstinence is food for the hungry, and even those already in the spirit world who accept Mother's message may begin their travel, or spiritual progress, toward a pure and sinless state.

Mother Ann also seems to have understood that visions of departed spirits were an effective method of convincing unbelievers. In several instances, she informs inquirers or recent converts that she has seen their "departed kindred" in vision. When Lot Pease told Mother about his family, he forgot to mention an elder brother, Samuel, who had died at sea when twenty-two years of age. "The next morning Mother came to him and said, 'You did not tell me right about your brothers. I saw your brother Samuel come to judgment last night'" (41). When Israel Chauncy visits Mother at Watervliet, she tells him. "Last night, when we were in worship of God, I saw a number of souls rise from the dead, and come into the resurrection of life. And when you [Israel] was here before, I saw your Mother; and when you was released . . . she was released also, and came into the resurrection. And now you must confess all the sins that you have committed, one by one." Later Mother tells him, "Israel, you have begun to bear for other souls, and you must never give out till the last soul is gathered in" (31).

Mother and the early Shakers clearly believed that the testimony and suffering of faithful Believers might redeem departed spirits and save them from damnation. Anxiety about the eternal state of one's parents might have been particularly acute among the Shakers, since biological parents, by the very act of begetting the future Shaker, might have condemned themselves to eternal torment. Mother's description of the fate of those who lived in "the flesh" is particularly vivid: "They are bound in prisons of hell, and their torment appears like melted lead, poured through them in the same parts where they have taken their carnal pleasure" (304). A belief in "bearing for the dead, or suffering for their sins," may have relieved Shakers' concerns about the eternal fate of their kindred.[8] Shaker narratives reveal a continuing preoccupation with

8. Daniel W. Patterson, "'Bearing for the Dead': A Shaker Belief and Its Impress on the Shaker Spiritual," *Shaker Quarterly* 8 (Winter 1968):122.

the fate of parents, particularly the mother. Believers frequently report that they, like Mother Ann, have seen their deceased parents in vision. The parents typically appear dressed in Shaker garb, an indication that they have renounced "the flesh" and are living as Shakers in the spirit world.

Mother Ann's visions predicting future events, especially the establishment of the Church in America, are especially influential on later Shaker literature. In such visions she most often reports seeing a concrete person, group of people, building, or place. Mother told her early followers that "while I was in England, I knew, by the revelation of God, that God had a chosen people in America; and I saw some of them in vision, while I was in England; and when I saw them in America, I knew them" (64). After coming to the New World, Mother reports that years earlier she had seen certain of her American followers in vision, and that she had similarly seen the Square House at Harvard several times: "Mother also testifyed . . . that she saw in vision . . . the people who afterwards embraced the gospel there; and that when she came in sight of the place, she knew it, and also the people that came to see her" (224).

Just as Mother recognized some of the first Believers as having appeared to her in vision, the converts themselves often report that, upon seeing Mother Ann for the first time, they immediately recognized her as the very same woman seen in a vision. When Elizabeth Chauncy dreamed of her husband, Israel, who had gone to visit Believers at Watervliet, she saw "Mother and the Elders and Israel with them, in the worship of God, and under great operations of the power of God. Israel appeared to be in great distress of soul and body, and his flesh was turned purple colour." After Israel confesses to a certain woman and asks her forgiveness, his flesh returns to normal. A few days later, when Elizabeth visited Watervliet, she recognized Mother as "the same woman she had seen in vision" (30). Believers remembered that Ebenezer Cooley saw a vision of "a woman whose appearance was very glorious, and her face shone as bright as the sun. In the beginning of the year 1781, he visited the Church at Watervliet; and when he saw Mother, he knew her to be the same woman whom he had seen in vision. She spoke to him and said, 'I have seen you before in vision. You must go forth and preach the gospel'" (26).

The memory of Mother Ann's spiritual gifts encouraged later Believers to value and record their own dreams, visions, and other unusual spiritual experiences. Although some of Mother's imagery does reappear in later narratives—the picture of those hungry for the gospel with "mouths wide open," for example—most incidents portrayed in her visions seem to have had little influence on the structure of Shaker narrative. Later Shakers do not experience, or at least, after the establishment of the order and structure of the Church, they rarely record, seminal revelations that might change the basic beliefs or organization of the Society. Only a few Believers record mystical union with Christ, envisioned in sexual terms, since the community deemed such experiences inappropriate to those chaste in mind and body. And although Shakers attributed visions of the sufferings of departed spirits to Father William and Elder John Hocknell,[9] few nineteenth-century autobiographers report appearances of lost souls.[10] Those visions of Mother Ann's, however, that present an image of a desired goal, whether a place or union with a particular person, and that imply the necessity for travel, did influence the development of the Shaker narrative. Throughout the nineteenth century Shaker writers report dreams in which they see a special person or a place. Often years pass before they actually meet the images of their dreams. Most often they recognize a Shaker brother or sister, or they see a Shaker building remembered from their dreams. These visions that foretell future events in the life of the dreamer are also important because they imply the need for narrative movement: the dreamer must travel great distances, overcome hardships, fight temptations, and resolve conflicts before the dream can be fulfilled.

While the stories about Mother Ann's visions justified the recording of spiritual experiences by Believers, the visions and say-

9. Believers remembered Elder John saying, "I saw the souls of three men, whom I knew while I was in England. They came to hear the word of God; but they had not finished their sufferings, and therefore were sent back to hell again" (228). Father William told a Believer, "I know the condition of souls that have left the body; and where I see one soul in the body, I see a thousand in the world of spirits" (230).

10. In the Era of Manifestations (c 1837–50) Shakers frequently see personages from the spirit land, often departed Shakers, who instruct them or admonish them about the failings of the community. Such visions, however, seem quite different in tone and intent from those of the first Elders which portray the torment of lost souls in hell.

ings of Father James Whittaker proved to be an even greater influence on the language and structure of Shaker literature. During the three years following Mother's death on 8 September 1784, Father James led the Society. Reminiscences about Father James invariably comment on his gift for memorable language. Shakers commonly remarked, "I love to hear that James Whittaker speak", and many of his sayings became proverbs, "words of wisdom and truth to the household of faith." [11] Father James's words to Believers were often sharp and stinging, as he exhorted them to lead strictly ascetic lives, to separate themselves from the world, and to enforce rigorous discipline. [12] How could the brothers and sisters at Hancock forget Father James's letter in which he accused the men of being "idle and slothful" and the women of being "idle hatchers of cockatrices eggs & breeders of lust & abominable filthiness as well as covenant breakers." [13] Years after his death, Believers still recalled the vivid sayings of James Whittaker. Fearful that recent converts to the gospel might be scattered and "fall back" to the world, Father James traveled throughout New England, even into Maine, preaching and encouraging Believers to be faithful to Mother's message. Many of the metaphors and images which fired the Shaker religious imagination throughout the nineteenth century owe their popularity to the memory of James Whittaker.

Father James derived the metaphors of his preaching and exhortation from the Bible, but he endowed them with specific Shaker meaning. He often describes these images as having appeared to him in vision. In perhaps the most commonly remembered of all the early Shaker visions, Father James sees the future establishment of the Church in America represented by the tree of life. "I saw a vision of America, and I saw a large tree, and every leaf thereof shone with such brightness as made it appear like a burning torch, representing the Church of Christ, which will yet be es-

---

11. White and Taylor, 70, 68.

12. Marini, 111–14, discusses these qualities and concludes that "Whittaker's fierce asceticism, personally abusive manner, organizational efforts at New Lebanon, and decision to end public evangelism were guided by an authentic charisma, but his inexperience and youth obviously hampered his leadership efforts."

13. Father James Whittaker, Letter to brothers in Hancock, Mass., 25 Feb. 1782, MS, OClWHi, VII:B–66C.

tablished in this land" (66). While the visions of Mother Ann are often abstract, those of Father James usually depict the spiritual world in concrete images which suggested a wide range of meaning. While Mother's visions tend to express mystical feelings of union with the divine, Father James's visions move toward the symbolic representation of religious experience. In Father James's vision, the tree of life is not an image of a natural tree which the dreamer, upon awakening, might discover growing in a new Garden of Eden. [14] Instead, the tree is understood to represent spiritual rather than physical realities. Believers were particularly fond of this image, which portrayed the growth of Shakerism as an organic process. They remembered Father James saying, "When you see the branches flourish, and bring forth fruit, then remember that the root is holy"(373). All Shakers, like the shining leaves or the fruit of the tree, were part of one living, growing organism rooted in Christ and Mother Ann. Metaphorically, the tree expressed the Shaker communal self-image.

The vision of the tree of life reveals how Shaker dreams and visions become the vehicle for symbolic expression of the spiritual state, of either the community as a whole or the individual dreamer. Accounts of visions, more often than accounts of ordinary experiences, feature the central metaphors of Shaker literature. Symbolic narratives were particularly appropriate for writers who made a radical distinction between the world of the flesh and the world of the spirit, for the Shaker expressed the relation between these two realms of experience through symbol and metaphor.

Visions, which permit communication between man and the divine spirit, also frequently provide the metaphors which link physical and spiritual worlds. Early Believers remembered Father James relating how "when crossing the sea, from England to America, he saw Mother and himself in vision; he was standing by the side of Mother, with his arm bound fast to hers, with a golden chain, which seemed to surround both their arms. This he viewed as a

14. The image of the Shaker community as a garden of Eden is also common in the spiritual. See "The Spiritual Relation," 159–60, and "The Wilderness Restored," 228–29, in Patterson, *Shaker Spiritual*. In their spirituals Shakers also represented themselves as trees, especially as the "bending willow." Another version of the tree of life image popular in Shaker songs, drawings, and narratives is the "living vine."

sign, to him, that he should never be separated from Mother"
(354–55). The image of the golden chain appears repeatedly in both
Shaker song and narrative. Although the chain image has been
interpreted as suggesting both sexual repression (a chastity belt)
and sadistic tendencies, the Shakers themselves offer a much richer
and more meaningful understanding of such images.[15] Mother Lucy
said that "Believers are held together in union, by a golden chain.
This chain is composed of the gifts and orders of God and every
order is a link in the chain."[16] Shaker spirituals portray the chain
as "a cord to unite us in bands of pure love."[17] While the chain
represents the love and union which bind the Shaker community
and which replace the "ties of natural affection," it is also one of
a number of images that present the boundaries within which the
Believer could enjoy a pure and sinless life.

Once again, Father James provided a metaphor for the Believers' need for protection from the dangers of "the world." After Mother's death, Father James envisioned the small band of Believers as
a "flock" which a wolf threatened to devour. In order to secure protection for the flock, it was necessary that Believers gather into
communities that excluded evil and temptation. Such communities, binding members together with chains of love and union, protected Believers from the outside world and from their own sinfulness. The search for such protection became one of the basic
themes of later Shaker narratives.

On the occasion of the first assembly of Believers in the new
meeting house at Lebanon on 29 January 1786, Father James offered the following benediction: "Blessed are all those that come
to the tree of Life, and have a right therein. Blessed are all those
that hate the garment spotted by the flesh. Blessed are all those
that are not defiled by women. Blessed are all those young virgins
that never were defiled by men" (376). This benediction, patterned
after the Sermon on the Mount, juxtaposes paraphrases from the

---

15. Louis J. Kern, *An Ordered Love: Sex Roles and Sexuality in Victorian Utopias—The Shakers, Mormons, and the Oneida Community* (Chapel Hill: Univ. of North Carolina Press, 1981), 108–12. Writes Kern, "Such close fettering is only a step away from a more overt sadomasochistic expression of feeling," 109.

16. "Sayings of Mother Lucy Wright," MS, OClWHi, VIII:B-114.

17. Patterson, *Shaker Spiritual,* 227.

book of Revelation and expresses metaphorically the core of Shaker theology.[18] In the Shaker interpretation, those who have a right to the tree of life and may enter the Holy City are the virgins, who wear pure white garments unspotted by the "flesh." Thus, the central images for the Shaker personal narrative originate in biblical passages, elaborated and reinterpreted by Believers in oral testimonies, songs, and religious writings.

While many of Father James's visions and sayings present metaphors through which later writers interpret their lives, another of his visions also preserves the first example of explicit narrative movement. Father James said, "I saw all the Believers travel, and then come to a stop, as up against a wall; and then they were brought into order; after which, I saw the old men and women travelling and bearing their own burdens" (396). As in most of the visions attributed to the founders of Shakerism, this vision does not refer to a significant event in Father James's own life but, rather, foretells the future of the Church. This vision, brief as it is, suggests the need for both physical and spiritual travel. Not only must Believers move to those places where the communities will be gathered and the ideals of the Society implemented, but at the same time individual members of the Society must continue their own "travel" in the spirit. Movement in time and space and from one condition to another is implicit in this abbreviated narrative. This vision, perhaps more than any of the others recorded in the 1816 *Testimonies,* suggests a model for those expanded and detailed accounts prominent in the testimonies and autobiographies of later Shakers.

In their visions, early Shakers elaborate the themes and metaphors suggested by the stories about Mother Ann and Father James. While Mother saw man's loss of innocence in the Garden of Eden, later Shaker writers portrayed the establishment of the Shaker community as a New Creation, God's restoration of a paradisiacal gar-

18. Father James paraphrases from the following scripture: "Blessed are they that do his commandments, that they may have right to the tree of life, and may enter in through the gates into the city" (Rev. 22:14); "These [the forty-four thousand with the Lamb on Mount Zion] are they which were not defiled with women; for they are virgins. These are they which follow the Lamb whithersoever he goeth. These were redeemed from among men, being the firstfruits unto God and to the Lamb" (Rev. 14:4); and "Thou hast a few names even in Sardis which have not defiled their garments; and they shall walk with me in white: for they are worthy" (Rev. 3:4).

den in the wilderness of America. Nathan Farrington, Sr., testified that he foresaw the building of the Lebanon Society. He "was one day taken in the visions of God, while in the field, gathering his Indian corn, and carried in the spirit to the spot where the meeting-house in Lebanon now stands. Casting his eyes eastward, he saw the mountain chiefly divested of its trees, from the place where he stood, even to the summit. Near the summit he saw the Lord Jesus Christ and Mother Ann by his side, with their faces towards the west; and they walked side by side, down the mountain, until they came within a few rods of where he stood, and then disap-peared. The vision then ceased and Nathan found himself in his cornfield again" (207). Farrington sees both the literal and sym-bolic clearing of the wilderness which must occur to make way for the holy community. Believers must remove the trees in order to build the Society at Lebanon; at the same time they must re-place the world of nature with the world of the spirit. Mother Ann and Christ travel from east to west; likewise, God's chosen people cannot find the new Garden of Eden in the Old World but must establish it in America. Instead of the natural trees of the Ameri-can wilderness, the tree of life grows in the Shaker paradisiacal garden. Thus, in the writings of many nineteenth-century Shak-ers, the clearing of the wilderness becomes a metaphor for a spiri-tual process: men and women must tame the wilderness within themselves.

The American experience clearly influenced how Shakers un-derstood themselves and their role in the New World. The first edition of *A Summary View of the Millennial Church* compares Shakers to pioneers in the wilderness:

> The first leaders of the Society may be compared to people going into a new country, and settling in the wilderness, where the first object is to cut and clear the land, and burn the rubbish, before the ground can be suitably prepared for cultivation. In this opera-tion, the axe and the fire are used with no sparing hand; and the falling of trees and the crackling of burning brush and useless rub-bish occasion much noise and bustle, and great confusion, espe-cially among the wild beasts and noxious vermin that infest the land. These are now obliged to flee for their lives, into some other part of the wilderness, or the fire will consume them. But when the land

is sufficiently cleared, and the rubbish consumed, and the wild vermin have all retreated, and the careful husbandman has securely fenced his field, he can then go on to prepare and cultivate his ground in peace; and if he is faithful to manage his business as he ought, he will continue to improve his premises, from year to year; so that in a few years, this once dreary wilderness will be seen to "blossom as the rose." [19]

From the early days Shakers, such as Nathan Farrington, believed that in America they were fulfilling the prophecies of the restoration of Zion: "The wilderness and the solitary place shall be glad for them; and the desert shall rejoice, and blossom as the rose" (Isaiah 35:1). In Shaker interpretation, however, the fruits of Zion's garden represent members of the community of Shakers. "A peculiar prophecy often referred to by Shaker historians is found in Psalm: 72 'There shall be an handful of corn in the earth upon the top of the mountains; the fruit thereof shall shake like Lebanon: and they of the city shall flourish like grass of the earth.' This handful of corn in the top of the mountains is to the spiritual eye of the Shaker beautifully fulfilled in the handful of true Believers at Mount Lebanon, the seed from which is to spring the harvest of redeemed humanity." [20] In Shaker understanding of the metaphor of the garden, the fruit contains within it the seed that is the gospel of Mother Ann. Those who believe Mother's message and follow her precepts are themselves the seed that, once planted in the world, will produce a great harvest — nothing less than the redemption of the world. Thus, Shaker writers often enunciated their mission in the world through organic metaphors which reflected theological concepts. They believed that revelation continues, and that every man or woman might experience it directly in his or her own soul. They also believed that religion, both in history and in the life of the individual, develops progressively, just as a tiny seed grows into a fruitful plant.

After the deaths of Mother Ann and the first Elders and the subsequent establishment of the order of the Society, Shakers in-

---

19. [Calvin Green and Seth Y. Wells], *A Summary View of the Millennial Church* (Albany, N.Y.: Printed by Packard & Van Benthuysen, 1823), xii.

20. White and Taylor, 81.

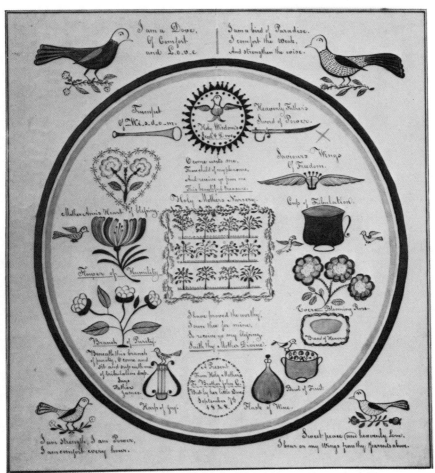

FIGURE 2: Spiritual drawing: "A Present from Holy Mother to Brother John C." Place unknown, 1848. (Courtesy of the Western Reserve Historical Society.) The emblems in Shaker spiritual drawings resemble the imagery in Shaker narrative. In the center of the circle, enclosed in a rectangular border, is "Holy Mother's Nursery," a redeemed garden where spiritual progeny flourish. Note also the images of spiritual nourishment: the "Bread of Heaven," "Bowl of Fruit," and "Flask of Wine."

35

creasingly regarded the reception of spiritual gifts less as evidence that a new millennium was at hand than as an indication of personal worthiness, of having successfully negotiated an individual move from one state of existence to another. Although Shakers perceived spiritual gifts primarily as signs of an individual's personal growth, of his or her "progress in the gospel," Believers might also receive communications from the spirit world that offered them special guidance. The earliest self-contained Shaker narratives are the records of such experiences.

"A Visionary Dream by Garrett K. Lawrence, Jan. 6, 1818," a popular narrative, was circulated widely among Shakers.[21] Lawrence, a "botanist and one of the chief promoters of the famous medicinal herb industry in New Lebanon,"[22] dreams that he is in a room where a number of Brothers are "viewing a very beautiful Partridge. It was all over spotted with the most beautiful yellow which glittered like gold, especially in its tail which was larger than its whole body, as it fluttered around." When the partridge flies out the door, Lawrence chases it but cannot find it. Returning to the house, he realizes he is naked. He slips "along slyly," afraid that he will be seen. He dresses quickly but does not wash his muddied feet. In the house the Brothers and Sisters are visiting with a stranger. Lawrence feels that the stranger "was truly the most beautiful man I ever saw in mortal clay. He appeared to be a perfect form of purity and innocence." When the stranger quizzes the Brothers and Sisters, "Whom think ye that I am?," they cannot identify him. But Lawrence answers, "'You are Father James Whittaker.' . . . Some of the brethren laughed at me, that I should think it was Father, since he was buried long ago, to which I replied, 'He has risen from the dead.'" When the stranger accuses Lawrence of having "given away in your feelings to unbelief—to fleshly affections and lusts," Lawrence admits that it is true. The stranger then advises him how to overcome the lusts of the flesh. "When these things come into your mind, you should turn your sense to your duty, & always have something that is beneficial and useful

21. Garrett Lawrence, "A Visionary Dream," Lebanon, N.Y., 1818, MS, OClWHi, VII: B–66C.

22. Edward Deming Andrews and Faith Andrews, *Visions of the Heavenly Sphere* (Charlottesville: Univ. Press of Virginia, 1969), 9.

to do." In a flood of tears, Lawrence feels a "gift of repentance." "All doubts were vanished from me. I awoke in tears, and continued crying for an hour, feeling that God was at work with me." Lawrence interprets his dream as follows:

> I saw that the nature of the flesh, or of man, was wild, and never could be tamed. And as the tail of the Partridge, was larger than the whole body, & seemed to steer & govern it, so it was with man, in the flesh—That it ever was, and still is, impossible, for him to be governed by reason . . . because the flesh never can, or will be purified. And then that nature may show its golden colors, and promise to its followers, pleasure, yet they never will find it, let their searches be what they may, but in the race will get naked, and their shame will appear.
>
> I furthermore saw, that by indulging a spirit of unbelief, and looking upon the things of nature with an eye of pleasure, & satisfaction, I had lost the beautiful garment of purity of heart, and that I walked naked before God, & his people, and my feet were dirty, so that my foundation was covered over with an earthly and sensual spirit; and that I must be washed, and made clean, by repentance, or never enter that happy mansion which the pure in heart enjoy.

Garrett Lawrence's narrative develops the motif of the recognition of a stranger, usually a holy man or woman who appears in a dream. Rather than seeing a person whom he later recognizes in real life, as Mother Ann had in her visions, Lawrence sees an apparition from the spirit world whose identity he alone knows.[23] His dream recalls Jesus' question to his disciples: "Whom do men say that I the Son of Man am? And they said, Some say that thou art John the Baptist: some, Elias; and others, Jeremias, or one of the prophets. He saith unto them, But whom say ye that I am? And Simon Peter answered and said, Thou art the Christ, the Son of the living God" (Matthew 16:13–16). Thus, in his dream Lawrence portrays Father James in the role of Christ, while he himself is Peter, the beloved apostle, the rock upon which Christ founded the Church.

Lawrence's identification of the stranger indicates that Father

---

23. The appearance of Mother Ann, Father James, and other early Shaker leaders becomes a commonplace in visions during the Era of Manifestations. Such appearances, however, were relatively rare during the early years of Shakerism.

James has reappeared on earth to give Lawrence spiritual advice. Lawrence had found it difficult to wean himself from the pursuit of sensual pleasure and had come to question the Shaker belief in the necessity of the virgin life. Father James appears in order to instruct Lawrence on how to overcome his carnal nature.

Lawrence's vision reveals how Shakers, in the years after Father James's death, developed the metaphor of "the garment unspotted by the flesh." In his vision Lawrence removes his clothes in order to run faster. The partridge that he pursues is an emblem of the natural world and of sexuality. He clearly associates nakedness with the lusts of the flesh, with desires that make him feel guilt and shame. The tail of the partridge, which "was larger than the whole body, & seemed to steer & govern it," represents the tendency of man to allow his sexual nature to control his life. Lawrence discovers that as long as he pursues sensual pleasure he will be unable to determine the course of his life. He finds that he can achieve control over his body, his nature, and his spiritual life only through total self-denial. Lawrence's vision thus expresses a common Shaker belief: that frustration and loss were the fate of those in the natural world and that those who pursue the "golden colors" of sensual pleasure are doomed to disappointment.

Lawrence's vision also shows the Shaker distrust toward the natural world. In the physical landscape and in the creatures that inhabit it, Shakers saw an image of the wild and disorderly nature of unredeemed man who selfishly pursued sexual gratification with no regard even for the "times and seasons" of procreation. The Shakers firmly believed that only a community based on divinely ordained laws could order and control nature in all its manifestations.

The Shakers viewed the community as the structure which protects those within it. It gathers the lambs and keeps out the wolves, or, to use another common image, it protects the new Adam and Eve from the serpent in the garden. At the same time, the New Zion is an example for the world of the possibility of living in the "New Creation." Shakers, no less than the Puritans, hoped to fulfill the scripture: "Ye are the light of the world. A city that is set on an hill cannot be hid" (Matthew 5:14).

Shaker narratives portray community members as the Saints in a New Jerusalem or the redeemed in a restored Garden of Eden. In either case, Shakers believed that only the sexually pure can inhabit the New Creation, and they appealed to Isaiah 52:1 for support in this view: "Awake, awake; put on thy strength, O Zion; put on thy beautiful garments, O Jerusalem, the holy city: for henceforth there shall no more come into thee the uncircumcised and the unclean." In Shaker interpretation biblical references to circumcision indicated God's requirement to pare away sexuality, and they believed that all members of the new order must be symbolically circumcised. Although in the time of Abraham circumcision was the external sign of membership in the tribe of Israel, in the "latter days" it became the sign of membership in the community of the redeemed. The Shaker autobiographer Issachar Bates, for example, who writes of submitting to the "circumcising knife," employs circumcision to describe metaphorically the change that occurred when he abandoned earthly pleasure for spiritual reward. Such sexual metaphors in Shaker writing often reveal less about individual sexual anxieties than they do about late eighteenth- and early nineteenth-century sectarian theology, which insisted upon a radical distinction between the damned and redeemed.[24]

While a number of basic metaphors in Shaker literature express belief in the need for sexual purity, others underscore the conviction that progress toward perfection can be obtained only through the confession of sin. Shaker literature presents confession as an intense fire which eats away the dross of past life and leaves only the pure, refined, precious metal. The fire which destroys man's carnal nature is most vividly described in a vision recorded by Elder Frederick Evans: "I saw a great fire, and a nude man, perfect in his physical organism, standing by it; he stepped into its very midst, the flames completely encircling his whole body. The next thing I observed was, that while he was perfect in *living beauty,* he was so organically changed that no 'fig-leaf' covering was required."[25] Shaker writers often describe passing through the "flames of con-

24. Kern's analysis fails to give sufficient weight to the religious context of sexual metaphors; thus for him Shaker use of the circumcision image indicates a fear of the castrating power of women. Kern, 79–82.

25. Frederick William Evans, *Autobiography of a Shaker and Revelation of the Apocalypse* (New York: American News Co., 1888; rpt. AMS Press, New York: 1973), 20.

fession" which burn away the desires of the natural man, eliminating the sexual instinct itself.

The Shaker believed that only the pure, those who had submitted to "the circumcising knife" and to "the flames of confession," might participate in the millennial community. To allow others inside the New Zion would be to risk admitting that old enemy, the snake, which led to man's original fall. In a vision Lydia Lyon clearly reveals Shaker perception of the necessity for protection: "The Saints were assembled within a beautiful enclosure, clothed in garments of beauty & loveliness, the walls of which was high & strong. They all appeared to be singing & dancing, & the sight was lovely beyond description. Outside of this enclosure a huge monster like a serpent appeared crawling around & trying the wall first in one place & then another, in order to get in & harm the Saints. The serpent was as large as a common stovepipe, extremely ill proportioned in form & ungainly in movement. Its color was variegated with bright spots of green & red, & it seemed deadly poisonous in its whole mass. But the Saints were well protected, & as no one seemed willing to admit so vile an enemy he remained without."[26] Lyon's vision reveals the need for the walls which protect Believers from the serpent, the agent of man's fall from paradise, which attempts to penetrate the new Garden of Eden. Lyon's vision graphically portrays the sexual nature of the monster that resides in the wilderness outside the Shaker community, and her use of color symbolism underscores this interpretation. Shakers usually interpreted green as the color of increase and red as the color of suffering. The green- and red-spotted serpent therefore suggests the regenerative life, which leads to both procreation and suffering. Within the protective walls of the Shaker community, however, the Saints cannot be defiled by the "lusts of the flesh." They are worthy inhabitants of the spiritual paradise, for they have put on "garments of beauty & loveliness" and have banished the monsters of nature.

In contrast to Lydia Lyon, who draws her images from the biblical story of man's fall, writers who are more familiar with Shaker

26. Lydia Lyon, [untitled autobiography], Enfield, N.H., 1862, MS, OClWHi, VI:B-37, 346.

theology and history portray the New Zion as the restoration of Solomon's temple. This notion was promulgated by Joseph Meacham, who divided the communities into three courts according to the description in Ezekiel 40–47. Yet even writers familiar with Shaker biblical commentary depict the New Jerusalem in the familiar images of the Shaker world. The streets of the New Zion are not paved with gold but are straight and narrow paths through the wilderness; the buildings are not bejeweled palaces but the plain white buildings of the Shaker community. Calvin Green records seeing "a very large building . . . like the ancient Temple. . . . It was formed in a manner I never before saw, being so arranged that any part could be finished & inhabited while new parts were being added." Green sees "nothing dazzling or splendid about it, as if for show, it was neat, plain, & simple, yet handsome, & adapted to the purpose of convenient habitations in all its parts." A spirit tells Green that the building represents "the New Jerusalem which is the 'Tabernacle of God with Men'—The decency & plainness of the Building signifies the meekness decency & simple plainness that becomes the true followers of Christ in all things."[27] The building in Green's vision reveals the complexity of Shaker metaphors, for it points in two directions at the same time. It is an image of the earthly community of Believers and reflects Shakers' belief in simplicity, utility, and lack of ornamentation. At the same time, it suggests an ideal spiritual world, a divine archetype which the earthly community seeks to emulate. Even the Tabernacle as it appears in the spirit world, however, is not a completed structure. The building of the New Jerusalem is a continual process, a process in which both the individual and the community must participate. Metaphors in visions like Calvin Green's serve two functions. On the one hand, they present Shaker theological beliefs by describing the divine archetype. On the other hand, they serve to confirm the Shakers' practical conviction that, as God's chosen people, they are to transform the earthly into the divine.

A vision by Nathan Williams clearly expresses the relationship that Believers understood to exist between the establishment of the

27. Calvin Green, "Parentage of the New Creation," Lebanon, N.Y., 1829, MS, OCIWHi, VII:B–66C.

Shaker community and the ushering in of a spiritual kingdom.[28] Williams's vision combines the themes of the garden and the Holy City, for the Shaker believed that the lost paradise could be restored only as a community. Williams, while away from Lebanon "drawing mill logs on Washington mountain," dreams that he is home in a "beautiful meeting." A spirit appears and asks Williams if he wants to go to "the Pleasant City." Just as the New Jerusalem is envisioned as a "city set upon a hill," so Williams sees that the Pleasant City rests upon a "little crowning." Writes Williams: "The buildings on each side of the streets, were all alike, two stories high, & about 100 by 50 feet, on the ground; they were as white as snow, & a great many of them. . . . There was on each side of the Street, a row of large maple trees, each about 2 feet thro the trunk, & 50 or 60 feet to the limbs. They were as white as snow, & I said, 'They whitewash these trees, don't they?' My guide said 'Look up & see.' I looked & saw they were white clear to the top. He then said 'Father Eleazar has the care of the Saints in this City,' & pointing to a house to the right of us, added, 'He lives in that house.'" When Brother Nathan meets Father Eleazar, they carry on a conversation that might have been spoken in the earthly Lebanon. Father asks him how he is. "I told him I was comfortable, & asked how he did. He said he was comfortable. I told him I was glad to see him. He said the same to me. I said 'You've got the pleasantest place that I ever saw.' He replied 'This is the Pleasant City.' 'What beautiful gardens you've got,' said I." The guide then gives Brother Nathan a tour of the gardens, and offers him some "little cucumbers" to take home to Eliza.[29]

The spiritual world of the Pleasant City is almost indistinguishable from Williams's earthly home in Lebanon. Indeed, the purpose of the vision is to reveal the relationship between heaven and earth. The only indication that Williams is in another realm is

28. Nathan Williams, "A Brief Sketch of His Life," Lebanon, N.Y., 1863, MS, OClWHi, VI:B-37, 50-51.

29. This detail in Williams's vision points out the difficulty of understanding Shaker symbol and metaphor without a knowledge of the Shaker interpretation of the Bible. Williams is alluding to Isa. 1:8: "And the daughter of Zion is left as a cottage in a vineyard, as a lodge in a garden of cucumbers, as a besieged city." Of course, Shakers would have identified the daughter of Zion as Mother Ann; the community which she establishes, then, is a vineyard, a garden of cucumbers, and a besieged city.

the whiteness of the trees, white from the trunks to the top limbs. As in the visions of Father James, the trees represent Believers themselves, the Saints of the City, who are pure and white, worthy inhabitants of the New Jerusalem. In this vision Williams feels a continuity and affinity between the life he already leads and the life to come. Lebanon is an image of the Pleasant City, just as the Pleasant City is an image of Lebanon, for Williams, like other Shakers, believed that the millennium had already commenced and that he was privileged to participate in it.

In the stories they told about Mother Ann and the early leaders of the Society, Shakers elaborated biblical images. In the visions they recorded, in the songs they sang, and in the language of worship, Believers attributed specific Shaker meanings to these images. While the meanings of certain images did not differ significantly from those in the literature of other Christians (for example, the use of white and black, light and dark), Shakers radically altered the conventional interpretation of many other images. Thus, nakedness in Shaker literature does not imply innocence and purity; it is a sign of guilt and shame, and underscores the need for the protection of the "clean white garment." Shaker writers thus drew upon a common store of figurative language which they interpreted and adapted to express personal experiences.

Since Shakers believed that gifts of the spirit communicated the divine to humans, it is not surprising that their descriptions of these visionary experiences contain the major symbols and metaphors of Shaker literature. As a basic form of early Shaker narrative, the vision was an important vehicle through which the metaphors of Shaker literature developed.

CHAPTER III

THE VISION
AS A
CONVENTION
IN SHAKER
NARRATIVE

Visionary experience is—or at least may be—the outward sign of a real experience. It is a picture which the mind constructs, it is true, from raw materials already at its disposal: as the artist constructs his picture with canvas and paint. But, as the artist's paint and canvas picture is the fruit, not merely of contact between brush and canvas, but also of a more vital contact between his creative genius and visible beauty or truth; so too may we see in vision, where the subject is a mystic, the fruit of a more mysterious contact between the visionary and a transcendental beauty or truth.

EVELYN UNDERHILL, *Mysticism*

When Shakers began to write about their personal experiences, they discovered that the vision was not only a source for metaphors and symbols, but could also be used to structure extended narratives. By the 1820s Believers were learning how to use accounts of spiritual gifts, which may have been written as short independent narratives since the latter part of the eighteenth century, as the focal point of testimonies and longer autobiographical narratives.

During the second and third decades of the nineteenth century, Shakers wrote numerous short testimonies that affirmed the writer's belief in the truth of Shakerism. In the first published edition of *Testimonies* (1816), editors arranged extracts from each Believer's statement to fit the life histories of Mother Ann, Father William Lee, and Father James Whittaker. The next volume of *Testimonies* (1827) presented each individual testimony as a single, separate narrative. Most of these narratives are four or five pages in length, and the location where the document was written, the date of composition, and the signature of the author follow each text.[1] It is in these documents, written during the 1820s, that Shakers first began to construct short autobiographical narratives.

Most testimonies begin with information about the author's birth and family. A popular alternate beginning relates the writer's first contact with the Shakers. The pattern that authors of these testimonies perceive in their past appears frequently in later autobiog-

1. [Seth Y. Wells, ed.], *Testimonies Concerning the Character and Ministry of Mother Ann Lee* . . . (Albany, N.Y.: Printed by Packard & Van Venthuysen, 1827). For convenience this text will hereafter be referred to as the 1827 *Testimonies* or the 1827 text.

44

raphies. They portray errors of childhood and youth, fears of hell and damnation, quests for the true religion, disillusionment with other religions, and finally, the discovery of a "way out of sin." Because each author speaks as one who has been personally convinced of the tenets of Shakerism, he or she feels it necessary to answer the question, as George Wickersham was later to phrase it, "How I Came to Be A Shaker."[2] As Shaker writers attempt to answer this question, they often describe visionary experiences that led to their conversion.

The testimony of Thankful Barce, mother of Shaker leader Calvin Green, reveals the development of Shaker narrative between 1816 and 1827. Barce was one of the first inquirers who visited Mother at Watervliet in the spring of 1780. The 1816 *Testimonies* contains no information about Barce's own life; it only records the words that Mother Ann spoke to her. For example, when Barce first visited the Church, "Mother asked her if she was sick of sin. She answered, that she thought she was. 'Tell me (said Mother) what you call sin, that you may be instructed: for the way to heaven is to leave the flesh behind, and be married to Christ'" (38). On another occasion, Mother tells Barce, "'You was a proud, haughty woman when you first came to see me; but you are a deal altered; and you must still labor and repent; and that work of God, which you have received, will carry you safely through, if you are faithful'" (314).

In contrast, the 1827 *Testimonies* presents Barce's personal story. It tells of the "great trouble of mind" which she experienced when young and of her conviction that there was "no peace for the wicked." Most significantly, Barce's testimony records a vision and its fulfillment. Barce relates that "one night, on my bed, I saw a very admirable woman. As she advanced along, I saw a very large flock of sheep following her. They appeared to be the most beautiful flock I ever saw, and were clothed with the cleanest and whitest wool that ever my eyes beheld. The woman advanced forward till she came to a large plain, where she halted; and I saw her bait the sheep with something that was in her hand; to my view it resembled salt. The sheep all seemed to gather round her and eat" (92). In 1780 Barce hears of "a strange people" who claim to live

2. George Wickersham, *How I Came to Be a Shaker* (East Canterbury, N.H., 1891).

without sin. She is determined to see these people for herself, since she has been unable to find any religion which protects her from sin. When Barce arrives at Watervliet, she is greeted by Mother Ann, who "sung very melodiously, and appeared very beautiful. . . . As I sat by the side of her, one of her hands, while in motion, frequently touched my arm; and at every touch of her hand, I instantly felt the power of God run through my whole body. I then knew she possessed the power of God, and I saw that she was the very same woman I had seen in my night vision, several years before" (93). When Barce realizes her vision has been fulfilled, she is convinced of "the work of God in this woman" (93). In the remainder of her testimony, Barce recounts her subsequent experiences with Mother and testifies to the "purity and innocence" of Mother's life.

The vision distinguishes Barce's narrative from less complex testimonies to Mother's good character. Instrumental in her conversion to Shakerism, the vision propels the narrative. The vision also symbolically reveals Barce's personal experience. In Barce's vision Mother is the shepherdess. She keeps the flock clean and white, feeds it, and, by implication, protects it from the wolves which might devour the sheep. While the similar vision by Father James predicted the future experience of the Society, Barce's vision foretells her own personal destiny. Like the sheep in the vision, Barce is drawn to Mother and nourished by her hand. The vision expresses Barce's desire to be protected and to be made clean and white and free from sin. When she visited Mother at Watervliet in the spring of 1780, Barce was unmarried and pregnant; she understood the vulnerability of the sheep without a shepherd. She found in Mother Ann and her gospel the protection from sin which other religions had failed to give her.

The testimony of Lucy Wight (not to be confused with Mother Lucy *Wright*) in the 1827 text also demonstrates how Shaker authors used the vision to construct more complex autobiographical narratives. After stating that had she lived in Christ's day she would have been his disciple, Wight recounts a vision:

> When I was about nineteen years old, I was taken very sick with a nervous fever, so that my life was dispaired of, both by myself and others. In the time of this sickness, I fell into a kind of trance,

and thought I died. Finding myself alone in the world of spirits, as I thought, and no one to help me, I was in great trouble, and prayed that some one would come to my assistance, and conduct me to a place of happiness. And there appeared to me a very pure, bright looking man, who conducted me to a house, as it seemed, where I saw a number of people who looked so pure and clean that I began to feel greatly ashamed of myself. Among the rest I saw a man who seemed to be walking the floor, under operations of the power of God.

The sight of such heavenly purity as these people seemed to possess, and the sense I felt of my own impurity and unfitness for such a place, brought excessive tribulation upon me, and I felt as tho I wanted to get away and hide myself. I told the people that when I was in the body, I thought when I died I should go to Heaven; but I could not find Heaven, because I had come there in my sins; and I asked them if there was not some place where I could go and repent of my sins and be saved, and not go to hell. They said there was; and I might go and repent. (65–66)

When Lucy Wight visits Believers in 1780, she witnesses the actualization of her vision: "The vision which I had seen in my sickness, more than four years before, came fresh to my mind. Here was the house and the people. I remembered the guilt and confusion I had felt in my vision, and now I had realized it. The man who came to me with outstretched hand, I found to be Elder John Hocknell; and I knew him to be the same man that I saw in my vision" (68).

In comparison with earlier examples, the vision of Lucy Wight reveals significant narrative development. Wight's testimony is not merely an account of a vision. It expands the personal context in which the vision occurs, during a period of great inner conflict and anxiety, and thus places greater emphasis on her individual history and personality. Her vision presents the interaction between individual concerns and familiar themes and images. No longer is the vision a set piece which an editor might lift out of context for a didactic purpose. Instead, Lucy Wight sets the vision within narrative time, and the vision functions to propel the central character forward in time and space. Wight moves from the home of her birth to a home among Believers at the same time as she moves from one spiritual condition to another. The vision, then, is a turning point in the narrative, bridging the two distinct halves of Lucy Wight's life history, her life before and after becoming a Believer. The account reveals the symbolic mode of perception, a distinctive characteristic of the Shaker autobiographical narrative, which unifies the story of the inner and outer life.

One of the earliest examples of the vision in Shaker autobiography is "The Infant Experience of James Bishop."[3] Bishop's narrative, written in 1835, is closely akin to the early testimonies, for he, too, relates memories of Mother Ann and the Elders. For example, Bishop describes how as an infant he was taken into Mother's arms. He kissed her "so ruggedly" that the next morning Mother's "cheek was quite red." Yet Bishop composed his narrative not so much to record such anecdotes as to preserve an account of a "night vision" he remembers experiencing as a child. Bishop draws the images which dominate his vision from Revelation 12:1, which he quotes on the title page: "And there appeared a Great Wonder in heaven; a woman clothed with the sun, and the moon under her feet, and upon her head a crown of twelve stars." In his vision Bishop symbolically portrays his own relationship with such a woman, Mother Ann.

Young Bishop dreams that he is lost in the wilderness. Seeing a "steadfast star," he understands that he must follow it and never lose sight of it, or he will be lost forever. His vision continues:

> After a long and painful travel, thro briers and thorns; over logs, rocks, and thro deep mire, which seemed to me to be nearly all night; often times almost lose sight of that beautiful star, or steadfast, being entangled in the brambles and mire; at length I found my way out of this wilderness swamp, which was to my great joy and solemn fear: here I found the bright star, or steadfast, to be a woman standing in the door of a house whose features shone like the sun in its meridian brightness. The door and every window in the house was illuminated with a similar brightness.
>
> There I was brought to a mortifying trial; when the light of steadfast shone upon me, I found my clothes were torn from me insomuch that I was almost naked, and covered with mud from head to foot.

3. James Bishop, "The Infant Experience of James Bishop. . . . ," Lebanon, N.Y., 1835, MS, OClWHi, VI:A-6.

My next exertion was, to find some way around the backside of the house; for I had not confidence to approach such a heavenly looking woman, and in such a bright light; but this would not do; the woman called to me and said: "You must come in at the door; for they that clime up some other way, are but thieves and robbers." Seeing no other way, I complied; and when I came to the door, she took me by the hand and led me to a back room, striped me of my raggs, and clothed me with a clean new dress; then led me to a table furnished with everything which heart could desire.

During my stay at that house, I was never able to express the joys comfort and satisfaction which I felt; I felt as tho I should never wish for any other heaven; for it was all life, power, love & joy; but, alas; when I awoke from sleep, I found myself the same old polluted sinner; then I could take some sense of my situation; that I was a poor lost creature; poluted from the crown of my head, to the soles of my feet.

I was ever confident that I should see the woman again in reality: and accordingly it proved so; when Mother came to see us, I knew her to be the same woman; and when I made my first visit at Water Vliet, I knew the place, and saw the same house illuminated as above stated, and the same woman standing in the door. (7)

Bishop's narrative brings together themes common to numerous personal narratives, from the early testimonies through later autobiographies. Like many Believers, he must traverse a wilderness. For Bishop, as for most Shakers, the wilderness is not a natural but a symbolic landscape. The branches which tear his clothes and the mire which soils him are the effects of his sins. In the wilderness Bishop is led by the light of the "steadfast star," identified with the woman in Revelation 12, whom Shakers interpreted as a figure of Mother Ann: "And the woman fled into the wilderness, where she hath a place prepared of God." The house which Bishop discovers, then, is the place prepared in the wilderness by God for both the woman and those who follow her light. The light which shines from the woman and from the house is the light of revelation which searches out and reveals sins. Thus, when Bishop sees himself in this light, he finds that he is naked and covered with mud, that he is polluted by the lusts of the flesh. In shame he seeks to enter the house through the backdoor, avoiding the bright light, but Mother leads him to a room where she strips him of his rags

49

and clothes him with a clean new dress. The Shaker would realize that the stripping away of the old life comes only through confession, and that in confession all the seeker's sins must be "brought to light." None can be hid if the Believer is to be worthy to put on the clean, white garment. When he regains his innocence through the purifying effects of confession, Bishop is ready to be nourished by Mother. This vision expands the conventional Shaker metaphors into narrative movement. It also emphasizes a recurring theme in Shaker literature: the need for maternal guidance and care. While the biological mother physically feeds and clothes her children, Mother Ann clothes them in garments of the spirit and feeds them from the tree of life.

The narrative movements in Bishop's vision, although expanded, are almost identical to those of Lucy Wight's vision and reveal the development of a prototypical visionary experience.[4] In both narratives the visionary must pass through a period of suffering. Bishop, who was only a child in the vision, represents this time symbolically as the "wilderness." Lucy Wight portrays it as an actual time of physical and emotional breakdown. Each finds guidance in the vision. A "beautiful man" leads Wight; Bishop follows the "steadfast star." Both narrators move into a spiritual world where they see a holy people and their habitation. The holy place in these visions, as in most Shaker narratives, is represented by a house. Both Bishop and Wight become aware of their own impurity and attempt to hide, but find they cannot do so. Although the vision gives both narrators a foretaste of the possibility of personal purity and spiritual nourishment, when they awake, they discover they are still the same as they were. The visions are not static but show the need for movement, for change in the individual's life. The vision also encourages the seekers, and when they finally meet Mother and Believers, it assures them that they have found the true people of God. The visions alone do not change the visionaries, but they increase their self-understanding and reveal the changes

4. In discussing the development of Shaker narrative, I have adopted some of the terminology used by Vladimir Propp, *Morphology of the Folktale,* 2nd ed., trans. Laurence Scott, introd. Svatava Pirkova-Jakobson, rev. and ed. with a pref. by Louis. A. Wagner, new introd. Alan Dundes (Austin: Univ. of Texas Press, 1968). In particular, the terms "narrative function," "initial situation," and "resolution" are derived from Propp.

which must occur if they are to find salvation. The true spiritual movement takes place beyond the vision, at a later time, when the narrators go to Believers, undergo confession, and begin to lead the pure life.

Although the basic narrative pattern of Bishop's vision is almost the same as that in Lucy Wight's, Bishop's account adds details and expands on themes only suggested in earlier visions. Bishop identifies the wilderness that he traverses, referred to at one point as Egypt, with the American landscape, containing both forest and swamp. His emphasis on following a "light" appears in many later autobiographical visions. Not only does Bishop feel himself unclean, as does Lucy Wight, but he represents his condition symbolically, describing his mud-covered attire and contrasting it with the white garments provided by Mother.

Bishop did not write the account of his vision immediately after it occurred. Some sixty years passed between Bishop's youthful conversion to Shakerism and the written description of these events. During that time the stories of the experiences of other Believers shaped Bishop's personal memories. His understanding of himself and his past came through metaphors and symbols familiar to him from years spent as a Shaker. The Shaker interpretation of biblical passages used to support the case that Mother was the Second Appearing of Christ influenced Bishop's portrayal of the "star" that he followed out of the wilderness. Believers, however, did not develop this doctrine until the first decade of the nineteenth century, some twenty or more years after Bishop's dream occurred. Bishop represents his past in ways the young person who experienced it could not have then expressed. The symbols, metaphors, and images which describe the conversion experience come out of Bishop's sixty years as a Believer.

During the 1830s and 1840s a number of Shakers wrote narratives that resembled expanded testimonies but included more autobiographical details. About the time that James Bishop recorded his childhood dream, Abijah Worster elaborated his earlier testimony to include more stories about his experiences during the early days of Shakerism. In 1845 John Rankin wrote a description of his early life and his memories of the Kentucky Revival at the turn of the century, the religious ferment out of which the western Shaker societies grew. In the following decade, Proctor Sampson described his life as a sailor before becoming a Believer, and David Rowley told of a remarkable conversion. In each case, the author composed an expanded narrative that included experiences that could serve as evidence on a particular issue confronting the Society as well as past experiences that were personally most significant. Almost invariably these authors describe some form of supernatural experience that crucially influenced their decision to become a Shaker.

Many Shaker authors, like Wight and Bishop, recall that visions occurred prior to conversion when the narrator was struggling to find the way to God. The writers often experience a deep sense of their sinfulness and worthlessness. Physical illness frequently occurs. During this period of great religious anxiety the Believers discern that the hand of Providence leads them. If a future Shaker is about to choose a path that would lead away from the community of Believers, divine intervention may occur. Believers often hear voices which repeat passages of scripture.[5] Abijah Worster records that when he was unable to find rest for his soul, he began frequenting the Baptist meeting. Like Paul, Worster hears a voice while "walking the Road." "The night before I was to have been taken into their church as I was walking the Road, and mussing on the scene these words dropt with weight on my mind, Arise ye and Depart, for this is not your Rest, for it is Polluted, it will Destroy you with a sure Destruction."[6] This message prevents Worster from committing a serious error.

Eunice Bathrick records a similar experience in her "Autobiography." Walking home from a Methodist meeting, she contemplates joining their society: "While I was walking slowly along and had almost concluded to become one of their number I was suddenly arrested by these words which were spoken from behind me. 'The people with whom you have met today are not the meek & harm-

---

5. This experience of hearing a voice is described frequently in Bunyan's *Grace Abounding* and illustrates the Protestant's reliance on the scripture for spiritual authority. Shaker autobiographers rarely hear voices quoting passages from the Bible after they accept the authority of the Shaker hierarchy.

6. Abijah Worster, "Testimony & Autobiography," Harvard, Mass., 1826, MS, OClWHi, VI:A-5, 48. Virtually identical is Worster's account of this incident in the 1827 *Testimonies*, 137.

less followers of Christ but if you would find salvation to your soul you must go and join the Shakers.'" Bathrick writes that these words were spoken to "her soul" and were not a "vocal sound." She replies, "'this I shall never do.' Then said the spirit hell will be your portion for you will never have another offer." These words convince Bathrick that she must become a Believer.[7]

Struggling to decide the future course of his life, John Rankin, Sr., receives a number of signs over a period of several years.[8] In his "Autobiography" Rankin relates that, although studying for the Presbyterian ministry, he continues to feel a great burden of sinfulness. Retiring to a "thicket where I had frequently spent sometime in solitary sorrow & intense meditation on my gloomy condition," Rankin prays to be delivered of his sin. Although he understands that God does not desire him to become a Presbyterian preacher, Rankin returns to his studies. But Divine Providence intervenes. Rankin becomes ill, returns home, and the Revolutionary War breaks out, so that it is impossible to continue his preparation. "I little knew what was moving on the wheels of Providence," says Rankin.

"Quickened" by hearing "new light" preaching, Rankin feels troubled by the doctrines of election and reprobation. A passage of scripture occurs to him "as if spoken to me viva voce. 'He which hath begun a good work in you will perform it untill the day of Jesus Christ.' As I proceeded on my way every nerve in my body seemed to be newly strung, & the most lively hope instantaneously sprang up in my soul, that at some future period I should obtain the object of my most ardent pursuit" (273–74).

When his hopes begin to fade again, Rankin for the third time receives divine encouragement. "I repaired to the fields in the solitary hours of the night, at a distance from man & under the shade of the full grown corn, I poured out my soul before God." A passage of scripture again occurs to him "as if spoken or ministered by a celestial messenger . . . 'Blessed are they who hunger & thirst after righteousness, for they shall be filled.' My consolation revived, my hopes were renewed, & I felt vigorous strength & resolution

7. Eunice Bathrick, "Autobiography," Harvard, Mass., n.d., MS, OClWHi, VI:A-5.
8. John Rankin, Sr., "Autobiography," South Union, Ky., 1845, MS, OClWHi, VI:B-37, 257ff.

to persevere in my pursuit, but did not know when or how the promise of God was to be accomplished in me" (275).

Such auditory experiences frequently hark back to biblical proto-types: Moses receiving the commandments on a mountain top or Paul's conversion "on the road." In both of these influential exam-ples, God reveals Himself primarily through His voice, and the revelation occurs in a natural setting. Perhaps for this reason the Shaker's experience of an "audible voice" often occurs outdoors: in a cornfield, in a "thicket," "on the road," or on a mountain. Addi-tionally, those, like John Rankin, who spent their youth in "the world" may have retained a romantic belief that nature was a con-duit for divine revelation. Although such a belief was incompatible with Shaker theology, these authors may have understood their early religious experience in non-Shaker terms familiar from their youth.

The "Religious Experience of David Rowley" presents a more detailed auditory experience, which Rowley calls his "trial upon the mount" (14).[9] Rowley has been "convicted of sin" and often prays alone in the fields. He has been meeting with various religious groups, but his soul remains dissatisfied. On a pleasant day in the spring of 1802, just after dinner, Rowley is praying under the apple tree in his yard when he feels a sudden impulse to cry aloud. Since he does not want to be heard by those inside the house, he is "im-pressed" to go to the top of a mountain and pour out his soul. Struggling through underbrush, he finally comes to a small clearing with a large rock. Although he begins to pray, Rowley discovers that his fervent feelings have disappeared. Suddenly he feels a strong pain in his right side. When he stands up the pain disappears, but when he continues praying it increases. Rowley is convinced that he is being "tried" by a diabolical spirit, and he vows to die rather than to give in to the evil one. Once he has made this determina-tion, the pain disappears.

> I was now filled with joy inexpressable, so that I sprang to my feet with shouts of praise and thanksgiving to God.
> A different scene now commenced, which, may be compared to the exhibition among the followers of Jesus at the day of Pentecost. (See Acts 2.) I leapt and ran about my little campground, shouting

9. David Rowley, "Religious Experience," Lebanon, N.Y., 1854, MS, OClWHi, VI:B–23.

with esctacies of joy beyond the power of tongue to describe. I clasped my hands, & swung them about, & danced into all kinds of antic conditions of body imaginable; so great was my releasement and perfect joy.—But the most predominant exercise was expressed by irresistable laughter. In this heteogenius esercise I continued untill darkness appeared. (11–12)

More than eight years pass before Rowley unites with Believers. Nevertheless, he views his Pentecostal experience as deriving from the same spirit that finally directs him to the Shakers at Lebanon.

While Abijah Worster, Eunice Bathrick, John Rankin, and David Rowley believed that divine intervention directed the course of their lives, their experiences were not true visions. The setting in which a vision occurs, in contrast to the scenes in which voices are heard, is most often indoors. Often the visionary retires to his room or his bed. Sometimes the vision occurs during sleep; on other occasions, the glimpse of the spiritual world comes upon awakening.

David Buckingham of Watervliet received, as a child, a revelation in the form of pure light.[10] In 1818, when his parents visit the Shakers, Buckingham and his younger sister are left at home alone. Night comes and a storm arises. Still the parents do not return. Young Buckingham is troubled and feels torn between two spirits, one for Believers and one against them. After retiring to his room and sleeping for two or three hours, Buckingham awakens to discover the room illuminated with a great light. Fearing that lightning has struck the barn and set it on fire, he looks outside, but all he sees is dark. Inside, however, a bright, white light fills the room. Buckingham concludes that he is standing in the presence of God. After praying and repenting of his sins, he is filled with peace. His parents return the next day, and he tells them of his experience the night before. They interpret their son's vision to be a sign from God; they are assured that the family is moving in His "light" and that it is God's will for them to become Shakers.

Visions may also occur after the narrator has become a member of the Society. The requisite condition for a visionary experience, whether occurring before or after conversion, is personal doubt

---

10. David Buckingham, [untitled testimony], Watervliet, N.Y., 1843, MS, OClWHi, VI: A-11.

and uncertainty. Visions, then, are possible at any point in the narrator's life. Both Nathan Williams and John Lyon record visions which help them to understand and accept their place within the Society. Although Nathan Williams had come among Believers as a child, he still felt the need to make a decision for himself as he approached his adulthood. Many of the young people were then leaving the Society, but Williams chooses "to serve God & follow Christ according to my understanding & faith, independent of any other being on earth" (13).[11] Yet he discovers that still more "trials" await him:

> This was a serious time with me. So much disappointment & adversity tended to discourage & try me severly. . . . There was no peace for my fallen nature, for I soon entered upon new trials of my faith & integrity, more deep and severe than anything I had yet encountered. The Elders of the Church offered me my choice, to come to the Church to live & be no body, or go to one of the Families & be somebody, meaning to take some official care & burden. I chose to come to the Church and be nobody, altho it seemed to me in those days that I was very unfit to be a church member; yet I undertook it. (18)

Not long after this decision Brother Nathan dreams the following:

> I was taken & put in prison in Troy. It had iron doors, & the walls were very high; they were formed of six stones, & each stone made a side. They were perfectly smooth & it was perfectly impossible by any means to scale the walls. I felt in a bad fix, & was mourning alone at my sad fate, when a good spirit came to me & asked "What's the matter? If you have the Gospel in you, you can be as happy here as anywhere — that makes you free." Then, feeling my justification, the prison walls disappeared & I felt myself a free man, & out of prison. (18-19)

In his own remarks about this vision, Williams relates it to fears that some Believers might be imprisoned for their refusal to fight in the War of 1812. From the personal context within which Williams places the vision, however, it clearly reflects his own conflicting feelings about committing himself to the Shaker way of life. His vision reveals a feeling that was perhaps difficult to admit openly

11. Williams, "A Brief Sketch of His Life."

FIGURE 3: Heart presented to Nathan Williams, Lebanon, New York. (Courtesy of the Western Reserve Historical Society.) This spiritual gift indicates that Williams was worthy of being "owned" by his Heavenly Parents, and it presents him with a shield of protection, a beautiful seal, and a crown of bright glory.

to himself or other Believers; for just as the walls protected the Believer from dangers, they also closed out the outside world. With the guidance of the good spirit, however, Williams learns that walls do not make a prison, that freedom is a quality of the spirit and does not depend on outward circumstances. The vision both expresses and resolves Nathan Williams's feelings about living the Shaker life.

After going to the Church family, Williams continues to have feelings of great unworthiness. In another "vision of the night" he again sees a prison, but this one threatens damnation:

> I found myself in an awful state, suspended in the center of what appeared to be the bottomless pit. To look down was all darkness, gloom, & horrid despair, sufficient to send a thrill of terror thro every feeling of my soul. It seemed to be about 15 feet wide — the walls built of solid smooth stones & no possibility of getting out I was down about 20 feet. I finally discovered that by great exertion & presure of my feelings upwards, I gradually rose. I found that I gained only by steady perseverance, for if I slackened my intense anxiety & the pressure in my feelings upwards, I then began to sink. This showed me my spiritual state: that it was only by a strait forward course of faithful crossbearing . . . that I could gain deliverance from this horrible & doleful pit of darkness. By a continual labor I reached the top, when I took hold with my hands, & lifted myself up. I got out, to my exceeding joy, & thanks to God for the means given by which I was able to effect my deliverance from this pit, which to my understanding, so forcibly represented my state of nature, & set forth how to rise with Christ in the resurrection of eternal Life. (20–21)

Williams's vision meshes the common image of hell as a dark pit with the Shaker metaphor of spiritual "travel." Williams understands that he must move upward, must scale the walls of the pit, if he is to escape damnation. Through his own exertions and self-denial, Williams discovers that he can "rise with Christ." The movement up out of the pit becomes representative of the resurrection, a rebirth from the life of the body to that of the spirit. The way out of such a prison, Williams discovers, is by overcoming temptations and one's sinful nature. Freedom is possible only when the natural man has been vanquished. After the time of this vision,

Williams relates that he undertook many "years of comfortable Gospel travel" (21).

The visions of Nathan Williams illustrate the difficulty of trying to establish universal meanings for common images in the Shaker literary imagination. The walls in Williams's visions at some times protect; at other times they imprison. Only in the context supplied by the autobiographer can the meaning of the visions be understood. In the personal narrative images often suggest more than one meaning. Because visions usually present a crisis in the life of the writer, the contradictory meanings of the images may express the conflicts experienced by the narrator. Thus the meaning of a single image may vary within a single narrative or even within a single vision.

Another frequently copied and widely disseminated autobiographical vision was that of John Lyon.[12] The circumstances of his life at the time he experienced supernatural manifestations closely correspond to those recorded by Nathan Williams. As a young man during the early years of the Society, Lyon, like Williams, was greatly troubled by the disorder and apostasy within the community. When many of his friends were "going to the world," Lyon was also tempted to give up the Shaker life. But just as Eunice Bathrick and Abijah Worster were "stopped on the road" and prevented from making serious errors, so supernatural intervention discourages John Lyon from becoming an apostate:

> In June, 1795, while alone in the field, hoeing, I was ruminating upon the beauties of the world, the prospects awaiting me in leaving Believers, and participating in the pleasures of sin, such as the lust of the flesh, the lust of the eyes, and the pride of life, when an audible voice spoke to me, the following words. "What will you do with your conscience?" This startled me, as I thot I might have been talking to myself, and was overheard by someone, in a hedge near by. I therefore left my work, thoroughly searched the hedge but could find no one; nor could I discover the existence of a human track. (7–8)

Lyon continues his work, and his thoughts go back to the pleasures of the world. Again he hears the voice. He returns to hoeing the

---

12. John Lyon, "Incidents in the Early Life of Elder John Lyon," Enfield, N.H., 1861, MS, OClWHi, VI:A-3, VI:B-36.

field, and a third time the voice speaks to him. At that point, Lyon says he knew that the voice was supernatural in origin. Thereafter, whenever he is tempted by the lure of the flesh or the world, he remembers this voice.

For the next three years Lyon did not experience any supernatural manifestations. Then "in August, 1798, as I was at work in the field, with several others, I suddenly heard a sound as a heavy rolling thunder, which seemed to fill immensity, and I heard a voice proclaiming 'Now is the time of the judgment, the time for every word, motive, intention, as well as every evil action, to be brot to judgment'" (10).

Even after John Lyon had determined to remain among the Shakers, he found it difficult to surrender his pride and will to the order of the Society. Lyon, like Nathan Williams, struggled against the restrictions of the Shaker life and portrayed the resolution of his conflict symbolically in a vision. [13] Feeling troubled and sinful, Lyon goes to his Elders for council, but in private he dismisses their advice. "One morning, in June, 1802, feeling in a miserable situation, I made one more effort to obtain help from my Elders, by going to them and opening my case as well as I could." The Elders give Lyon the following advice: "Turn your sense from the world, & from your nature, attend to your duty, and labor for the gifts of God, and it will help you to overcome." As soon as he is away from the Elders, however, Lyon again follows his own "lead." Thus, the initial situation which prompts Lyon's vision is his difficulty in accepting the Shaker life.

Lyon is careful to note the precise time and circumstances of the vision. "At about 10, Oclock, while at work, and alone," he is "taken from all sense of the things of time." The vision opens with Lyon's perception that "the whole heavens were filled, seeming to roll backward and forward, and in every direction." Looking to the east, Lyon perceives a "bright streak of light, as fine as a hair, in perpendicular position, appearing about eight feet in length." He hears a voice which instructs him, "Go to that light." Although Lyon knows that he must pursue the light if he is to find salvation, he

13. Ibid., VI:A-3, 17-24.

discovers that his "travel" is dangerous. The passage from one condition to another entails crossing a "vast deep gulf with almost perpendicular banks and there appeared to be timber extending across in form of a bridge . . . ; this timber was covered with planks, and other timber thrown on, promiscuously, having many holes; some of this covering appeared rotten, so much so that I thot it a dangerous place, and required the greatest care to cross it." As he starts to cross the gulf, "every vestage of light was withdrawn," and Lyon is left "in horrible darkness" except for a "little streak." "I then began to look this way and that and to feel about for something firm, upon which to place my feet, but, could find nothing upon which I durst rest my weight, only where I stood. I therefore remained where I was, and on looking for the streak of light, it was gone! — O, the horror I was in! I was enveloped in darkness, and durst not stir, and, if I did I knew not which way to go." Once more, Lyon gropes for the light, trying to avoid the fatal "holes," but again he loses it. A third time, he finds it but discovers that "a very little deviation" from the right path puts him into the dark once again. "I not only despaired of again finding the light, but, also of keeping sight of it, if I should find it; therefore, I thot I might as well give up to die where I was. To go forward was impossible, and to go back, I could not think of it, for that was equally impracticable."

Lyon thus feels himself in a state of near paralysis. Having begun on the Shaker "way," he feels there is no possibility of turning back to "the world," yet he finds himself unable to make spiritual progress as a Shaker. Unable to keep the light in his sight, Lyon almost despairs. "Nothing mitigated my distress and I began to cry and beg, that I might have help, if there was any for me, and, also, for knowledge why I did not, or could not keep sight of the light, when I had it." Only at this point does he surrender his self-will and beg for divine aid. This action is the crucial turning point in the vision. "I was then told, energetically, that, in all my distress heretofore, I had not come low enough to ask for instruction. I said, 'I will.' 'And this shall be my course, both now and forever.' . . . Accordingly, my first work was to find the streak of light, and place myself in the direction of it, so I set myself to work, moving in all directions, as I had done before, with this difference, to think of nothing but the light. I did not then try to look about in the dark, or to feel my way with my feet, but moved as rapidly as I could."

Lyon's vision reveals the only way he can continue as a Shaker. He must not let his mind dwell on the holes in the timber. He must put away thoughts about the "lusts of the flesh" and the attractions of the natural world. He must not allow himself to be led by his senses; he must not "feel" his way in the dark. Instead he must concentrate on the things of the spirit, symbolized by the supernatural light. "Having placed my eyes directly on the light, I set out with a determination to reach its source, and, to pay attention to no other object, whether it was in myself or elsewhere! Thus I moved under this determination. Without any difficulty, I arrived at the place from whence the light proceded."

Having reached this decision, Lyon is permitted to see the heavenly world, the spiritual New Jerusalem, the source of the light of revelation.

On my arrival here, I found the light was emitted thro an aperture. There appeared to be a wall that I could not cross, so that I could not procede any further, and, it was so dark, I could not see of what it was composed, But, there were two pillars inserted in the wall, and placed as near each other as they could be, and not touch; thro this aperture, between the pillars proceeded the streak of light. The appearance of the pillars was like polished silver, seven or eight inches square, by eight feet long. These pillars were so constructed, that, by placing my eyes close to the joint between the pillars, I could look thro, and see a hemisphere of light, and such brightness as nothing on earth can describe. It was brighter than the sun, yet such was my sight, I could look upon it without its dazzling my eyes; it was the most delightful scene my eyes ever beheld, and, I hoped I should never be compelled to leave it. Accordingly I kneeled down and placed by head against the pillars, where I had a full view of the light, and brightness which came thro them to this dark world.

How long I was in this situation, enjoying this heavenly view, I know not, but after an interval of time, I heard the same sound which I heard at the commencement of the vision; it came rolling thro the heavens, and seemed to fill all things. I heard this, for a time, which seemed to close the vision, and I returned to the scenes of earth, and found myself upon my knees, having wet with tears, a place some ten or twelve inches in diameter. I arose, went to see the time of day, and found I had been in this trance, about 4 hours!

Although a wall separates the world of nature from the world of the spirit in Lyon's vision, the Shaker who puts away all thoughts of the natural order may bask in the brightness of the spiritual world. Shakers would recognize the two silver pillars through which light streams from the "aperture" as Christ and Mother Ann, the divine parents who support and sustain their followers. Shakers also referred to Mother Lucy Wright and Father Joseph Meacham as the "first pillars." In these two leaders the spiritual authority of the community resided, and it is to them that John Lyon must submit in order to continue his spiritual progress. He has learned that in order to banish the "world of the flesh" he must yield to his "lead," and he must relinquish his individual will to that of the community. After the vision Lyon reports that he was released from trouble, for he realized that God had appointed only one lead. He understands that in the past he had set himself up as a judge over others, and that when he had come to the Elders he had doubted that he was standing before the throne of God. Elder John Lyon concludes his narrative, "Instead of vexation I found peace; instead of perplexity in trouble, I found comfort & consolation. All I had to do was, to hear this word, & obey it. This from a lover of the New Creation!" (34–35).

Lyon's vision, like the visions of other Believers, follows a familiar narrative pattern and suggests a predictable form for the Shaker personal vision. In testimony and autobiography the Shaker describes the initial, personal context in which the vision occurs. Usually the visionary needs to make a religious decision; sometimes he or she needs to surrender to the laws of the Society; at other times physical or mental illness requires healing. Most writers describe both the temporal and physical setting of the vision. Many give not only the date but also the hour when the vision occurred. Auditory experiences most often occur outdoors: on the road, on a mountain top, in a field. Pictorial visions tend to occur indoors:

after falling asleep (such a dream was called a "vision of the night"), after being awakened from sleep, during or immediately after powerful worship.

The opening of the vision may be signaled by sounds (most often thunder), supernatural lights, or bodily sensations. Often the visionary reports being removed from "all sense of the things of time." Some narrators describe a feeling of leaving the body, of soaring above it and looking down on the physical self.

Narrators typically recount experiences of travel and travail. They often must traverse a wilderness or a swamp; some climb mountains or cross rivers. They must surmount obstacles, overcome dangers, and avoid temptations. Often a guide in the form of a beautiful person, a spirit, a light, or a star accompanies the visionary. Visionaries who encounter difficulties in their travel must remember to request divine aid and not to depend upon their own powers. They must pray, or seek advice from their spiritual guide. In another version of this motif, the visionary remembers a relevant passage of scripture or recalls a religious promise which renews faith and courage.

At the end of the journey the visionary arrives at a holy setting. Usually otherworldly people or buildings come into view. The pure people are often dressed in white; sometimes they are dancing and singing. Some visions represent them as white sheep or as shining trees. When the visionaries see a house, they most often describe it as plain and white and square in shape. In other visions, the holy place appears as a paradisiacal garden or the New Jerusalem. Whatever the details of the setting, its purity and holiness impress the narrator, who intensely desires to become a part of the people or community. Particularly in the visions of men and women who are already members of the Society of Believers, the glimpse of the spiritual world gives the narrator a deeper understanding of Shakerism. In visions which are said to have occurred before the author joined Believers, the narrator feels excluded from the holy setting and realizes his or her unworthiness. Shaker writers commonly use images of nakedness or uncleanliness to express such feelings. The realization of their imperfection and sinfulness shames the visionaries, who often attempt to hide or run away. These efforts to conceal their spiritual condition always fail; sometimes the narrators recount submitting to the "searching light" or to the "flames of confession." Often they receive instructions from their guide, who tells them how to become like the people in the vision. Although not yet allowed to join the holy community, the narrator receives hope that such union will be possible in the future.

When the dream journey ends, the visionary returns to the temporal sphere where the vision began. Often a period of several hours has passed. Those who were already Shakers at the time of their vision report that their spiritual experience has resolved some anxiety or conflict. Some find that they are able to surrender their pride and self-will; others discover that they can accept the restrictions of the Shaker life. In some cases the narrator specifies that the vision helps to subdue the "lusts of the flesh." Those who are not yet Believers when the vision occurs feel themselves still sinful and polluted afterward. Although they have yet to resolve their initial doubt, these authors in retrospect feel the vision reveals how they may be saved from sin. In such narratives the vision often predicts a future event: the journey to Believers which the narrator re-enacts in real life or the recognition of persons or places seen in vision.

Although the number of narrative elements included in any one vision varies considerably, the basic sequence of the narrative remains constant. The individual imagination of the narrator, his or her unique personal experience, and images drawn from Shaker culture interact to create a meaningful symbolic structure. The Shaker personal vision as it appears in testimonies and autobiographies follows a predictable pattern influenced by the visions of Mother Ann and the early Believers and shaped by Shaker theology. Individual Believers molded their experiences, including visionary ones, to fit the conventions and expectations of Shaker culture. While the content of the vision might be drawn from the Believer's own past history, its form expresses the shared beliefs of the community.

Not only was the structure of the vision itself predictable in Shaker narrative, but the function of the vision within the narrative became a convention of Shaker literature. Often the vision constituted a ready-made turning point in the narrative. Revealing the way to Believers, the vision transformed the narrator from one spiritual state to another. The basic structure of Shaker autobiographical literature was the contrast between the life of the flesh and the life of the spirit, between life in the world and life as a Shaker, and the vision was the device Shaker writers used to mark the transition between these two states.

Long time therefore abode they speaking boldly in the Lord,
which gave testimony unto the word of his grace, and granted
signs and wonders to be done by their hands.

ACTS 14:3

Shaker autobiography flourished in the mid-nineteenth century, yet from the early years of the century Shaker testimonies
had contained autobiographical information. The recurring formu-
lations of the Shaker personal narrative — the use of a standard religious vocabulary, the selection of the materials deemed appropriate
to autobiography, and the use of the vision as a structural device —
are all rooted in the recorded testimony. Oral testimonies, a feature of the worship of Believers, may also have influenced the development of the Shaker personal narrative.

Only a few nineteenth-century documents claim to preserve testimonies verbatim from oral renditions. Although transcribers may
have shaped such texts, the form of these testimonies nevertheless
differs dramatically from those that Shakers composed first as written narratives. Testimonies that have been transcribed from oral
presentations often use the present tense, and they tend to emphasize the feelings of the speaker. Frequently sentences begin with
the first person pronoun. Short sentences and parallel constructions are common. These testimonies show little if any tendency
toward narrative development. The following testimony by Jemima
Blanchard, with an annotation that it was recorded as it was spoken
in meeting, is typical.

> I love & bless my good Ministry.
> I love & bless my good Elders.
> I love & bless all my good brethren and sisters.
> I feel thankful that I have lived to see this blessed day.
> I pray that I may feel a thankful spirit for the love

> and kindness and charity which is bestowed on me by
> all my kind and good elders and brethren and sisters.[1]

Although Shaker authors' familiarity with such oral testimonies may have influenced their writings about their religious experience, any attempt to establish such a relationship is fraught with difficulties. In the first place, texts which claim to have been recorded from oral presentations are too few to provide adequate data for such a study. Second, the remnants of oral testimony exist only in the form of written documents. Finally, texts that purport to preserve oral testimonies may constitute a distinct genre of religious literature, although, like the written texts, they were designated by the Shakers as testimony.

Tracing the development of Shaker testimony from oral to written forms is next to impossible. Since the orally preserved stories about Mother Ann and the early Believers were not embodied until the 1816 *Testimonies,* these examples are many steps removed from the oral originals. "The basis for the 1816 text was 'Mother's Sayings'; this was a manuscript collected by Elder Rufus Bishop around 1812."[2] This manuscript was itself most likely a reworking of written documents, testimonies, anecdotes, and letters which early Believers submitted to Elder Rufus. Therefore, any study of the development of Shaker oral testimonies would require access to original documents, untouched by the pens of editors, which have not survived. With the exception of those few texts which claim to have been set down verbatim from oral presentation, the surviving Shaker testimonies reflect a written tradition.

Shaker autobiographical narratives likewise owe more to written literary precedents than to oral traditions. The structure of Shaker autobiography was most clearly influenced by the written testimonies, particularly the collection published in 1827, in which many of the testimonies were miniature autobiographies. At the same time, the images and metaphors which inform the autobiographies are similar to those which dominate the testimonies of the 1840s. Believers wrote these testimonies during the Era of Mother's Work, when spiritual manifestations functioned to purge the Society of

---

1. Jemima Blanchard, [untitled testimony], Harvard, nd, MS, OClWHi, VI:A-8.
2. Swain, 3.

accommodations to "the world" and restore Shakerism to its original ideals. These documents contain little personal information, but they typically employ highly metaphorical language when recounting spiritual gifts. Many authors detail the "beautiful & heavenly presents" they have received: gold chains, rings, diamonds, pearls, rare fruits, and precious wine. Such "gifts" are signs to Believers that they have established the New Jerusalem where the "vain imaginary things" of the material life have been replaced by "the durable treasures" of the spiritual world. In the later months of 1843 and the early part of 1844, the Elders requested that members of the United Society express in writing their convictions that the spiritual manifestations were divine in origin.

One of those Shakers who responded to this request was James Wilson of Lebanon, who on 13 December 1843 set down his personal testimony to the validity of Mother's Work.[3] In 1866, nearly twenty-five years later, Wilson wrote his autobiography.[4] An examination of the similarities and differences between these two texts demonstrates how Shaker autobiography developed from the written testimony.

Although in its broad outlines Wilson's testimony is similar to many which date from this period, his narrative is atypical in several ways. In the first place, it is more lengthy and more complex than most testimonies of the 1840s. Additionally, Wilson was one of a handful of Believers who portrayed a significant conversion experience in a testimony ostensibly composed to support the spiritual manifestations. Unlike those who had been brought up among Believers, Wilson united with the Society as a fully mature adult, married, with a number of children. While those who joined Believers when very young reveal little of their own personalities in their testimonies, Wilson's narrative exposes a self-assertive, sometimes even cantankerous, character. Wilson's pre-Shaker experience, his complex personality, and his dramatic conversion to Shakerism may have motivated him to write a more detailed testimony than

3. James Wilson, Sr., [untitled testimony], Mt. Lebanon, 1843, MS, OClWHi, VI:A–6. The testimony is unpaginated. Wilson was born 22 July 1794 and died in January 1870. He united with Believers in 1827.

4. James Wilson, Sr., [untitled autobiography], Lebanon, N.Y., 1868, MS, DLCMs, no. 149. The autobiography is unpaginated.

the Elders expected. These same characteristics may account for Wilson's desire to offer an even more elaborate version of his life more than a quarter of a century later.

Wilson's testimony, like most others of the same period, begins and ends formulaically. He opens with the statement that it is his "duty and priveledge" to relate his experience as a Believer. He closes with the assertion that the current spiritual manifestations are divine in origin. Within this framework Wilson describes the experiences in his own life that lend credence to his ability to judge the genuineness of the gifts then being received by Believers.

After a conventional beginning, however, Wilson's testimony proceeds to recount the author's idiosyncratic concerns. He relates that his father had been wealthy but "took to dreanking & making bad bargains." Wilson determines that he must "have a trade to work at," and "with hard pleading" he persuades his father to apprentice him to a blacksmith. Wilson's apprenticeship becomes a great trial, for the blacksmith was "a stranger & he proved a drunkard & often from hoom, & his wife was about as bad so that I many times have been distressed with hunger almost to the point of starvation & when I could not stand it any longer I would then go hoom to my parents & then not having judgment would eat without discresion & in this way I got broke down so that I was like an old man before I was thirty, & cripled & diseased so that I could scarsly git about." Wilson then describes his search for the true religion, his disillusionment with religious groups, particularly the Methodists and the Quakers, and his increasing conviction of the sinfulness of the sexual relation. Indulgence in sex and food were the two great sins which, in Wilson's view, bound him to the life of the flesh. Gluttony and lust, Wilson felt, have been intertwined since the fall of Adam: the eating of the apple represented, to Wilson as well as to other Believers, man's fall from sexual purity. Wilson feels that before becoming a Shaker he was "as much lost in eating & dreanking . . . as in the flesh."

Wilson briefly notes his marriage, without giving details of its circumstances or naming his wife. Instead, he emphasizes his growing disillusionment with sexual relationships. "I was young at the time & expected to take much comfort in the Maried life & I beleave I did as much as is common, But I found myself terebly disapointed, which I beleve all souls will acknoledge when they get to see themselves & is honest enuf to own the truth." Marriage, Wilson discovers, further separates him from God, and he finds it difficult even to pray. Although he attempts sexual abstinence, he is "soon overcom with the meny temtations that surrounded" him. He tells his wife of his conviction against "the works of the flesh," but she advises him to keep this conviction to himself. She fears that "the peopel would cawl me a Roman Catholic if they new my mind & feellings."

Disillusioned by religious solutions to his "trobel and dispair," Wilson is attracted to the theories of Robert Owen and becomes a member of the ill-fated utopian community at Valley Forge.[5] After the failure of the community, some of its members visit the Shakers, since they have heard that Believers also share all goods in common. When one of the visitors returns, he tells Wilson about the Shakers' temporal arrangements; and then, writes Wilson, "He . . . told me he had something yeat to tell me & he did not know how I would like it. . . . They dont marry said he but live a virgin life." Wilson, contrary to the expectation of his friends, who know nothing of his aversion to the sexual relation, is convinced that the Shakers must be the true people of God. The reports that the Shakers dance in their worship trouble Wilson, however. At this point in his testimony Wilson records a vision which leads to his conversion to Shakerism:

> Now I was wounded for sarton, Now my former convictions . . . came hoom to me like a dart, My feelling I canot express of sorrow & gladness both. . . . But dancing seemed to stager me. . . . This I could not see into, untill I seen the gospel of god in vision or visions clean & pure Just as they appered to me when I first saw them. . . . I thought I was taken into a beautifull place where I never had been before, & was taken down into the loer part of an old

5. For further information about the Valley Forge Community, see Calvin Green's "Biographic — Memoir — of the Life and Experience — of Calvin Green," Lebanon, N.Y., 1861-1869, MS, OCIWHi, VI:B-28, 415, 416, 418, 427, and 473. Green provides additional information in "Journal of a Journey to Philadelphia and Its Vicinity — May, 1828," MS, OCIWHi, V:B-98-98A. See also George Wickersham's narrative in which he lists over twenty-five persons who came from Valley Forge and remained Shakers, and the autobiography by Jane Knight, *Brief Narrative of Events Touching Various Reforms* . . . (Albany, N.Y.: Weed, Parsons and Co., 1880).

building which I afterwards found to be our old dwelling hous in [?]
There I seen great preparations for eating which I thought would
come right as I was very hungry so I waited with a great deal of
pashions a long time Still expecting to git sumthing to satisfy hunger
which by this time had becom two distresing to bear any longer but
nothing apperes to be ofered to me although I see a great feasting
having plenty, so I didn't know what to do, I was in a strange place &
knew not where to go nor what to do, I seen no prospect of gitting
enything to eat heer & I was now distrest with hunger so much that
I could not stand it eny longer & live unles I had sumthing to eat & I
had waited heer so long & got nothing & no prospect of gitting enything so I at length thought I could look sum where els, & when I
began to look around I found myself surrounded with a great high
wall & no way for me to gitt over so I thought I had got into a bad
situation could not git away nor git nothing to eate & about starv-
ing. However I thought there was no other way for me & perhaps I
might git something to eat yeat, & whiles I was pondring over thes
things in my own mind I began to notice myself & I found that I was
very black & dirty & the more that I looked at myself the blacker I
appered to myself & others around me & I begun to feel ashamed &
mortifyed & the more I looked at thoes around me the cleaner &
whiter they appered to me which still increased my mortifycation till
I felt so bad that I did not know what to do & by sum means I was
waked up & shortly after I was brought into the same situation &
place where I awoke, & I seen those beautifull clean white people,
again with an increas of beauty & in a beautifull looking valley I
now scenced them to be & myself as before, black & dirty, & they
went fourth in beautifull bands in dancing they first began in slow
Marching & got into quick moves & whiles I was standing agaising
I thought that I seen a beautiful looking angel flying alonge over thoes
in the dance & looked upon them with a smiling countenence &
looked angry at me which increased my troble, he had something in
the hand like a large paper with writtings upon it & was the Laws of
this people, as I was told & he signafyed to me that if I would obey
thoes laws I might unight with this peopel & my dirty black garment
would be taken of me & I would have a clean white garment as they
had & no sooner said then don & I was taken right in amongst them,
so I awoke or come to myself having lost all prejedest feellings against
dancing which never trobled me since, & Just as I was taken into the
dance after I opened my mind, I wonted to unight in the dance but
give away to backward feellings untill I was whirld right into it.

The controlling images of Wilson's vision are the same as those previously introduced into the testimony. In the first part of the vision, Wilson perceives a great hunger in himself while the beautiful people feast on great abundance. The search for food represents Wilson's search for the true religion. Spiritual nourishment, Wilson's vision reveals, cannot be found outside the walls of Zion. It is offered only to those who join together within the community and accept its laws. During Mother's Work Believers often received gifts of spiritual food, and Wilson could be certain that those who read his testimony would readily understand the import of such images.

The second group of images in the vision represents Wilson's feelings of overburdening sexual guilt and shame which have pressed down upon him for twenty years. In the vision he sees himself as "black & dirty" while Believers are pure and white. Although stripping away the old, filthy garments and putting on new, clean, spiritual garments is another common metaphor in Shaker narrative, Wilson's use of it here is less routine and more personally intense than in most other Shaker testimonies. Both hunger and uncleanliness describe the condition not merely of James Wilson but of all men in the world. Wilson's personal concerns are articulated in his vision in images acceptable and understandable to other Believers.

In order to partake of the feast and to receive clean new garments, Wilson must be worthy; he must be cleansed from all sexual pollution and must accept the laws of the community, including the need for a virgin life, which the heavenly mediator reveals to him. Once he does this, Wilson is instantaneously whirled into the dance of Believers. The last sentence of the vision in the testimony, "I wonted to unight in the dance but give away to backward feellings untill I was whirld right into it," does not distinguish between the visionary experience and the real-life experience of uniting with Believers. Through the use of the metaphor of the dance, Wilson is able to refer simultaneously to both.

Wilson's vision presents in symbolic form the two poles of Shaker experience: the law represents self-denial, restraint, and individual control; the dance suggests self-expression, release, and the merging of individual identity with the group. The dance also represents Wilson's social union with Believers: he accepts their beliefs, he joins in their worship, and he shares both his temporal and spiritual concerns with them. On another level, the dance symbolizes, as Shaker theologians explained, "the one spirit by which the people of God are led."[6] The dance, then, is a powerful image expressing the change that occurred in James Wilson's life. It connects his life before becoming a Believer, one of despair, hunger, and uncleanliness, with his life as a Shaker, one of hope, nourishment, and purity. The dance portrays a metamorphosis, the radical transformation of a man into the opposite of what he had been before.

Without giving any further information about his conversion to Shakerism, Wilson concludes his testimony by asserting his "good sound faith" in the spiritual manifestations and his willingness to accept instruction from any "instrument" chosen by God. Thus, Wilson's testimony alternates individualized descriptions of personal experience with the stock phrases of Shaker testimony. He expresses his thankfulness for the Shaker life, "for my good hoom today" and "my priveledge in the blessed way of god." Frequently he resorts to the clichés of Shaker parlance: "I truly am lost for words to express my feelings." Later he asserts that he is neither "ashamed nor afraid" to testify, and he is willing to lay down his natural life for his beliefs. The frequency of such phrases in the testimonies of this period suggests not only that the authors may have been familiar with both oral and written testimonies of other Believers but also that appropriate expressions may have been suggested to the writers.

Shortly before his death in 1870, between 1867 and 1868, James Wilson wrote an autobiography. Whereas his testimony had been prompted by the request of the Elders, Wilson composed his autobiography out of a personal need to recapture and understand his past. In addition, like many Believers who wrote narratives during the last years of their lives, Wilson probably intended his story to be an example to younger members of the Society. While the goal of testimony was to record the writer's firm conviction on a specific issue, such as the character of Mother Ann or the sanctity of the spiritual manifestations, the purpose of autobiography varied according to the concerns of the individual author. Autobiog-

6. Patterson, *Shaker Spiritual*, 99–101, cites Shaker theological justification for the dance.

raphy gave more leeway for authors to display their particular temperaments and emphasize issues they deemed personally significant.

While Wilson's testimony and autobiography cover the same major events in the author's life, the autobiography gives a much more detailed account of Wilson's apprenticeship to the blacksmith, his religious search (including information about his visits to the Dunkers, the Moravians, the Swedenborgians, and the Rappites), and his marriage. In the testimony Wilson casually alludes to "my woman" without first telling the reader of his marriage. The autobiography, on the other hand, elaborates on Wilson's feelings about courtship and marriage. He implies that he began to feel that he sinned "against God's tabernacle, my own body" when he was about thirteen years old, confirming the connection between his feelings of defilement and the onset of puberty. Both sexual indulgence and overeating, Wilson implies, are sins of which he is guilty. He relates that he was several times engaged to be married, but each time he became extremely anxious and broke the engagement. Like Adam, Wilson tends to blame "wimmen" for his fall into sin, and he accuses them of "spoiling" him, using a term which can be equally applied to both women and food.

Wilson describes his conviction that people marry in order to gratify lust, and he expresses a common nineteenth-century belief that only procreation justifies the sexual relation and that sexual activity which only satisfies selfish desire is sinful. Wilson finally decides to marry "for love," but he tells of his almost immediate disappointment in marriage. He dwells at great length on his anguished and tormented condition and his feelings that he is polluted by sex. While the basic content of the autobiography is similar to that of the testimony, in the later narrative Wilson expands his material, provides more details about the facts of his experience, and greatly increases the emphasis on his feelings. In the autobiography Wilson's wife becomes a more fully developed character, and Wilson gives more information about their relationship. He portrays Margaret Wilson with great sympathy, saying they lived together peaceably for many years and that her conduct during his many illnesses was exemplary. Margaret, he relates, never troubled herself about religion, and out of loyalty to him she accompanied him to Lebanon and became his "sister in Christ."

75

In his autobiography Wilson describes his mental state before his conversion much more fully than he does in the testimony. Although the various religious groups Wilson joined before becoming a Shaker asserted that he was "saved" from sin, Wilson still feels himself terribly polluted, and he expresses his feelings of worthlessness in excremental images, writing that he was "fit neither for the land nor the dung hill." Before his conversion to Shakerism, Wilson had reached a point of total despair and felt there was no remedy for his condition. His experience strikingly parallels one type of conversion delineated by William James:

> When you find a man living on the ragged edge of his consciousness, pent in to his sin and want and incompleteness, and consequently inconsolable, and then simply tell him that all is well with him, that he must stop his worry, break with his discontent, and give up his anxiety, you seem to him to come with pure absurdities. The only positive consciousness he has tells him that all is not well, and the better way you offer sounds simply as if you proposed to him to assert cold-blooded falsehoods. . . .
>
> There are only two ways in which it is possible to get rid of anger, worry, fear, despair, or other undesirable affections. One is that an opposite affection should overpoweringly break over us, and the other is by getting so exhausted with the struggle that we have to stop — so we drop down, give up, and don't care any longer. . . . Now there is documentary proof that this state of temporary exhaustion not infrequently forms part of the conversion crisis.[7]

In this exhausted state of mind Wilson experiences his vision of the Shaker life. He records in great detail his physical and mental condition when the vision occurred: "I was much trobled in my mind on account of my shaterd state of mind as well as physical derangements. . . . My folks told me, that I layed about three weeks, & most part of the tim not able to turn myself on the bed, & all that I eate in that tim woudent much exceed one meal for a workin man, & slept scarsly any, as they said, & when I began to recover the vishon came to me." Wilson's state of physical exhaustion, mental despair, and almost total helplessness is similar to that described

7. William James, *The Varieties of Religious Experience: A Study in Human Nature* (London, N.Y.: Longmans, Green, 1952), 208.

by religious mystics before they experience illumination. In such phases, termed "desolations and nights," "the clarity of the mind's judgment seems to fade, and the life runs for a time, and perhaps for a long time, in a maze of doubt and uncertainty which to an observer and to a reader bear a strong superficial resemblance to the phases of psychological illness." Mystics also portray feeling a "sense of instability and moral impurity," a feeling which James Wilson's autobiography explores in depth.[8] Freed from the constraints of the testimonial form, Wilson in the autobiography examines the full spiritual and psychological context in which his vision occurred.

While Wilson's autobiography describes the context of his visionary illumination at much greater length than does the testimony, it adds only a few, relatively insignificant, events to the narrative. In fact, most of Wilson's additions are explanatory and discursive, and consequently they retard the narrative movement. In the autobiography Wilson not only observes where he was when the dream occurred but also gives information about who was with him and their reactions to his condition. At one point he awakens from his dream "in the most distrest situation I ever was in all thrue my life." The people asked "what was the mater with me I made such a mornful distresing nois whils sleeping, & they thot it best to awaken me so that I might git relest from the troble I was in." At this point Wilson inserts an incident that did not appear in the first vision. The devil comes to him, while awake, to tempt him to doubt the dream: "The enemy . . . whisperd to me & imprest it on my mind in the folowing maner, You have ben seking after religon all your life & never found that which satisfied you, & you are fixing to go to the Shakers, & you will be as bad of ther as you always have ben, for you never will find that ther which will satisfy you, for it isent to be found, you have ben hungry & seking somthing to satisfy your hungry felings all thrue your life & never found any thing that could satisfy you, & you wont find it among the Shakers." Wilson feels that if it had not been for God's protection he would have gone "clear out of [his] senses"; but he resigns himself to God's

---

8. David Knowles, *What is Mysticism?* (London: Burns and Oates, 1966), 68–69, quoted in Louis Jacobs, *Jewish Mystical Testimonies* (New York: Schocken, 1977), 8.

mercy, and once again falls asleep and continues his dream. In recounting his dream in the autobiography, Wilson adds rational explanations for the actions of the participants. He explains to his readers why he did not immediately go up to the people he saw: he was afraid of intruding. He explains why he had to draw nearer to them: his sight was dim and his hearing was dull. He explains why he did not speak to them: he was bashful. And he worries that at times he may have no rational explanation for details of the vision: he admits that he does not know how he could see that his own face was black and dirty. Wilson, as autobiographer, feels obligated to offer explanations for details that in the testimony he allowed to speak symbolically for themselves.

Wilson also expands the vision in the autobiography by adding information about his feelings. Not only does he see himself as black and dirty, but he describes feeling that he is not as good as the pure people whom he observes. He assures his readers that, even though he came to Believers in a state of impurity, he did want to be pure and good. Wilson also abstracts from concrete details. For example, he now remembers the people's countenances as having been "cheerful and pleasant." In the autobiography Wilson quotes the words of the Angel to him: "This roll contains the laws of this people you see, down in the low valley. And if you will obey these laws, you can gather into my fold, & become as one of those I saw down in the valley." Once again, Wilson is anxious to express his emotions: "No sooner said than cheerfully don, as all my powers & facultes instently bent & strongly inclind towards obediens to the marsefull & kind offer maid me by the blessed savour." Wilson now identifies the Angel of the vision in the testimony as the "Savior." In the testimony pictorial and symbolic descriptions predominate. In the autobiography the account of the vision tends to be both discursive and sentimental.

Wilson does add one major incident to the vision in the autobiography. When he seems to have lost all possibility of obtaining food, Wilson feels "detarment on doing . . . somthing for myself as ther was none that will lend a helping hand to me in so grate a tim of need as I thot it was with me, . . . & on looking around to see a clear pasedge out from this peopel, I soon discovered a high wall over which I coudnot see any pasedge whatever . . .

finally there was a lader presented to my vu, & at the very place where I had ben looking so much to find a way over the wall, . . . I vewd the lader putte clos having suspishons of its being strong enuf to carey me over the wall safe, that was so mensly high, & on taking a clos examinashon of the lader I discovered it to be entirely too short at the uper end as it dident reach near the top of the wall, & it was a poor consarn at the best, being totering & flimsley, about able to bear its own heft but not mine." In resisting this temptation, Wilson makes clear the theological meaning of the ladder. The low valley where Believers reside is the "valley of humiliation," which each Believer must experience before beginning the ascent toward spiritual perfection. Wilson must begin his spiritual travel at the bottom of the ladder. At the same time, he must accept "Zion's walls"; he must welcome the protection from sin which the community provides. He also implies that within the community he has been tempted to accept an easy, but ultimately false, path of spiritual travel. Several times in the vision Wilson states that, although most Believers appeared clean and white, there were some exceptions who, like him, were dirty and ragged. He suggests that, even at the time he is writing, some members of the Shaker community have not been purified of their carnal nature. Such passages reflect Wilson's displeasure with the changes that had taken place in the Society during the years after he composed his testimony. In the autobiography he is especially harsh on those who were attempting to justify expanded relations with "the world." Wilson, then, inserts the incident of the ladder into his later rendition in order to address a specific problem facing the community of Believers in the 1860s.

Wilson's choice of contrasting metaphors, the dance and the ladder, reveals his changing concerns and perceptions about the Shaker life. In the testimony the change from the carnal man to the spiritual man is instantaneous and complete, and the dance is a symbol of ecstatic and total union. "No sooner said than don, & I was taken right in amongst them." The vision concludes symbolically and joyously with Wilson's immersion in the spiritual world of Believers. In the autobiography, however, Wilson deletes this ending. The lack of such a symbol in the later vision suggests that Wilson, after almost forty years as a Shaker, is no longer concerned with the propriety of dancing in religious worship. It also suggests that Wilson's recollection of his vision is to some extent shaped by his theological understanding and his experiences in the intervening years. Wilson implies in his autobiography that the road to perfection is long, that change is gradual, that the first steps are humility and the acceptance of the law, and that the journey does not end at the moment of conversion. Each Shaker must continue his or her "travel" toward saintliness. By its very nature, testimony demanded a strong, unequivocal affirmation of the change that had taken place in the writer's life; thus, in it Wilson is able to focus exclusively on his spiritual state. Believers would deem details of difficulties, doubts, trials, and temptations that occurred after the acceptance of Shakerism as out of place in a testimony to the certitude of the author's faith.

Aesthetically, the vision in the testimony is more appealing than the one in the autobiography. The changes Wilson made when he composed his second narrative — the addition of rational explanations, the emphasis on his emotions, the increase in didacticism — reduce the intensity of the original vision and lessen its religious appeal. Rather than the miraculous change from a life of the flesh to one of purity which Wilson portrayed in the testimony, the autobiography describes a process of spiritual development that is often retarded by temptation and sin, and sickness of body and mind. While in the testimony Wilson more clearly delineates the moment of revelation, in the autobiography he more fully explores the complications of religious development.

In autobiography the Shaker author feels justified in continuing the story of his life beyond the initial conversion experience. Thus, after the vision is presented, Wilson goes on to relate his struggles against his carnal nature and his lifelong fight to overcome his obsessions with food and health. The need to recount his physical history, as well as his religious development, led Wilson in the later narrative to adopt a more realistic and less symbolic mode of presentation. The autobiography, then, may more accurately reflect the complexities of real life. Although symbolically altered by his vision, Wilson in reality finds that he must ascend the ladder of spiritual perfection gradually, that he must begin at the bottom, not at the top, and that his progress, although sure, will be slow.

Wilson's autobiography relates his slow recovery from his physical and mental breakdown. As soon as he is able, Wilson makes his way to Believers at Lebanon, but when he arrives he is still so ill that the Elders will not allow him to confess his sins until he becomes more "rational." In this distressed state, Wilson dreams that he is working in an "old building" containing machinery which flings him back and forth and which he thinks will surely kill him. Calvin Green appears and stops the machine, rescuing Wilson. Shaker readers would immediately recognize the "old house" that imprisons Wilson as the body with its needs and desires working at cross-purposes with the spirit. Wilson, the reader understands, needs to escape the "machinery" of his reproductive and alimentary systems, a machinery over which he has lost control. Soon after this dream the Elders allow Wilson to begin the confession of his sins, and Wilson discovers that this is his avenue of escape from the anguish of his former life.

Nevertheless, Wilson continues to be preoccupied with food. He is convinced that in order to cure his physical and spiritual disease he must starve his carnal nature. Despite the opposition of some Believers who fear he will kill himself, Wilson, with the support of Elder Richard Bushnell, covenants to live solely on bran bread and water for forty days, thus reenacting Christ's experience in the wilderness, where he resisted the temptations of the devil. Fasting for Wilson represents a purgation of the body which parallels the spiritual purification gained through confession. During the remainder of his life, Wilson gives up all animal food except for occasional milk and cheese, and he fasts periodically. In the late 1830s and early 1840s fasting became a common method of preparation for spiritual gifts among the Shakers. Wilson was proud to have received knowledge about the need for vegetarianism, abstinence from strong drink, and the benefits of fasting before other Believers received these directives. He devotes long sections of his autobiography to the eating habits considered proper for Shakers, and he strongly opposes eating meat, which he equates with "cravings for the flesh." Clearly James Wilson never completely overcame the obsessions of his early life. And yet from the Shakers Wilson acquired a religious vocabulary and a theological understanding that allowed him to interpret his personal problems within the wider context of the need for spiritual regeneration. Thus, compared to his testimony, Wilson's autobiography presents a fuller psychological portrait of a man caught in a destructively obsessive behavior he feels powerless to control. Through his Shaker experience Wilson regained command of his life and he spent many productive years among Believers.

While the reader might credit Wilson's expansion of his material and his increasing didacticism to the garrulousness of old age, the differences between his testimony and autobiography are more fully explained by the expectations of each literary category. For an inexperienced and unskilled writer like James Wilson the testimony offered a strictly prescribed form, a structure which could be superimposed upon personal experience. The autobiography, on the other hand, was a much looser genre with a much less clearly defined tradition. Thus, when a Believer of limited education turned his efforts to autobiography the result, as in Wilson's narrative, is not infrequently a rambling, repetitive narrative.

The autobiographical form offered a number of advantages to the writer who wished to relate a story more complex than would comfortably fit within the limited structure of the Shaker testimony. In the autobiography authors could concentrate on the external events of their lives, on experiences which might lack specific religious meaning. The larger format of the autobiographical narrative was also better suited to exploring the complexities of individual personality and the details of personal history. In the case of James Wilson, although the theme of the quest for food appears in embryonic form in the testimony, it is never fully developed. Wilson needed the larger framework of the autobiography to work out the theme as it affected all stages of his life. Autobiography, then, was a form in which an author like James Wilson was free to express fully his personal concerns and to impose an individual pattern on the course of his religious experience.

In adopting the more expansive autobiographical form, however, the Shaker author often sacrificed the intensity and aesthetic unity of the testimony. The shorter form of the testimony, the more rigorous selection of incident and event which it demanded, made the testimony an appropriate vehicle for the symbolic and metaphorical portrayal of experience. To be sure, Shaker autobiographers also frequently made use of these devices. Because of the length of most autobiographical narratives, however, as well as desire to include a wider range of personal experience, most autobiographers found it impossible and undesirable to connect every event and detail to an overarching symbol or metaphor. The Shaker autobiographies that most clearly imitate the form of the testimony tend to present their material metaphorically.

Although hundreds of Shakers wrote testimonies, relatively few of them also composed fully developed autobiographies. No extraordinary experience was necessary for a Believer to write a testimony; the author needed only a command of the current religious language of Believers and a knowledge of the specific issue concerning the Society at the time. Of course, the most interesting testimonies do more: they record spiritual manifestations or other particulars of individual experience. Some also describe dramatic conversion experiences. Those authors who do portray a striking change in their lives, as James Wilson did, are the ones who later compose autobiographies. Thus, while the age at which a person joined the Society matters little in the testimony, it has a great impact on autobiography. Almost all Shakers who wrote autobiographies joined Believers either as teenagers or adults. In either case, they were old enough to remember clearly their former lives in "the world" and to describe non-Shaker experience when writing their life story. Only a handful of those who joined Believers before the age of ten wrote autobiographies. Of these, Calvin Green, who was born among the Shakers, structured his narrative around his role as a Shaker leader rather than around a conversion experience. A few others who joined the Shakers when young—Giles B. Avery, John Lyon, and Isaac Newton Youngs—penned autobiographies. Although these men could not relate a dramatic story of how they came to be Shakers, each of them did record a crisis of faith, a period of doubt and uncertainty, which he had to overcome before being firmly established in his beliefs. Thus, while a conversion experience or spiritual crisis is not essential to Shaker testimony, such experiences are at the heart of the structure and meaning of Shaker autobiography.

CHAPTER V

THE FORM OF
SHAKER
AUTO-
BIOGRAPHY:
ALONZO HOLLISTER
AND HIS REDACTION
OF JAMES WILSON'S
"AUTOBIOGRAPHIC
MEMOIR"

It must be remembered that in autobiography structural needs cannot, as in poetry and fiction, freely generate appropriate materials. There is a *donnée* which preëxists the form, a body of subject matter that can be hewn down like a block of marble but not filled in at will like a blank piece of canvas.

Wayne Shumaker, *English Autobiography: Its Emergence, Materials, and Form*

Shakers printed and distributed few narratives for "the world," leaving most in manuscript form, and they rarely copied their own work. The task of copying often fell to a person with some experience and skill in writing who, because of special stature within the community, was permitted access to the records of the Society. In the latter half of the nineteenth century, Alonzo Giles Hollister (1830–1911) was the most prominent scribe among the Shakers. Inveterate scribbler, copyist of innumerable Shaker manuscripts, and prolific writer of Shaker tracts, Hollister not only copied the writings of his contemporaries but collected, preserved, and transcribed Shaker documents from the early years of the Society. He reproduced the biographies and autobiographies of many leaders of the Society, including Mother Lucy Wright, Calvin Green, William Leonard, Richard Pelham, and John Dunlavy. He compiled a collection of Shaker autobiographies, "Autobiographies of the Saints, or Stray Leaves from the Book of Life," and he gathered several collections of testimonies which had not appeared in published volumes. Hollister himself was a prolific writer of Shaker tracts.[1] An examination of Hollister's role as copyist and editor of Shaker manuscripts tells us much about what the Shakers themselves thought about the literature they created.

1. Hollister's interest in the preservation of Shaker materials also led him to assist John Patterson MacLean in his efforts to collect Shaker manuscripts and to preserve the memory of the Shaker experience, and he aided MacLean in the preparation of the first bibliography of Shaker imprints. See John Patterson MacLean, *A Bibliography of Shaker Literature . . .* (Columbus, Ohio: Fred J. Heer, 1905).

Hollister's account of his own life, recorded in his autobiography "Reminiscences, by a Soldier of the Cross,"[2] helps us to understand his role in shaping those Shaker narratives which he copied. Although Hollister's personal narrative provides no paradigm for Shaker autobiography, it does reveal his emotional involvement with Shaker literature and shows that Hollister's life was centered on his role as a scribe for Believers. His own autobiography is a carelessly written first draft which he never copied or rearranged into a coherent narrative. It shows little thematic or chronological order, and toward the end it breaks down into diary form with dated entries. Hollister gleaned much of the most interesting material — descriptions of Shaker meetings, dances, and messages, especially from Negro and Indian spirits — from written sources rather than personal experience. At one point Hollister notes that he records not only "what I saw and heard" but also what "I have learned since, by free access to the records, as for years I have had a quantity of the manuscripts in charge" (174).

Indeed, Hollister shows less interest in his own life than he does in the lives of other Believers, giving very little information about either his own family or his childhood. Hollister tells us that his father was a factory worker who brought his family of four sons to Believers.[3] After briefly mentioning his youthful pastimes, Hollister gives a very short and very typical description of his spiritual experience: "Between the ages of 18 & 20, I was given to know & understand, to my complete convincement, & soul's satisfaction. Then came the testing, three years of trial & service, at times, seemingly as keen as I could endure. And tho sometimes near fainting, my purpose remained single & my aim true, & God & His holy Messengers enabled me to go (or) pull thru" (176). Hollister, it seems, never experienced any period of great religious doubt or any decisive spiritual crisis. He was a faithful Believer who directed his energies and interests away from himself. Rather than receiving

2. Hollister, "Reminiscences . . . ," Lebanon, N.Y., [ca. 1908], MS, OClWHi, X:B-31. Page references in this chapter refer to this work, unless otherwise indicated.

3. Hollister gives some confusing details about what happened to each brother. Lorenzo John left the Society and died two years later; Orlando left at age 21 and died at Salt Lake City, Utah, at the age of 38; Henry, who was born in 1838, was with Believers at Shirley when Hollister was writing.

direct spiritual revelations, Hollister observed and recorded the spiritual manifestations experienced by others. His temperament was that of the scholar, not the religious visionary.

Hollister outlines the jobs he performed at Lebanon. As a youth he worked in the shoe shop and in the garden. From 1855 to 1856 he managed the farm. From 1860 until 1907, when he took over the medicinal business, he worked in the extract department. Through all these years Hollister was also writing. Working evenings, Sabbaths, and holidays, he produced an amazing quantity of material.

Hollister devotes several pages to a description of his efforts to finance Believer publications, despite the opposition of some members of the Society. Often he used his own money acquired through the sale of Shaker literature.[4] At other times he sold "old metal sacking" and "some roots of no value to us" (234). His brother Henry, after "he turned his face again Zionward," would occasionally send him five dollars, which went toward the printing of tracts. In an expression of gratitude, Hollister lists the names of those who aided his efforts to publish and disseminate Shaker materials.

Hollister's "Reminiscences" is most alive when discussing his literary activities. Excited over Rebecca Jackson's "Autobiography," he even includes long passages from this document in his own autobiography. Her writings, he feels, are the most inspired of those that have come to his attention.

Reading, writing, and copying Shaker literature were undoubtedly the chief pleasures of Hollister's life. He reports proudly that he has read all of the Believers' publications, some of them many times (230). And he is pleased to relate his role in supplying the Yale University Library with Shaker publications (241). Concerning these activities Hollister says: "The writing & publishing abroad of Shaker literature, & the correspondence resulting, brot a large amount of sunshine into my life, & compensated in some measure for my seclusion & loss of comradeship" (235).

As an orthodox Shaker and as a scholar, Hollister was also keenly aware of the changes and the decline that had taken place in the

---

4. Evidently Hollister was allowed to use personal funds during this period, another indication of the changes that were taking place among Believers during the later years of the 19th century.

Figure 4: Alonzo G. Hollister, Lebanon, New York, copied and preserved Shaker spiritual narratives.

Society during his lifetime. Under these circumstances he seems to have felt the need to preserve records of the Society as it had been in its prime. Hollister writes: "Tho intensely disgusted with the changes, deviating from the true order of Believers, my faith, & obligations to obedience, have never weakened nor changed. My reading, writing, printing, & circulating Shaker literature after, 1883, formed an element for me, in which I felt contented & part of the time supremely happy" (235–36).

In his "Reminiscences" Hollister strives for the objective tone of the historian, but occasionally he describes incidents which provide some insight into the needs and personality of the man. Once when returning from a visit to Alfred, Maine, Hollister absent-mindedly gets off the train one stop too soon, and consequently misses his connection. He is forced to walk several miles to the next train stop and arrives at the train station near Canterbury so late that no one has waited to meet him. Refusing to hire trans-portation and thus waste Believers' money to pay for his own mis-take, Hollister walks to the Society at Canterbury. Arriving at his destination late at night, he is tired and greatly humiliated. Hollis-ter relates that, even after the passage of many years, he still cannot recall this incident without great shame. "My mind was tense with excitement, fearing I would make some mistake. And sure enuf, I made one for which I have not got over smarting & do not expect to while life & memory lasts. Seasickness past away in the morn-ing. But this, after 18 years, gives me heartache. . . . It seemed to me that the spirits I had sucked into my brain while reading the newspaper, had hoisted me bodily out of the car & put me down by the track" (210–11).

To a man such as Hollister even the minor infraction of reading a newspaper might result in grave consequences. Missing the train becomes almost a symbolic warning of the dangers of too great an involvement with "the world." Hollister's extreme anxiety and his desire to be "home" take on a sense of urgency which, in an-other context, might be incomprehensible. Modern readers can understand that this incident, seemingly inconsequential, perhaps even pathetically amusing, reflects Hollister's fears of diverging from the "straight and narrow" path, his feelings of inadequacy in the outside world, and his sense that security could be had only among his Shaker brothers and sisters.

Hollister describes a second incident which reveals his uncomfortable relation with "the world." On a trip to New Haven, Connecticut, pranksters, who pretend to be interested in purchasing one of "Skeene's Biblical Charts" which Hollister is peddling, lure Hollister into a bar. Hollister is slow to realize that he is being made the butt of a joke. Only after the jokesters hide his Shaker hat and refuse to give it up does Hollister understand that they are making fun of him. Reflecting on this incident, Hollister recalls a dream of having been in "semi-darkness — looking out thru a window" and of seeing a pack of wolves "headed toward me, as if anxious to seize me" (243). Thus he assures himself that Divine Providence, having prepared him, allowed him to escape the band of ruffians in New Haven. Even for an educated Believer like Hollister, who had more frequent contact with the world than most Believers, life outside the protection of the Shaker community was full of snares and perils, and even a respected leader, a man of reserve and dignity, could be an innocent among wolves. These anecdotes reveal how keenly Hollister felt that contrast between life in "the world" and life as a Shaker.

In his "Reminiscences" Hollister portrays himself as a man committed to Shaker belief, comfortable and secure within the community of Believers, and fortunate enough to have discovered his true vocation even within the restricted options available among the Shakers. Not only was Hollister an orthodox Believer, whose autobiography indicates a strong desire to be accepted as a worthy representative of Shaker ideals, but he was also intimately familiar with Shaker doctrine as it had been expressed in Believers' writings. Hollister's understanding of Shaker literary and religious tradition, as demonstrated by his redaction of the autobiography of James Wilson, significantly influenced the textual and editorial decisions he made as he copied Shaker narratives.

After Wilson's death in January 1870, his papers fell into the hands of Alonzo Hollister. Hollister notes a "little curiosity,": having made several attempts at copying Wilson's manuscript, he was "so bothered . . . out of the sense of it" by the "queer spelling" that he "gave it up, for other more inviting employment."[5] Hollister continues:

> When I first began to copy, it soon brot such a sense of burden, that I laid it by, thinking perhaps I never would, unless I got out of other employ. Yet I felt unwilling to part with it untill I could find time to make some extracts that I thot would be interesting, as well as valuable testimony. The second time I found heart to take it up, it was with an interested feeling that continued to the end, & I feel richly paid for the labor & time spent in transcribing. Nor have I this last time, found it difficult to read. Moreover, I generally have felt unusual clarity of mind, in writing most of the additions inclosed in brackets. (167)

Hollister here reveals two important aspects of his role as a Shaker copyist. First, Hollister implies that he did not feel obligated to reproduce all of Wilson's writings, but that he felt it his job to select the most "interesting, as well as valuable testimony." Moreover, Hollister felt free to make additions to the original text, although he did indicate through the use of brackets which passages he had contributed to the autobiography.

A comparison of Wilson's holograph and Hollister's copy reveals that Hollister added numerous comments of his own, but brackets clearly indicate such additions.[6] Hollister provides explanatory material, clarifies proper religious belief and practice, and attempts

5. James Wilson, "Autobiographic Memoir . . . ," Lebanon, N.Y., 1868, MS, OClWHi, VI:B-34, 167. Hereafter all page references within the text refer to this work.

6. The holograph of Wilson's "Autobiographic Memoir" is preserved in the Library of Congress Shaker Collection in MS 149. The available evidence confirms that Hollister was working from this group of papers when he transcribed Wilson's autobiography. Hollister's own description of Wilson's manuscript corresponds to that now in the Library of Congress: "The manuscript of the author from which this memoir was copied, with some verbal corrections, was in several fragments, marked or numbered, & the last was marked as above for continuation, & whether it was ever finished, or whether a portion of it was lost in passing thro so many hands, before it lodged in mine, I am not able to say" (167). Moreover, the Library of Congress manuscript contains a number of corrections penciled in above passages that have been crossed out. The corrections do not seem to be in Wilson's hand, and they correspond to changes which Hollister has made in his copy of the autobiography. There seems little doubt, then, that the Library of Congress manuscript is the holograph of Wilson's "Autobiographic Memoir" which Hollister transcribed. For the sake of convenience and clarity, in the following discussion the Library of Congress MS 149 will be referred to as the holograph, and any reference to the "Autobiographic Memoir" (the title having been supplied by Hollister) will refer to Hollister's copy.

to place Wilson's frequent criticism of the state of the Society into a wider context. His most lengthy addition to Wilson's "Memoir" is a separate essay on original sin which bears minimal relation to Wilson's narrative. Such topics are obviously of more interest to Hollister than to Wilson, who was theologically unsophisticated and limited in his understanding of Shaker doctrine. Hollister's contributions to Wilson's narrative clearly reveal that Hollister viewed himself as a Shaker historian and a defender of orthodoxy. In this role, he never hesitated to intrude on Wilson's narrative in order the better to preserve those ideals espoused by Believers; he was, however, careful to keep his intrusions separate from Wilson's text.

Hollister also realized that, in its original condition, Wilson's miscellaneous arrangement of papers, written in phonetic spelling with numerous grammatical errors, would have gone unread even by the most curious and scholarly of Believers. Hollister therefore felt it his task to correct Wilson's manuscript and put it into readable form so that it might serve as "valuable testimony" to the Shaker life. Hollister corrected spelling and grammar, modified vocabulary and eliminated colloquialisms, added punctuation, and broke the narrative into sentences and paragraphs. He also condensed passages. Despite these changes, Hollister's faithfulness to the meaning of Wilson's original text is impressive. Wilson's repetitive and digressive style might have tempted a less conscientious editor to indulge in major rewriting of the narrative.

The additions to Wilson's narrative and the modifications of his language disclose Hollister's understanding of the basic structure of Shaker narrative. Many of the changes that he makes indicate a deep concern with establishing the time frame, the before-and-after structure, within which Wilson relates his personal experience. For example, in describing his disillusionment with the Valley Forge community, Wilson says: "My experience had taught me . . . that mankind were too selfish to live together [in their natural state] & support a joint interest" (97). Hollister's bracketed addition points out that Wilson modified this opinion after becoming a Believer. Hollister compels readers to note that a community of joint interest is possible, but only when based on the proper spiritual, rather than natural, foundation. At the same time, Hollister suggests that Wilson's opinions have changed as a result of his Shaker experience, that his understanding as a Shaker is not the same as his understanding when he was in "the world." Throughout Wilson's narrative Hollister attempts to clarify the point of view, clearly distinguishing between the perspective of the natural man (Wilson before joining Believers) and the spiritual man (Wilson after becoming a member of the Lebanon community). On another occasion, Wilson says, "I could not find [untill the Shakers came] any people that I thot were" God's people (139). Again Hollister's bracketed addition insists upon a distinction between past and present experience. Hollister is often impatient with a contemporaneous rendering of experience, always fearful that the reader might fail to realize that such views held in the past were incorrect. Through his own personal experience as a Believer, as detailed in his "Reminiscences," and through his familiarity with the traditions of Shaker narrative, Hollister realized that the contrast between life in "the world" and life as a Shaker was at the heart of any Shaker testimony or autobiography. Hollister also seems to have grasped intuitively that the relationship between these opposing experiences could be presented most effectively through metaphor and accounts of spiritual experiences.

Thus, as he read the autobiography of James Wilson, Alonzo Hollister understood that, although it contained the raw materials for a religious testimony to the superiority of the Shaker life, Wilson's rambling, repetitious narrative obscured its essential spiritual message. Therefore, Hollister felt justified in rearranging the material found in Wilson's manuscripts in order to highlight the relationship between the physical and spiritual experience of James Wilson. Hollister thus became an interpreter of Wilson's language, helping the reader to understand the religious significance of the pattern inherent in Wilson's life. In other words, Hollister saw, as Wilson did not, that effective Shaker autobiography needs a metaphorical structure.

Hollister must have soon discovered that the quest for food was a dominant theme in Wilson's life and writings. The need for spiritual nourishment was a congenial metaphor to express Believers' understanding of man's condition, and the metaphor appears in a number of songs, testimonies, and even poems. The following song, for example, which originated at Alfred, Maine, in 1837 was widely known by Believers:

> I hunger and thirst, I hunger and thirst after true
>   righteousness.
> In what I've obtained, in what I've obtained, my soul
>   cannot rest.
> An ocean I see, without bottom or shore.
> O feed me—I'm hungry; enrich me—I'm poor.
> I will cry unto God—I never will cease
> Till my soul's filled with love, perfect love and sweet
>   peace.[7]

When he began copying Wilson's narrative, Hollister was working with a group of autobiographical papers, not with a single, unified manuscript. Since Wilson's holograph appears to have had two separate beginnings, Hollister chose to begin his copy of the "Memoir" with Wilson's account of his near starvation when he was apprenticed to the blacksmith. Both Wilson and Hollister agree that this experience was seminal and that it greatly influenced the course of Wilson's life, but in Wilson's holograph this incident appears in the middle of the narrative. By placing it at the beginning of Wilson's autobiography, Hollister sets up the comparison between physical and spiritual nourishment which creates a metaphorical structure for the "Autobiographic Memoir." Through this structure the reader can better grasp the range of meaning implied in Wilson's quest and the complex relationship between the physical and spiritual life of the author.

Even though Wilson's obsession with natural rather than spiritual food often exasperates the reader, the theme of the quest for nourishment gives Wilson's autobiography a rudimentary structure, which was latent in the original manuscript but which is revealed fully only in Hollister's redaction. Because Wilson's search for the proper food is concretely rooted in his individual past, the

---

7. Daniel W. Patterson, Notes, *Early Shaker Spirituals Sung by Sister Mildred Barker with other members of the United Society of Shakers, Sabbathday Lake, Maine,* Rounder Records 0078, p. 8. Edward and Faith Andrews in *Fruits of the Shaker Tree of Life* (Stockbridge, Mass.: Berkshire Traveller Press, 1975), 75–76, print a poem which in theme and imagery is similar to Wilson's vision of the Hidden Manna.

metaphor succeeds in holding together an otherwise rambling narrative and linking Wilson's life before becoming a Believer with his life as a Shaker. Neither Wilson nor Hollister has imposed an external terminology on the author's experience. Rather, from a wide variety of religious symbols current among Believers, Wilson has chosen those which truly express his personal needs, and Hollister, by his arrangement of Wilson's materials, has emphasized this choice. Indeed, Hollister was able to apply the metaphor of nourishment as a structural device in Wilson's narrative precisely because the image did not emerge from the recesses of the individual imagination but from Shaker culture. Hollister certainly understood the symbolic import of Wilson's hunger, and in his redaction of Wilson's manuscripts he hoped to make this meaning clear to the readers of the "Autobiographic Memoir."

Another modification by Hollister tightened the structure of Wilson's original. In the original manuscript Wilson sandwiches the conversion vision (discussed in detail in the preceding chapter) between another vision about a departed Believer and a description of his experiences among the Methodists. Rather than occupying a central position in the narrative, the vision comes toward the end of the manuscript. In such a position it loses much of its impact. Hollister places the conversion vision at the center of the narrative, thus allowing it to function as a turning point in the autobiography, the climax of Wilson's search for the true people of God.

By his crucial centering of the conversion vision, Hollister attempts to create a balanced temporal structure for Wilson's narrative. He divides Wilson's life into the years before he became a Believer, years full of errors, misconceptions, illness, and mental confusion, and the ones after uniting with the Shakers, when Wilson found himself on the road to mental, physical, and spiritual wholeness. Hollister, it seems, was less concerned with actual chronological sequence than he was with shaping Wilson's narrative so that it reflected theological concepts and established conventions of Shaker narrative. With the conversion vision placed at the center of the narrative, Wilson's autobiography moves downward, until he reaches the depths of illness and despair. Only when Wilson has reached the "valley of humiliation" and has experienced "mortification" can his spiritual progress begin. In this condition Wilson is ready to receive instruction and encouragement from divine sources. After he receives the vision, Wilson begins his "travel" upward, toward hope, physical renewal, and spiritual reward. In the section following the conversion vision, Wilson, even in Hollister's copy, often returns to incidents in his earlier life, but the reader understands these events in terms of his former life rather than his life as a Shaker.

Near the end of his copy of the "Autobiographic Memoir" Hollister records a vision of "Spiritual Bread—or the Hidden Manna." (In the text below, the bracketed words were written above the lines of the narrative and may indicate corrections Hollister made as he reread his copy.)

In the forepart of the summer, 1868, it appeared to me that I was taken out of this shattered house I have lived in so many years, & I found myself in a large & beautiful room in the spirit world. How large I cannot tell, for I only saw one side, or end of it, where was a large & beautiful door. And there was a very large assembly of beautiful looking people, & all, as far as eye [I] could see, were dressed in white. And I did not know, neither do I now, as there was either male or female there, for they all appeared to be one. I thot that just previous to my arrival, they had been singing & dancing, & had taken seats upon what seems to me now were long benches. They all appeared to be looking at me & their heavenly countenances were pleasing & comforting to me, so that I took many good views of them—for their familiarity [easy gracefulness] took away much of my diffidence, & I felt in a great measure at home with them altho they seemed not to have much to say to me, nor I to them.

I have been led to think since, that my gift was not with them in particular, but with Father James—which was to encourage & strengthen me to bear my afflictions of body & mind, which I labor under, & expect will continue while I remain in this feeble & delapidated tenement of clay. . . .

It appeared that I got hold of a long piece of good bread, similar to our coarse wheat bread. . . . It was baked in loaves about three inches thick & cut into long, square strips. As I held a large piece in my left hand while eating, it appeared to be crumbling & falling to pieces in my hand. As my hand covered not more than half of it, I ate fast, to diminish its size, & prevent the crumbs from falling upon the beautiful floor. But I was soon much surprised, to find that notwithstanding the length of time I had been eating, there was no diminution, as it retained the same size & appearance neither could I see any crumbs fall on the floor, for it all hung together loose as it was. The taste was delicious — sweeter & more pleasant than our bread, which I thot was good enough for anybody. Standing on a table close by me, was a large bucket full of the same kind of bread. Neither did I see but one kind of bread, which I have thot since the vision, was a plain simple testimony against the many kinds of bread we have at every meal we eat, & also of the many varieties of food set before us at one time. It is a great temptation to eat too much. . . .

When about in the height of my labors, the door I have mentioned, opened, & in came Father James. . . . As soon as he entered the room he raised both hands & came towards me with open arms. I knew what it meant, & I raised my arms in the same manner & advanced to meet him. When we embraced, both his arms were above mine, & I struggled to get my left arm above his, that I might have a better chance, & he gave way a little to assist me, & when we got arranged right, as I thot, we had a real hugging match. It was truly comforting to me to be in Father's company, & be embraced as I was by that heaven born soul. I thot he did not appear to me as he now is but as he was when living in this world, & since the vision, I have thot that was the most suitable way for him to meet me in my present situation.

The earthly part was left behind, so that I saw with my spiritual eyes when I appeared in the spiritual world. (164–66)

The vision of The Hidden Manna symbolically reveals the spiritual progress which James Wilson made after his union with the Society of Believers. This vision also appears in Wilson's holograph, but Wilson places it in the middle of the manuscript. Wilson thus fails to focus the reader's attention on the import of the vision. Without having read Wilson's description of his conversion, the reader is at a loss to understand the significance of his vision of spiritual bread. In Hollister's copy, however, it is clear that the concluding vision answers the questions which had been posed by the devil in the conversion vision, questions which had haunted James Wilson in the years before he joined the Shakers. The devil had suggested to him: "You have been seeking after religion all your life,

& never have found that which satisfied you. And you are fixing to go to the Shakers, & you will be as bad off there as you always have been; you will never find that there which will satisfy you, for it is not to be found. You have been hungry, & seeking something to satisfy your hungry feelings, all thro your life, & never found it — & you wont find it among the Shakers for it is not there."

Through the vision of the Hidden Manna Wilson asserts that he has found the nourishment that will satisfy him, and that has satisfied him for many years. His fears of starvation have been put behind him. No matter how much or how greedily he eats of the spiritual bread it does not diminish. Wilson has found his Holy Grail, his horn of plenty.[8] No longer does he feel himself to be a stranger and wanderer in this world as he did before coming to Lebanon. Now he feels "at home" among the beautiful people. When Father James hugs Wilson, the readers of the "Memoir" know that James Wilson has been accepted as worthy to be "owned" by the first witnesses who are now in the spirit world.[9]

Hollister's copy of Wilson's autobiography ends with an anecdote about Believers who were laboring to build a dwelling house on a quagmire during the early days of the Society. Suggesting the analogies between the physical body (house) and the spiritual house and between physical food and spiritual food, which have recurred throughout Wilson's narrative, the anecdote is a fitting conclusion to the memoir of a faithful Believer nearing the end of his earthly pilgrimage.

> And some of the Brethren being hard at work in a time when provisions were scarce, when four, five, & sometimes six, if I mistake not, had often no more for their temporal support than would suffice one or two hard working men. Yet they kneeled with hearts

8. Roger Sherman Loomis, *The Development of Arthurian Romance* (New York: Norton, 1963), discusses these themes in medieval romance. Spiritual nourishment in much of Christian literature was associated with the Eucharist, the partaking of the body and blood of Christ. Chastity was one of the chief qualities required in order to seek the Holy Grail (113). Wilson restates themes found in earlier religious literature but adapts them to his personal concerns and to Shaker beliefs.

9. David R. Lamson, *Two Years' Experience Among the Shakers* . . . (1848; rpt. New York: AMS Press, 1971), 81, describes the "hugging gift": "The elder says, 'I feel as though I wanted a little gift of hugging.' The brethren then gather up into one clump, and the sisters into another, and have a general embrace."

devoted to God, & then partook of their scanty fare, & eat it all up, leaving no crumbs, & they felt satisfied therewith & did not desire any more. And their scanty morsel held out, & with the blessing of God, afforded them sufficient strength to perform this service. This being often repeated, they became established in the living faith of God, Christ, & Mother, & pressed forward against wind & tide. They took for their pilot, Mother Ann, who always conducted them to a safe harbor of peace & comfort. And all who will volunteer in her service will be as sure to fare, the same, as the Sun is to rise in the morning. So then let us in obedience bless Mother & she will bless us. (166–67)

In Hollister's copy of Wilson's "Memoir," the concluding anecdote becomes a parable which sums up the individual experience of James Wilson. Even though the texts of Wilson's original and Hollister's copy are almost identical word for word, Hollister's re-arrangement of the material has enhanced the meaning for the reader. Hollister has shown that Wilson's narrative contains a beginning, a middle, and an end. The initial situation is sexual defilement and lack of food; the middle describes a quest for nourishment and sexual purity which culminates in the conversion vision; and the ending is the vision of spiritual bread and the parable, which relate the individual experience of a single Believer, James Wilson, to the experience of the Shaker community. The rewards promised by Mother Ann and the early witnesses have been fulfilled in Wilson's life, and, by implication, are available to those who follow him.

Even in Hollister's version, the "Autobiographic Memoir" of James Wilson cannot be considered a masterpiece of Shaker narrative. Nonetheless, Hollister's arrangement of the narrative does reveal a thematic coherence not obvious in the original text. Emphasizing the key experiences in Wilson's life that are most relevant to understanding his spiritual travel, Hollister, without doing violence to Wilson's meaning, creates a structure for a narrative which would otherwise have been confusing and uninteresting. Hollister's copy is not only artistically superior to the original, but it also provides a better portrait of James Wilson and a clearer exposition of his testimony.

Both his own writings and his acknowledged additions to Wilson's "Memoir" confirm that Hollister was deeply concerned with the explication of theological issues and felt bound to defend and clarify the orthodox position. Hollister strongly believed that Shaker literature, including autobiographical narratives, should serve a didactic purpose by clarifying proper belief and providing examples of proper behavior. Therefore, it is not surprising to find Hollister intruding into the text he was copying by acknowledged expansions of content or unacknowledged rearrangement of incidents. When he felt that the original author had neglected an opportunity to make a theological point about an incident recorded in the narrative, Hollister was tempted to add homiletical commentaries. When there was the possibility that an author might misrepresent the Shaker perspective, Hollister did not hesitate to bracket his own clarifications. Perhaps most significantly, when he saw an opportunity to illustrate the efficacy of Shaker belief by tying real-life events to the spiritual development of the autobiographer, Hollister reorganized incidents and experiences in the narratives he transcribed. In Wilson's case, by simply relocating the visions Hollister was able to demonstrate that one who undertakes spiritual travel must first deny the self, that is, undergo mortification and humiliation in the "low valley," before the process leading to perfection could begin. Deeply grounded in Shaker theology and intimately familiar with the conventions of earlier Shaker narratives, Alonzo Hollister reveals in his restructuring of James Wilson's "Autobiographic Memoir" a presupposition shared by many Shaker writers, copyists, and readers: that Shaker narrative, in its structure as well as in its content, should reflect the theology of Believers in Christ's Second Appearing.

PART TWO

EXAMPLES OF
SHAKER
AUTOBIOGRAPHY

"Enfield Village," in J. W. Barber, *Connecticut Historical Collections.*
(New Haven: Durrie and Peck and Barber, 1838.)

CHAPTER VI

METAPHORS
OF TRAVEL:
THE SPIRITUAL
JOURNEYS OF
JANE BLANCHARD
AND
WILLIAM LEONARD

This book will make a traveller of thee,
If by its counsel thou wilt ruled be;
It will direct thee to the Holy Land,
If thou wilt its directions understand.

Pilgrim's Progress

Whether recounting the stories of immigration, the settling of the frontier, the escape from slavery, or the return to the old country, Americans often made the journey a central episode in their first-person narratives.[1] Shakers were as drawn as other Americans to the metaphor of travel, but they gave it a distinctive meaning. In Shaker parlance, the term *travel* frequently retains its original meaning of "travail" and signifies both the physical and mental labors required to bring forth spiritual gifts.[2] In its expanded meaning, *travel,* or *travail,* connotes a journey on which the soul moves toward perfection. For many Shakers such travel begins with the confession of sins and the acceptance of the "gospel way." Often an autobiographer notes at a spiritual turning point that "from this time I date the beginning of my gospel travel." Shakers believe that such spiritual travel must continue throughout their lives. "Of major concern in the day-to-day Shaker exhortations to holiness in life's journey are the conditions of one's travel: the difficulties of the way or path to be traversed; the transformation of the difficult path into one more easily met; the weight of the burdens

1. Albert E. Stone, "The Sea and the Self: Travel as Experience and Metaphor in Early American Autobiography," *Genre* 7 (1974):279–306, explores the metaphorical use of the sea voyage in three American autobiographies. Sidonie Smith, *Where I'm Bound. Patterns of Slavery and Freedom in Black American Autobiography,* Contributions in American Studies, No. 16 (Westport, Conn.: Greenwood, 1974), describes the use of the journey in slave narratives and in black autobiographies.

2. Early 19th-century Quaker writings such as the *Journal of the Life and Religious Labours of Elias Hicks* (New York: I. T. Hopper, 1832; rpt. New York: Arno, 1969) also preserve a similar use of "travail."

borne by the traveler; those things which assist the traveler in his path."[3]

Many Shaker autobiographies, however, describe a more familiar sort of travel, an actual journey which occurs as the writer searches for the true people of God. Jane Knight recounts her family's many moves in a search for safety and security during and after the War of 1812; Mary Antoinette Doolittle describes her journey over a mountain to see her grandmother and her visit with the Shakers along the way; Richard Pelham undertakes a journey because he is restless and dissatisfied with his life, and in retrospect he realizes that Divine Providence was leading him to the Shakers at Union Village, Ohio; Proctor Sampson makes a connection between his voyages as a sailor and his religious quest; and John Rankin, finding his religious life in North Carolina spiritually sterile, travels to Kentucky where he participates in the great turn-of-the-century frontier revivals.[4] In each case, the journey that ends in finding the Society of Believers is a central episode in the autobiography. In this context the journey is not so much a spiritual quest for internal perfection as it is an external search on which the seeker must rightly interpret the signs and warnings of Divine Providence. Yet in the best of the Shaker narratives such concrete journeys often assume metaphorical, and, in certain instances, almost allegorical overtones. Two such autobiographies are those of Jane Blanchard and William Leonard. Choosing from the wide variety of metaphors and images available to the Shaker, these two authors selected the journey, as a metaphor for a spiritual pilgrimage, to express the pattern of their lives.

As the focal point of their narratives, the journey furnishes both a spatial and a temporal framework for their autobiographies. For both Blanchard and Leonard "vision and memory remain the es-

---

3. Virginia Weiss, "A Travel into Warfare: A Consideration of the Figures of the Heavenly Journey and the Internal Combat with Evil in the Shaker Experience," *Shaker Quarterly* II (Summer 1971):52.

4. Jane D. Knight, *Brief Narrative* . . . ; Mary Antoinette Doolittle, *Autobiography* . . . (Mt. Lebanon, N.Y.: The United Society, 1880); Richard Pelham, "Sketch of the Life . . . ," North Union, Ohio, 1862, MS, OClWHi, VI:B-45-48; Proctor Sampson, [untitled autobiography], Lebanon, N.Y., 1853, MS, OClWHi, VI:B-17; John Rankin, "Autobiography."

sential controls, time and space the central problems, reduction and expansion the desired goals."[5] Thus these two authors emphasize the time spent on their journeys and severely condense the description of other experiences. Leonard, for example, carefully notes the exact moment when he resumes each stage of his extended journey to Believers, often telling not only the month, day, and hour when his travel began but also describing the position of the sun in the sky and the weather. The months which often pass between legs of his journey, however, he vaguely summarizes. At one point he simply notes, "After a year had passed, I left." Leonard likewise devotes many pages to describing the wild and beautiful landscape through which he passes on his travels, but he writes little or nothing about the towns and settlements in which he resides for many months along the way. By strictly controlling temporal and spatial references, Leonard never allows the focus of the narrative to shift away from the journey. Blanchard constricts her autobiography even more, for she concentrates on the description of three richly meaningful days in her life: her vision at age sixteen which foretells her future quest, her actual journey to Believers, and her final visit to her natural relations. The discipline imposed by strict attention to the unities of time and place augments the aesthetic and religious impact of Blanchard's narrative.

Contrary to an assumption that successful autobiographies are written only by authors who themselves do not fully know beforehand the conclusion of their narratives, Blanchard and Leonard demonstrate that impressive spiritual autobiographies may indeed be written by men and women who at all times retain a firm sense of how their life histories will end.[6] Although the end itself to a great extent predetermines the presentation of past experience, in the case of Blanchard and Leonard the lack of conflict and tension within the narrative does not act as a limitation. Particularly in

---

5. William Howarth, "Some Principles of Autobiography," *New Literary History* 5 (1974): 364.

6. Roy Pascal, *Design and Truth in Autobiography* (Cambridge: Harvard Univ. Press, 1960), 181–82, asserts that "good autobiography is always more than a mere exposition to the public of something already known"; he considers works that convey no sense of discovery to be failures.

the case of Blanchard, the very strong sense of an ending allows her to shape her life almost as a well-wrought artifact, a beautiful memento of the perfect Shaker life. For both authors the journey comprises the central episode of their narratives and becomes emblematic of their entire life.

> Thus I continued struggling along, up hill & down, thro
> sloughs & mudholes, coming in contact with stumps & stones
> & rocks of offense — thro dark night & cloudy days — passing
> once in a while over a short piece of good road — then over
> waters of affliction, the tempest raging & angry billows roar-
> ing & beating against my little boat.
>
> ISAAC NEWTON YOUNGS, [UNTITLED AUTOBIOGRAPHY]

IN "A SKETCH OF HER EXPERIENCE," Jane Blanchard freezes two important moments in her life, a vision and a journey, which express symbolically the whole essence of her existence.[7] Blanchard uses other events in her autobiography merely as connectives either to frame or bridge these epiphanies. So uninterested is Blanchard in describing any other moments in her life that she leaves readers without any evidence, within the sketch or elsewhere, of the context in which the autobiography was composed; there is no information as to its date, the status of the author, or her motivation for writing.[8] Because of this singular lack of attention to details, Blanchard's narrative rises above many others as a paradigm of the Shaker experience and invites readers to partake imaginatively of that experience.

Jane Blanchard's "Sketch" opens with a brief description of her childhood. Like many other Shakers in their autobiographies and testimonies, she describes her parents as good people who taught her to be kind, to be truthful, to pray, and to attend religious meet-

7. Jane E.S. Blanchard [1824-?], "A Sketch of Her Experience Previous to 1868" New Enfield, N.H., n.d., copy made by Alonzo G. Hollister 25 July 1875. Blanchard's "Sketch" is included by Hollister in his "Autobiography of the Saints or Stray Leaves from the Book of Life," 2:307-17, MS, OClWHi, VI:B-37. Hollister likely added the quotation that precedes Blanchard's narrative: "And he shall send his Angells, & shall gather his Elect from the four winds." Unless otherwise indicated all page references within the text refer to this work.

8. Although Blanchard's name is included in the Western Reserve Historical Society membership file, it notes only the date and place of her birth, 12 March 1824, Norwich, Windsor Co., N.Y., and the fact that she went to the Church Family in 1886.

ings. Still, Blanchard feels she is unable to overcome a sinful nature. At sixteen she experiences great fears of hell and death. In
prayer she asks, "Is there any way out of sin?" (307). She receives
the answer in a vision:

> After I laid my head on my pillow & closed my eyes, I saw some-
> thing in the form of a head. It whispered in a low voice "Are you
> willing that I should lay my head by the side of yours?" I paused
> a moment and then answered If you are willing to you may.
>
> It remained silent for a few minutes, & then whispered, "Will
> you go with me? . . . You can if you try. Don't you want to go." I
> said I would go. It started & I followed. It was as white as snow,
> & went thro the air like a feather. We went over mountains, hills,
> & woods untill at length, we came to a large building, & entered
> into a small hall & then into a small room, where there did not
> seem to be much. We then commenced going upstairs, & after as-
> cending four flights, we entered a large room, where the floor was
> as white as snow. There were benches on the sides of the room.
> I seated myself & viewed the room all over. It was white & beautiful,
> & a chandelier hung in the center. Soon a large company of persons
> entered, who seemed all of a height. A part of them stood in the
> center of the room & sung powerfully, while a larger part of them
> flew around the room so swift that I could hardly see them. I never
> saw anything so heavenly before. I felt as tho I was in heaven in
> reality. They were clothed in white from head to foot, & were all
> of a height—They flew around the room like spirits, & turned like
> tops. Some spoke very lengthy, firm & solemn.
>
> While I was in deep thot to know what I was there for, this spirit
> or head, as it appeared to me, came & asked if I would like to be
> there. I replied that I would, but could not be like those who were
> there. It told me I could if I wanted to, but I would have to go back
> & get ready, for my time had not come. O what a feeling came
> over me at the thots of going back. I burst into tears & felt as tho
> my heart would break.
>
> It started & I followed, over brush & fence, mud & mire, untill
> I reached my father's house. When I awoke, I was on my bed in
> my own room. . . . When I was alone, I meditated & cried to God,
> that if there was any place on earth like that which I had seen, that
> I might live to see it. (307-9)

As in the visions of many Believers, a spiritual guide leads the
seeker to view the heavenly life that awaits the faithful. For Shakers

this future blissful state is not only possible after death but is attainable in this world as the millennium unfolds among God's true people. While visions in Shaker autobiographies often encapsulate the experiences of the authors, in Blanchard's case the vision predicts a future in which she must persevere on the "thorny path" in order to reach the community of the blessed. At the same time, the vision encourages her to pray for Divine Providence to aid her travel and assures her of the ultimate rewards of faithfulness.

Two years after her vision, in 1843, while recovering from a serious illness, Blanchard visits the family of George Adams who had once lived with the Shakers. Having returned from a journey, Adams "talked about the Shakers, a subject quite new to me, for I had never heard of such a people before. . . . He said that when he was a boy he lived with John Lyon, & as he was doing something one day, while playing with the boys, that John did not approve of, he caught him by the arm and shook him as a dog would a woodchuck. I told him I supposed he deserved it. He said he did, & more than that, for he was so wild that he could not stay" (310). Blanchard is extremely interested in Adams's account of these people. When he reveals that the Shakers "are a strange people; they do not believe in a married life," Jane immediately exclaims, "Well! that is just the life I want to live & I mean to go there & see them. Said he O silly woman! You would not be willing to live as the Shakers do" (311). But Jane Blanchard silently vows that she will visit the Shakers and decide for herself whether to adopt their manner of life.

On the following day, she leaves Adams's house and starts for home with a woman companion, but something tells her that if she goes home now she will never go to the Shakers. As she begins her homeward trek, Jane Blanchard is suddenly "stopped in the road." The motif is familiar in Shaker narratives and ultimately derives from the biblical account of Paul's conversion.[9] "All the time we were talking, something kept whispering in my ear Do go to the Shakers; you will be sorry if you dont. I tried still harder to

9. The motif of being stopped in the road appears in some early Shaker narratives as well, of course, as in the New Testament's account of Paul's conversion. The sister of Thomas Brown in his *An Account of the People Called Shakers . . .* (1812; rpt. New York: AMS, 1972) was stopped in the road, as were Abijah Worster, Issachar Bates, and Eunice Bathrick.

believe it was foolish for me to think of such a thing. As I walked along I was suddenly stopped as tho some one held me by the arm. The woman took hold of me & asked me if I was faint. I could not speak—I felt cold and the water dropped off my face. I felt as tho the spirits had got me fast, saying 'Go to the Shakers & we will help you on your way'" (311).

Jane Blanchard returns to George Adams's house, and the next morning, 3 May 1843, she begins her journey to join Believers. This journey is both physical and spiritual and will test Blanchard's determination and her fitness for future "travel in the gospel." Walking over muddy and lonely roads, Jane Blanchard begins her pilgrimage. She does not know the way to Enfield, New Hampshire, and must trust in Providence to guide her. When she asks a man for directions, he tries to persuade her to return home, saying that the Shakers "are the meanest people on the earth—they drown their children—tie them to a tree & whip them" (312). Although he finally tells her which road leads to Enfield, Blanchard is afraid that she has been intentionally misdirected. Within two miles, however, she meets another traveler, who assures her that she is on the right path.

The difficulties of her journey have only begun. The spring rains have washed away a bridge. Forced to retrace her steps, she finds herself actually heading toward her home rather than toward the Shakers. Discouraged, she begins to weep and wonders whether Providence is directing her toward her home rather than toward Enfield:

> I began to think it was a judgment upon me, because my parents did not know where I was. . . . I started for home, but soon found I could not walk. My whole body was so weak I could hardly stand. What can this mean? Thot I. Am I being punished for my sins? Nay, this was but a trial of my faith. . . . I prayed earnestly to know which way to go. Soon I heard a voice saying "Go to the Shakers, then you can walk; I will help you." I came to myself a little & started on, & found I could walk with a great deal of strength. But as there had been a freshet, the roads were muddy—Trees were blown down, or torn up by the roots—some lay across the road—some I had to crawl under & some over. I had to walk on logs, over brush—& on walls & fences in order to get along the best I could. (313)

Just as in her vision, Jane Blanchard travels over "brush & fence, mud & mire" (309). Beautifully described by Blanchard, such metaphors are not unique to her autobiography but appear frequently in Shaker speech, narrative, and song. "The journey motif . . . had long been conventional for marches" which were consciously emblematic, the song texts of the marches explicitly stating the symbolism of spiritual travel.[10] During the period of Mother's Work, the journey was even more explicitly dramatized by the twice yearly pilgrimage to the Holy Mount. Shakers remembered the ascent to the Holy Mount in terms appropriate to spiritual travel: "It was a holy, a joyful day, — lifted above earth and earthly tasks and burdens; the long climb, its rocks and cliffs, its stumbling places and its dark, forest depths, all typical of the hard, burdened, shadowed path through earth life, up the spiritual steeps of redemption. . . . Yet each step of the way must be trodden by each one for himself. His own, her own, work of climbing must be done alone."[11] Jane Blanchard, thus, is drawing upon symbols and images which permeate her culture and using them to portray an individual experience as representative of the experience of all Shakers.

Each detail of her journey to Enfield conveys meaning on two levels. The bridge that has been washed away is not only a physical impediment but indicates Blanchard's need for courage and perseverance. It also signifies a spiritual temptation to return home and avoid the suffering and hardship necessary for spiritual travel. This is but one of several tests that Jane Blanchard must pass in order to finally unite with Believers.

The episode of the missing bridge points to another serious problem of spiritual travel: How can seekers know that they are reading God's signs correctly? Blanchard wonders, What if God is trying to show her that she should return home? Jane Blanchard's answer is the same as before, when she was anxious over her spiritual state: Pray earnestly to God and He will guide you.

Blanchard stops at a house for water. She finds a woman with four small children begging for bread, but there is no food in the house. Although Jane Blanchard has only two small cakes, she di-

10. Patterson, *Shaker Spiritual,* 368.
11. White and Taylor, 231.

vides them among the children. "I did not think nor feel as tho I should ever want anything myself, nor know how far I should have to go. But I putt my trust in God, believing this promise would be fulfilled. 'They shall run & not be weary—they shall walk & not faint'" (313). Once again Blanchard is utilizing a well-known metaphor of Shaker life, the contrast between the need for physical and spiritual nourishment. On her journey, Jane Blanchard sees the sufferings of those living the carnal life in a world that lacks both spiritual and natural food. By sharing her only provision and trusting God to provide for her needs, she is tested and found worthy. In retrospect, Jane Blanchard sees that she has been supplied with nourishment more fulfilling and sustaining than the food of "the world."

A bit further on her journey Blanchard comes to a crossroads and is perplexed over which path to follow. The only people nearby are at a tavern, and she is afraid to approach them lest they realize she is a stranger and harm her. Blanchard fears both the storms in unredeemed nature and the passions in unredeemed men. Both roads are surrounded by woods, and she worries that Enfield may still be far away. Avoiding the main thoroughfare, Blanchard travels through a wet field and finally arrives at a small building, the Square House. She sees a boy on horseback and asks him where she might find the Shakers. He tells her to proceed to the next building and ask there. "Everything was calm, & still as the hour of death. I knocked at the door untill my knuckles were lame, & no one bade me enter. Sure enough, thot I, no living mortal is here. What could I do? Could I think the Spirits had deceived me, & led me this thorny path to a deserted place?" (314).

The atmosphere that Jane Blanchard evokes in describing her arrival at Enfield is reminiscent of a fairy tale, where the traveler finds herself in an enchanted land. Indeed, Blanchard implies that she has finally arrived in another world, a holy spot where spirits, not mere mortals, dwell. "Again my heart swelled with grief, for I felt as tho I could walk no further. I reentered the road & started for the church when I heard a door open, & looking around, I saw two girls standing here" (314). Rather mysteriously, the girls tell Blanchard that everyone is away "picking wool." Blanchard thinks this odd since it is May. She asks if she may stay overnight, and the girls invite her in and give her food. "While in this sorrowful mood & looking out at the window, I saw the Brethren & Sisters coming from the ch.h. [church]. They looked as if they had been to a funeral instead of picking wool. . . ." (314). Later Blanchard learns that the entire Society had gathered to hear the reading of the Holy Roll.[12] It is 1843, and Jane Blanchard has arrived at Enfield, New Hampshire, at the height of the spiritual manifestations.

Blanchard does not portray the mood of the community as the quietly joyous one often conveyed by other autobiographers. Rather, she repeatedly associates the solemn stillness with death. The inhabitants of the society seem to move through a shadowy realm like silent spirits. At Enfield, Blanchard suggests, the world of the flesh and all its joys are truly dead.

Still, Blanchard has not firmly resolved to become a Shaker. She does not reveal her real name to those at Enfield but calls herself "Elizabeth Snow." In her choice of a pseudonym Blanchard reveals her desire to become "white as snow," like the people in her vision (308–9). When night comes, she is still troubled and cannot fall asleep:

> O the sorrows of that night. I walked the floor in deep sorrows of heart. It seemed that there was no sorrow like my sorrow. Surely I had become acquainted with grief. Away from my parents; among a strange people whom I knew not, I still cherished the thot that He who had called me was sure. I prayed to my heavenly Father & all the good Spirits that they would make known to me my duty, & enable me to conquer the will within my own heart. . . . Soon I heard the joyful news of the gospel. Then thot I, My Redeemer liveth. He heard my prayer when I was weak, And sent my food prepared; The waters bubbled at my feet And thus my life was spared.[13] (315)

By once again resorting to prayer, Blanchard receives comfort and guidance.

She is pleased to discover an acquaintance among the Enfield

12. Philemon Stewart, *A Holy, Sacred and Divine Roll and Book* (Canterbury, N.H.: The United Society, 1843). A volume of inspired writings, the Holy Roll was the object of some controversy among Believers.

13. Although it does not appear in verse form in the autobiography, the last sentence appears to be a quatrain extracted from a Shaker spiritual.

Shakers, and on the following day her friend, Amanda, opens the testimony of Christ's Second Appearing to her. A few days later Blanchard begins the confession of her sins. Although she now wishes to remain with Believers, the ministry instructs Blanchard to return home and settle her worldly affairs. As in her vision, when her guide requires her to go back into the world after she has been led to the beautiful white house, she now must return one last time to her worldly relations.

Blanchard's homecoming is like a funeral. Indeed, the young woman she had been only a short time ago is now dead. In her place, a solemn sister in Shaker garb greets her natural relations. "On our arrival my father came to the door, & I spoke & called him father, saying that I was as ever his daughter. I believe this astonished him as much as tho one at that time has risen from the dead . . ." (316). Once again, Blanchard is given the strength to resist the temptations placed before her and refuses to heed the pleas of her family to forget the Shakers. "When informing them that I had made my choice to spend the remainder of my days with the Shakers, such a house of mourning I never before saw" (316). Blanchard portrays her initial visit to the Shakers, and particularly her confession of sins, as the death of her carnal nature. Her final visit to her family thus becomes a symbolic transition from one state of existence to another.

Jane Blanchard's autobiography is not complex in its organization. Yet in the symmetrical construction of the vision and its fulfillment and in her effective use of the metaphors of travel, nourishment, and rebirth, Blanchard creates an aesthetically satisfying and harmonious narrative in which all details contribute to a tightly woven whole. Because it depends so little on non-Shaker perceptions of experience and because its informing metaphors and images are so deeply rooted in the Shaker vision of the purpose of life, Blanchard's "Sketch" is a paradigm of the Shaker religious imagination. The final paragraphs of her autobiography, masterpieces of poetic juxtaposition, are representative of the best Shaker literary style:

> The world was nothing but vanity to me now. I could take no
> more pleasure living with my parents. I rent the ties of natural affec-

tion which cost me many tears, & turned my face Zionward. I bid adieu to nature's charms, for which I feel thankful, & can say in truth and sincerity, Go to the flames all carnal enjoyments which yield to my hungering soul no support.

I was eighteen years of age when the gospel first reached my ears. To me it was Good news & Glad tidings, Salvation to my sin sick soul. My treasure is here—my home & all my interest. Here are my gospel relations whom I love above every other. As the Lord liveth & as my soul liveth, I will never leave thee nor forsake thee. For here I find an hundred fold of the blessings of life, with all the assurance of life Eternal in the world to come.[14] (317)

Couched in highly lyrical yet familiar Shaker forms, Blanchard's conclusion repeatedly contrasts the experiences of past and present and constantly sharpens the distinction between the millennial life and her previous non-Shaker life. Blanchard regards her new world as but an extension of herself, one so familiar that it can be addressed directly as "thee."

14. This paragraph echoes lines from several songs, including "My treasure is in Zion, my interest is here," and "Here's my home, my all & treasure." See Patterson, *Shaker Spiritual,* 308, 329.

> Between the call and the work of every inspired leader lies
> a wilderness. It may be in Judea as for Jesus, or in Arabia
> as for Paul and Mohammed; it may be a prison cell as
> for Bunyan, or in personal solitude in crowded city streets.
> To all who act for God in some special way comes a so-
> journ in a wilderness. The seed is buried in the earth, ap-
> parently forgotten; silent, unguessed forces, educative and
> preparative, are at work, unseen by all but God.
>
> ANNA WHITE AND LEILA TAYLOR,
> *Shakerism: Its Meaning and Message*

MANY SHAKER FIGURES OF TRAVEL are similar to those found in
the writings of John Bunyan. Since there is virtually no evidence
of any direct influence, the similarity can be attributed to common
scriptural sources, but Bunyan uses such "figures" allegorically
whereas the preferred usage among the Shakers is metaphorical.
"As a rule, the variant uses of any single figure in the Shaker and
Bunyan texts are to be accounted for by multiple scriptural uses,
and by the nonallegorical character of the Shaker writing. And
it may be safely said that both are heavily, if not totally, dependent
on scriptural sources."[15]

The "Autobiography" of William Leonard does contain both direct and indirect references to Bunyan.[16] Leonard's narrative is
perhaps the only Shaker autobiography to be influenced by the
author's knowledge of *Pilgrim's Progress* and *Grace Abounding*. In the
American Bunyan literature, "when the pilgrimage was transferred
to the American continent, it was confronted by an environment
radically dissimilar to that of the conventional English pilgrimage.
Jerusalem no longer waited at the end of the difficult way: if it
were to appear, it must be created, constructed, shaped."[17] This,
however, is not true of William Leonard. Although often presenting himself as a Christian searching for the Celestial City, Leonard

15. Weiss, 50.

16. William Leonard, (1803–1877), "Autobiography," Harvard, Mass., n.d., MS, OClWHi,
VI:B–5. All further references to this work will be included in the text. For published works
by Leonard, see Mary L. Hurt Richmond, *Shaker Literature: A Bibliography Compiled and Annotated by Mary L. Richmond* (Hancock, Mass.: Shaker Community, 1977), I, items 862–63.

17. Smith, *John Bunyan in America*, 10.

writes a narrative that is shaped as strongly by the American landscape as by the ultimate goal of his journey. Unlike most American writers who directed their characters in Christian's footsteps, Leonard did not have to construct a personal, individual New Jerusalem; he found the holy spot already flourishing in the Shaker community at Harvard, Massachusetts.

Leonard's pilgrimage to the Shakers began as a search to replace the void left in his life by the early loss of both his parents. His father disappeared before Leonard's birth, and his mother died when Leonard was nine. Leonard knew little about his own father, who possessed a restless, adventuresome temperament, much like the later Leonard himself. "My Father, was a native of London; I never saw him, he never saw me" (6). As a youth, Leonard's father had run away to sea and was impressed on a British warship. Although he managed to escape, he was soon "pressed" again and sailed for the West Indies. In port at New Brunswick, Canada, the elder Leonard met and married a young widow. Soon after his marriage, he set sail to London in order to visit his father but was once again "pressed" into service on a warship, and never returned.

Leonard and his mother moved to New York City, where many Methodist revivals were taking place. Images of the joys of heaven and the torments of hell fired Leonard's youthful imagination. At age seven his conscience troubled him, and he often dreamed of death and judgment.[18] One night, while awake, he saw "the monster before me, as plain as I ever saw anything in the light of day . . ." (15). When he was nine, his mother became very ill and for six weeks before her death she labored "in the spirit" and testified to hundreds who came to her bedside. After his mother's death Leonard lived with his grandmother. Still tormented inwardly by his childish sins, Leonard one night experienced a "night vision or dream," which he later realized had been predicting his future:

> Retiring to rest one night, and feeling sensible that I had failed
> to come up to the advise of my departed Mother, before I awoke

18. Bunyan's description of his childhood is similar: "Even in my childhood he did scare and affright me with fearful dreams, and did terrifie me with dreadful visions. For often, after I had spent this and other days in sin, I have in my bed been greatly affected, while asleep, with the apprehension of Devils, and wicked spirits . . . ," *Grace Abounding to the Chief of Sinners* (Oxford: Clarendon Press, 1962), 6.

from my slumber, I dreamed that the judgment day, of which I had heard my friends and others, so frequently converse about had commenced. The heavens blackened and thro' this blackness innumerable bodies of angels descended, with trumpets which when sounded seemed to reach thro' vast creation. I looked steadfastly upon them, till fully aroused by a sense of my danger. I then looked in every direction, and found myself standing on a vast plain. I saw the dead rising around me in every direction. They were coming up to judgment.

My fears were now in the most lively agitation. All my short comings arose vividly before me. I had no doubt remaining of my being sentenced to final misery. But on looking anxiously around, to see if there was no chance for my escape, I discerned at a distance, a gentle rise of land, and on a hill side a plain white building.

Somthing now whispered to me, that in this building the heavenly order resided. I now found myself struggling thro' the uprising host around me, and with some labor I succeeded in gaining an entrance in this building. I assended a flight of stairs and came to a square room. Around this room seated closely together, were a large number of females. . . . They were seated in silence, looking thoughtful, but composed and happy.

They were dressed in the exact attire of the Sisterhood among Believers even to their caps, and were sitting in the same order, they usually sit in, in their union meetings.

Directly in front, and facing me, I saw my Mother seated, about in the center of the number. She looked steadily at me, not reproachfully, or compassionately, but with a manifest lack of that natural affection that exists in the bosom of a Mother.

I was in great distress and fear, but the profound silence of the place utterly forbid my giving utterance, to a word or sound. But as my Mothers eyes were strangely fixed upon me, I sought by every look, gesture, and such motions and appearances, as a child can exert, to attract her attention as my former Mother; but all to no purpose. And soon I found myself outside of that singular, silent habitation, where all was peace and tranquility. I felt, I did not, (in the condition I was then in) belong there. Among that select few, none could describe the tranquility; every where outside, none could describe the commotion, distress, and confusion.

My anguish could not be imagined, when I again found myself on that great plain. Every thing now assumed a different aspect. To me, it was horrid to contemplate. In the West, the whole horrizon was lighted up by a boiling sea of liquid fire from beneath. Into this ocean of flame the whole earth was steadily moving like the downward course of a mighty river; bearing with it a countless number doomed to be swallowed up in these boiling embers of destruction.

I stood and gazed wildly, and found myself irresistably borne onward, till I felt the scorching heat, like the [?] of the desart, from this boiling ocean; and being unable to restrain myself longer, cried out in the agony of despair, and awakened from my slumbers. I was bathed in a cold perspiration; and so real was the vision, that I thot for months after, I had made one of the most remarkable escapes from endless destruction. (19–23)

Although the general outline of Leonard's dream is common in Shaker visions, *Pilgrim's Progress* may have influenced some of the details. Like Christian, Leonard dreams that judgment is imminent and he seeks to escape destruction. Like Christian, he must journey across a plain and finally ascend a hill to enter the Holy City. The Celestial City in Leonard's narrative, however, is not one of golden streets and buildings; nor is it filled with angels carrying harps and wearing golden crowns. Instead, Leonard's New Jerusalem is an image of the Shaker community: a "plain white building," simple and austere. The inhabitants of this holy place are Shaker sisters sitting in a single straight line, as if in a union meeting. Leonard evidently takes his place opposite the women in one of the chairs reserved for Shaker brethren. Inside the white building all is orderly, peaceful, and tranquil; outside the building the world is full of "commotion, distress, and confusion."

Like many Shaker autobiographers, Leonard discovers that he cannot remain in the holy place. Like Christian in *Pilgrim's Progress,* Leonard wakes from his dream with the knowledge that the vision has revealed the path he must follow to avoid destruction. Shaker theology shapes the landscape of Leonard's vision; escape from destruction is possible only by entering into the protection and order of the Shaker community.

Although Leonard's vision shows the influence of Bunyan, his dream conveys personal anxiety, when his recently departed mother appears as a Shaker sister. His dream betrays childhood fears that his own sinfulness caused his mother's death and that his mother has rejected him as unworthy of her continued love. Separated from her in this life, Leonard wants desperately to be worthy to join her in the afterlife. The search for "that natural affection, which I sought, but could not find" (23) becomes in the following years a restless quest which merges the desire for spiritual salvation and the need for a home and a mother.

Leonard's depiction of his spiritual life before he begins his journey to the Shakers is clearly influenced by *Grace Abounding*. Like Bunyan, Leonard fears that he has committed an unpardonable sin against the Holy Ghost.[19] "Before, and at this period, I had heard other persons talk, of sinning aginst the Holy Spirit; and perhaps, before I was seven years old, I fell under a strong temptation, to utter some sentence of great disrespect, against the God of heaven" (24). When he succumbs to this temptation, Leonard enters a period of great despair, similar to that depicted by Bunyan in his autobiography. Leonard's description of his condition is also reminiscent of Mother Ann's statement before her revelation of the origin of sin: "In my travail and tribulation my sufferings were so great that my flesh consumed upon my bones. . . ."[20] Leonard records: "I was especially for the first three months after, in a state of gloom and despair. So much so, that I used to examine my flesh and it seemed to me that it wasted from my bones" (25).

While still despairing, Leonard falls from a pile of boards onto a wharf. He escapes drowning only because a man holds out his foot, and by grasping it Leonard pulls himself from the water. "I then felt that this was a providential escape from the terrors of a burning hell" (26). He nearly drowns a second time, and on another occasion he almost dies by falling down a precipice. In retrospect, Leonard views each of these events as a remarkable deliverance. Just as Bunyan in *Grace Abounding* realizes that he has been providentially preserved, so William Leonard sees the hand of God in his past life.[21]

---

19. See Bunyan's account of his sin against the Holy Ghost in *Grace Abounding*, 41–46.

20. White and Taylor, 17.

21. In *Grace Abounding*, 7, Bunyan also notes three providential escapes from death. Like Leonard, Bunyan nearly drowns twice, once falling into "a crick of the Sea" and another time falling "out of a Boat into the Bedford-River." On a third occasion, Bunyan escapes being stung by an adder in the road.

Leonard, then, draws upon precedents found in *Grace Abounding* and in the writings about the life of Mother Ann and adapts them to the story of his own life. His use of the patterns of spiritual autobiography, however, does little to convey the personal struggle he experienced after his mother's death. It is only when Leonard begins to describe his teenage years—his movements from one job to another, his lack of home and family—that readers begin to understand his quest for a holy community.

In New Brunswick, Leonard's grandmother apprentices him to a shoemaker with whom he spends six very unhappy years. His master, although originally from the lower classes himself, has recently become wealthy and treats the apprentices like servants. Leonard discovers that New Brunswick, after the defeat of the British in the Revolutionary War, was settled by loyalists who hoped to reinstitute a society based on social class. Even in such hardship, Leonard finds the workings of Providence, for he says that if he had been permitted "more agreeable surroundings" he would have formed ties both to the place and the people; but having no such bonds, he is not hindered from searching for God's people.

After being released from his indenture, Leonard lives with various families, once working on an uncle's farm, another time living with friends, but never finding a permanent haven. During this period he becomes increasingly disillusioned with the professing Christians he meets. One is a converted sinner who becomes a leading exhorter in the church, but when Leonard lends him money, the man refuses to repay it. Another is a preacher who gained a lucrative "calling" at a local church through underhanded dealings. Although Leonard has promised to follow wherever God "opens" a way, he discovers that neither the Methodists nor the Baptists live the life they proclaim. Leonard begins his journey in a state of spiritual unrest. "I viewed it then somwhat, as I have fully realized it since; that an overruling providence, headed my plans, sundered my ties, cut off my hopes, and compelled me to wander abroad" (68). Leonard attributes his determination to travel to "inspiration." When he begins his journey, he has no destination in mind but sets out over some of the most rugged and beautiful territory in northeastern America.

When the spirit of departure came upon me, I felt it like a tide of inspiration. Like myself, I must not delay the time, tho the worst season of the year, I could have selected for traveling. I determined to make directly for the City of Frederickton, the seat of government, in New Brunswick. The main road to that section, lay thro' intervale lands, that was buried many feet beneath the spring freshet. The other margin of the river, was rough high land, seldom used for traveling. . . .

. . . I took an overland rout on foot, as no stages, or other vehicles, run from the head of Belile Bay where I started from, to the broad waters of the St Johns River. By the night of the first day, found myself at a hotel on the intervale side, sixty miles below Frederickton, opposite Gage town.

It was one of the most wild, romantic scenes, that ever met my vision. As far as the eye could reach, up and down that river might be seen, hundreds of overgrown shade trees, strongly rooted over that extensive intervale contry, and the tide runing in circles among the branches. It was a season, when few attempts were made to cross over. The river at that place was between one and two miles in width, and the waters were wild and rapid. (68–69)

Despite the dangers of crossing the river, Leonard is determined to continue the journey he has begun. Making a "liberal offer," he persuades a young waterman to attempt the crossing with a canoe. "The sun was up; the sparkling waters, rapid currents, and forests of tree tops glittered in the sun beams. It was a wild adventure, and one that produced in me a thrill of delight" (69–70). Successfully reaching the other side of the river, Leonard prepares to resume his journey "over many miles, of rough contracted road, and rude mountainous country" (70).

Leonard's account of his trip around the lakes and across the rivers of New Brunswick, through the province of Quebec, to Bangor, Maine, and finally to Boston, Massachusetts, contains some of the best natural description to be found in any Shaker narrative. Leonard, unlike most Believers, does not choose details of the natural landscape that may be interpreted as figures of spiritual realities. Rather, he delights in remembering the beauty and power of the untamed North American wilderness, but at the same time he never loses sight of the spiritual significance of his journey. Over forty pages long, and placed in almost the exact center of the "Autobiography," Leonard's journey is the structural focus of his narrative and represents the turning point in his life.

After arriving at Frederickton, Leonard finds work as a shoemaker. He never informs his readers how long he remained there, although he does mention that after a year had passed he left his first employer and joined the best shop in the city, where he became a first-rate bootmaker. The details which Leonard provides about his stay in Frederickton all highlight the spiritual inadequacies of his situation. His companions are "worldly," and he is determined to resume his travels. Following the banks of the river toward Quebec, Leonard receives the aid of Providence. He stops for directions at a farm, where he meets someone he had helped long ago who is happy to assist him. When he seeks accommodations for the night at another farmhouse, he discovers the relative of a friend. The next night, a fellow traveler invites Leonard to spend the night at his home. There Leonard learns that his companion's father-in-law had known and cared for him as an infant. In each of these incidents, Leonard discerns providential signs that he is moving in the right direction.

Leonard tarries several months in the vicinity of Woodstock, Canada, but soon he feels confined and desires to continue his journey. "But I was anxious to proceed, to a land that was more densely populated. For that whole mountainous region, with its wild narrow river, which generally run between rough high banks, its few inhabitants, on the margin scattered here and there, seemed to me, like a gloomy prison house" (91). Once again, Leonard's urge to travel comes at a bad time of the year. It is the first of January, ice covers the rivers and streams, and no road is passable. Yet Leonard, never deterred by external obstacles, sets out to cross the border into the United States. He arrives at a new American settlement, Holten Plantation, and prepares to proceed to Bangor, Maine. "And now, the distance of one hundred and sixty miles, of wild country, thro which a surveyor had never laid out a road, lay between me and the City of Bangor; but I determined to go forward . . ."(92).

Since there are no roads, Leonard must wait two or three weeks for the mail carrier who can act as his guide through the wilderness. He begins the journey with the mail carrier on horseback.

In order to get from the home of one settler to that of another he "had to cross a soft bog . . . over a mile in width" (93). Many spiritual autobiographers, especially those familiar with *Pilgrim's Progress,* would invest such a natural "bog" with religious significance, presenting it as a "Slough of Despond." A Shaker author like Jane Blanchard might interpret such an impediment as God's test of her perseverance. Leonard, however, seems reluctant to look for spiritual meaning in the natural landscape. His narrative focuses instead on the beauty and novelty of traveling through the wilderness in winter.

When Leonard and the mail carrier arrive at the river, "it was frozen sufficient, to try our skill in skating. . . . We came to falls and rapids, and had to travel miles thro the forest" (94). As he skates, Leonard observes the lumbermen "drawing out their countless logs" (94). The following day, Leonard and his companion reach the Penobscot River:

> The river was open and running rapidly, but was frozen quite out from the shore. We descended it about six miles, breaking the ice into large fragments, as we flew over it; and at sunset ascended a hill and tarried at a station house. Next day, as we were now on the main river, and my course down was a plain one, I let my traveling companions pass on, and descended alone & more at leisure. I amused myself, at viewing the rough scenery, that extends sixty miles down that broken water course. Some parts of the River was frozen quite out, at others not so far, which gave me ample opportunity, to examine Islands, ledges, rips, and waterfalls. In passing one hundred miles up that stream, you pass over three hundred Islands. (95)

The next day Leonard travels in the company of a group of Indians and arrives in Old Town, where he describes the great falls, the huge mills which "with their majestic gangs of saws take those tremendous logs to pieces" (96), and the clear, sparkling waters in which one can see "the bottom fifty feet down" and "witness the immense crowd of [?], shad, salmon, herrings etc; that rush up the river, to spawn during the greatest run. I have stood, and looked at the foot of the falls, over a broad sheet of water, where it seemed, that there were as many fish in quantity, as there was water. And before they pass this great ledge, the fishermen obtain large quantities of them" (97).

Such passages in Leonard's "Autobiography" closely resemble wilderness descriptions found in nonreligious American literature. Leonard celebrates the abundance of the land. As he describes it, the natural world stands independent from man and his religious strivings, yet in the wilderness Leonard is alone more than ever. Nature cannot satisfy his longing for a place in the world of men.

Leonard spends the winter in Old Town working as a shoemaker. When spring arrives, he resumes his trek, passing Bangor and continuing to Prospect, where he works until the next spring:

> I found that situation, did very little to enliven my feelings; and, as yet, I strove to believe, that happiness was, to a greater or less extent, to be found in location.
>
> The unvarnished truth is, My soul was depressed, I felt that I was a child of wrath. I had no confidence in the gratifications of this world for happiness, whither I practiced them or not. I knew by bitter experience that they were empty, vain, & worse than worthless.
>
> I felt no eliment, nor pleasure in worldly Society. There seemed to be, almost an eternal separation between us. I had lost all confidence in the religionists around me. I felt my soul in a despairing, almost dying state. That fall, I walked long routs in my leisure hours, thought much, and reflected bitterly. At times I felt my lost sinking condition, till it seemed almost insupportable. (102–3)

In near desperation, Leonard seeks a resolution to his anxiety. He reads dozens of books in the local library, searching for answers to his personal crisis. He makes friends, but finds that friendship will not alleviate his discontent. He tries to pray, but finds that he can hardly "connect ten rational sentences together. I almost longed for annihilation. I felt the strongest separation between myself, and every thing on earth . . ." (103).

In this state of almost total alienation, feeling himself a part of no family or society, Leonard first hears of the Shakers. "One Saturday feeling weary of life, & heartily sick of every thing around me, I threw my cloak over my shoulders, put on my hat and gloves and walked up to the town of Acton five miles off." While he is visiting friends there, the conversation turns to stories about the

Shakers: "While this conversation was being made, there was a strange unaccountable feeling, passed over my whole being. It fairly aroused me. I enquired how far off they lived? She answered one Society at Shirley was about seven miles off, the other at Harvard about ten. It was now Satturday at noon, and the thought darted thro my brain, that I had better walk up there, see them, spend the Sabbath, and enquire them out" (104).

So William Leonard sets out on the last leg of a journey which has taken him more than three years to complete. When he arrives at Harvard, Leonard comes to a dilapidated house, the South House, where the curtains are drawn. It is dark outside, but he sees light inside the house. Everywhere there is an impressive silence. He enters, not knowing even if Shakers profess Christianity. Joseph Hammond and Mary Grosvenor greet him. In conversation, Eldress Mary soon opens the Testimony of Christ's Second Appearing to him:

> She was in possession of a good flow of language, was quite polished in her method, & manner; presented her ideas pointed, and clear, & showed up Adams fall, as clear as it took place. And tho' I considered this (according to my former ideas of propriety) rather than a singular subject for a female to introduce into general conversation, I was deeply interested in it.
>
> She fairly uncovered man's first iniquity. But when she entered into his total disregard of times, and seasons, of his repeated . . . beastly connections, to beget one offspring; and contrasted it with the more orderly cohabiting, of all the lower tribes of animals, I was suddenly struck down; from all opposing argument, as tho the sentence of death had been read to me, to consign me to the gulentine. (108–9)

Leonard sees that in order to begin a new life he must first give up the old. He feels himself, like Paul, converted from darkness to light in a "twinkling of the eye." After several more visits, Leonard determines to "go thro' it," but the Elders advise him first to fulfill his obligations to his employer, and then in the spring to confess his sins and come to the Society at Harvard. Leonard, before his final union with the Shakers, compares himself to Christian in *Pilgrim's Progress:* "My sins tho' not out breaking felt like pilgrims burden" (125). In order to relieve the burden of his sins, Leonard must

FIGURE 5: Shaker Village, Harvard, Massachusetts, where William Leonard ended his spiritual journey. (Courtesy of the Western Reserve Historical Society.)

arrive at the Celestial City, in his case Harvard, Massachusetts, and begin the purifying work of confession. Leonard relates that he was "under continual mortification. By the aid of strong memory, and extreme conscientiousness, I was months closely engaged in the work of self examination, and coming to the light" (127). The "travail" does not cease with Leonard's arrival at his destination, but now continues as an inward spiritual journey.

In his conclusion, Leonard notes that for a year and a half after uniting with Believers he was under the care of Elder Joseph Hammond, who had been instructed by Hannah Kendall, who had received the testimony directly from Mother Ann. Thus Leonard regards himself as a direct spiritual descendant of the founder of Shakerism. The anxiety of separation from his natural mother, so clearly revealed in his childhood vision, is stilled. Unable to be reunited in this life with his own parents, Leonard finds union with his spiritual parents.

Although Leonard's use of the journey to depict a crucial period in his life was influenced both by *Pilgrim's Progress* and by metaphors of travel found in Shaker testimonies and songs, Leonard, unlike Bunyan and other Shaker writers, does not present each detail of his travel as an image of spiritual reality. Instead, Leonard's presentation points to a complex attitude toward Shakerism and is a key to the basic structure of his autobiography: the contrast between his life before becoming a Believer and his life as a Shaker. Leonard calls attention to this contrast in his introduction to the "Autobiography," where he describes the conditions of his life as he begins to write the narrative. He faces "a long, dreary winter" with "many new trying duties to perform." He anticipates "seasons of solitude, and lonliness," and he resolves to fill whatever moments he has free from "unremitting care and toil" to write his life story (5). In comparison with his present life, Leonard's early life was filled with wild, "romantic" adventures. Before becoming a Shaker, Leonard demonstrated resourcefulness, courage, and daring as he struggled against the circumstances of his birth and as he conquered the natural obstacles that confronted him in his travel. Among Believers, however, every day is much like the one before; life is orderly and predictable. There is little need or opportunity for great risks or heroic deeds.

The "Autobiography" thus holds two perspectives in tension: Leonard's love of the disorderly natural world and his need for the order and stability of the Shaker community. Unlike most Shakers, who interpret nature in purely theological terms, Leonard's view of nature is influenced by a nineteenth-century romantic sensibility. He celebrates the American wilderness — its beauty, its fertility, its power. The wild disorder of nature thrills him. Leonard's view of the natural world thus contrasts sharply with that of other Shaker writers. The American landscape in Leonard's "Autobiography" is not an unredeemed wilderness, filled with evil, which constantly presents trials and temptations to the traveler. The hazards of Leonard's travel are physical, not spiritual. But if Leonard does not view the natural world as fallen, neither does he look to it for religious salvation. The natural world, Leonard implies, cannot offer the security of a home, family, or community.

Leonard's reluctance to reject completely the natural world creates a conflict within his autobiography which he never fully resolves. The believing Shaker sought to overcome both the external world of nature and man's carnal nature. The Shaker regulated, ordered, and controlled nature so that man might live fully in the spirit. Thus, as the Shaker community turned the wilderness into the garden, it converted the natural man into the spiritual. The spirit of the wild, natural landscape is the very same spirit which Leonard must repress within himself. After becoming a Believer, he must strive to live "out of nature." He must confine his experience to the interior landscape of the austere white house of his vision. Never again can he venture on romantic journey into nature. As a Shaker, his adventures must be internal, not external; his travel must be spiritual, not physical; his goal must be personal perfection, not the Celestial City.

On one level Leonard's autobiography expresses the conventional Shaker belief that contentment is not to be found in an earthly setting but in a state of mind. On another, more emotional level, however, the narrative reveals Leonard's keen sense of what he has forfeited by choosing the Shaker way. Consequently, William Leonard leaves readers of his "Autobiography" wondering whether his internal, spiritual travel has been as exciting or satisfying as the journey of his youth. Whatever difficulties Leonard may have encountered in his spiritual journey, he nevertheless found a spiritual home and a family among Believers.

The autobiographies of Jane Blanchard and William Leonard demonstrate how the Shaker author could structure a narrative around an important journey which, viewed in retrospect, could be regarded as a spiritual pilgrimage. At the same time, these narratives reveal how two authors who chose similar structural devices could nevertheless create distinctive autobiographies. Each autobiography bears the imprint of the particular personality of its author.

Both Blanchard and Leonard divide their narratives into three sections: the first portrays the writer's early life, the second describes the journey to Believers, and the third presents the writer's relationship with the outside world after converting to Shakerism.

In both narratives the vision is the central event in the writer's early life. While Blanchard's vision gives her assurance that she will be part of God's people in the future, at the same time it reveals how she should interpret the predicted experience, her journey to New Enfield. The image of the holy community that Blanchard sees contrasts with Leonard's vision of the Shaker community. Like Leonard, Blanchard must enter a building and climb the stairs, but once inside the Shaker meeting room Blanchard is impressed not by the peace, tranquility, and order of the Believers but by the religious ecstasies the holy worshippers experience. The motions of the spirits are disorderly; the Believers fly around the room swiftly and turn like tops. It is the spiritual energy and the freedom of expression that attracts Jane Blanchard. To a young woman who had little opportunity for adventure in the world, the Shaker life seemed to offer both excitement and spiritual salvation.

Leonard's vision, on the other hand, does not reveal a symbolic landscape in which the trials of his future journey take place; rather, it depicts the fate of those who fail to make the journey: the pit of fire and brimstone. Leonard's dream also highlights the contrast between the disorder of the world, the City of Destruction, and the order and harmony within the Shaker community. The biological family in Leonard's experience is fragile, its security constantly threatened by the deaths of family members. Leonard thus seeks an enduring community, one based on spiritual rather than biological ties. In his autobiography Leonard asserts a basic premise of Shaker belief: enduring relationships must be based on spiritual love, not physical. Thus, it is the order and stability of the Shaker community which deeply attracts William Leonard. Writing many years after the vision occurred, Leonard does not attempt to interpret the dream for the reader, yet in the autobiography the vision clarifies Leonard's compulsion to travel, his unhappiness in the world, and his satisfaction in his Shaker home.

Leonard and Blanchard portray their journeys differently. Leonard's depiction of his travel is influenced by written sources and by romantic ideas which found little acceptance within the Shaker community. Blanchard, on the other hand, understands her journey through the natural world in purely Shaker terms, in images and phrases drawn from Shaker songs and testimonies. While Blanchard describes only those events or objects which have specific religious value, Leonard is much more responsive to the world around him for its own sake. Although at all times aware that he is writing about a spiritual quest, Leonard feels the need to describe a beautiful world condemned by Shaker theology. The persons and events, and especially the trees, rivers, and cliffs, are sharply etched in his memory even when they have no specific spiritual meaning. The third parts of the two narratives reveal additional differences. Blanchard ends her relationship with the world, including her own family, and describes her last visit with her kin as a funeral. As the funeral imagery indicates, this Believer has resolved the tensions between the values of the larger society and the values of the Society of Believers. She has totally rejected, or buried, the values of "the world." Blanchard's narrative thus lacks tension or drama; its beauty lies in the serenity of its author's vision. Blanchard's narrative is as tightly bound in time and space as her life was circumscribed by her Shaker commitment. By the end of her journey she has achieved contentment. Her achievement is inward, spiritual, and self-contained. Although narrow, the Shaker way could also be beautiful. Leonard's narrative also describes a travel toward personal salvation, but it betrays the author's desire always to actively shape his destiny. Leonard continues to reach out to the world beyond the Society, looking for an affirmation that his own journey was but a model for others. Even after he arrives at his destination,

Leonard is impelled toward further achievement; he wishes to influence and lead others to Shakerism. Not surprisingly Leonard became a respected leader of the Harvard community and the author of theological tracts, while Jane Blanchard is known to us only through her splendid testimony to the Shaker life.

CHAPTER VII   I sing what was lost and dread what was won.
THE SEARCH   W. B. YEATS
FOR A
NEW WORLD:
THE AUTOBIOGRAPHY
OF JOHN M. BROWN

Jane Blanchard and William Leonard employed journeys to guide
and shape their autobiographies. They used their travels not only
to delineate the spatial and temporal boundaries of their life stories
but to convey metaphorically a spiritual progression from one condition to another. Other Shaker autobiographers also give accounts
of traveling long distances in search of a new spiritual or social
order. Of these, several were immigrants. In 1843, during the Irish
potato famine, John M. Brown (1824–1875) came to the New World
in search of material fortune; he found, instead, the Society of Believers in Lebanon.

The membership rolls at Lebanon list sixty-seven immigrants who
joined Believers between 1788 and 1873, only nine of whom came before 1840. Most, like John Brown, arrived during the 1840s and 1850s,
periods of economic hardship in both the Old and New World. Of
the forty-five immigrants who joined the Lebanon community during
these two decades, many were children. New immigrants, surprised
at the scarcity of jobs in America, the land of plenty, frequently
found themselves unable to support their families. Thus, parents
often left children with Believers while they searched for work and
sought to establish a new home. Although an occasional immigrant,
such as William Offord, joined Believers for strictly religious reasons,
such motivations seem rare. Of those who came to Lebanon during
the 1840s and 1850s, only eight spent their adult lives as Shakers.
Among these were John Brown and his friend Amelia Calver.[1]

1. [Membership Roll of Lebanon and Watervliet], Lebanon, N.Y., MS, OClWHi, III:B–18.

133

John Brown differed from the typical immigrant who joined the Society of Believers, for of the sixty-seven immigrants at Lebanon he was the only native of Ireland. In his "A Biographic Sketch & Religious Experience," begun in 1866, Brown tells the story of the incomplete metamorphosis of an Irish Protestant into an American Shaker.[2]

Brown's autobiography also illustrates the difficulty some Shaker writers experienced in integrating the two kinds of life they had lived—a worldly one and a spiritual one. The authors had to select events that would reveal how they moved from one condition to another. The reader of Shaker autobiographies usually knew beforehand both the beginning and the end: the initial situation is the author's life before becoming a Shaker; the resolution is the reward of the Shaker life. The reader's interest centered upon how the author related these contrasting perspectives, holding "*what was* up to view in light reflected from *what is.*"[3]

Some Shaker writers use metaphors appropriate to both phases of their lives, as does James Wilson. Many use the vision as a device to move the protagonist from one realm of understanding to another. Still others describe a journey that underscores or parallels spiritual development. Shaker authors most typically unite the beginning, middle, and end of their narratives through the use of one or more of these narrative conventions.

Such technical conventions also express specific theological beliefs. Committed Believers did not perceive their lives, or the life of the community, as static. Rather, they interpreted all events in terms of the ever-unfolding progress of their belief. Shakers were convinced that the seeker who is open to divine signs and revelations would be led upon an evolving path toward the community of Believers and toward personal perfection. Unlike the spiritual autobiographies of other religious groups, especially the Puritans, who were influenced by the doctrines of predestination, the Shakers did not believe that the state of the soul could be fully discerned at any

2. Mount Lebanon, N.Y., 1866, MS, OClWHi, IV:B-35. The manuscript is in Brown's own hand, and the last page is dated 30 January 1871. Page references given in the text refer to Brown's "Biographic Sketch."

3. Wayne Shumaker, *English Autobiography: Its Emergence, Materials, and Form* (Berkeley: Univ. of California Press, 1954), 114.

point in life, that each moment could reveal election or damnation. Instead, Shakers presented the past as the story of the author's gradually increasing understanding of the nature of true religion. The types of metaphors and the structural devices used by Shaker writers reflected this theology. Thus, they not only aided writers in making connections between the past and the present; they also served a thematic function by illustrating the possibility of progress and the rewards awaiting the Believer.

Such integration of the past and the present posed little difficulty for authors who had completely rejected their former lives, for whom "the world had lost its charm." For others, like John Brown, renunciation of "the world" proved much more difficult. Interestingly, sexual denial seems less troublesome to many Shaker writers than foregoing the excitement and variety of life outside the Shaker community. Even as devoted a Believer as Alonzo Hollister at times felt intellectually and socially isolated, and William Leonard remembered his adventures in the wilderness nostalgically. Yet both of these autobiographers, while expressing occasional discontent with the Shaker life, affirmed that their choice was correct.

Unlike these secure and successful Shaker writers, John Brown, an unassimilated Irishman, strived to write a conventional Shaker narrative but ultimately was unable to force the Shaker perspective upon the raw material of his experience. The disunity of Brown's autobiography illustrates both the customary form of Shaker autobiography and the difficulties encountered by a complex personality attempting to fit the story of his life into the expected pattern. Brown divides his "Biographic Sketch" into two parts. The first is a spiritual autobiography which breaks down toward the end into year-by-year journal entries; the second is designated by Brown as "Appendix."

In his introduction Brown sets forth his intentions in writing his autobiography:

> Beloved Gospel Friends, I feel a desire for perpetuity; — I want to live, — live forever. — Live for God, and for the cause of human redemption on the earth.
>
> I want to speak encouragement, and to minister strength today, and in all time to come. —
>
> I feel impressed to write some about myself, altho' a delicate sub-

ject, because I am aware egotism is not commendable. But as we are justified or condemned, only by our motives, I feel the promptings of that spirit, which sustains me in my integrity[4]. The duty which appears before me is to leave upon record, a concise history of my experience, proving the truth of that Scripture, Rev. 12.10. "Now is come Salvation & Strength, & the Kingdom of our God, & the power of his Christ, etc." (2)

From the outset, John Brown's motivations for writing his autobiography appear complex. He wants to demonstrate his willingness to submit to the order of Believers, but at the same time he betrays a strong desire to be remembered, not as an example of the righteous man, but as an individual. Brown, unlike many Believers, does not claim to be writing at the request of others; in fact, there are indications, here and in some of Brown's other writings, that the Elders did not always look favorably upon his need to write about himself.[5] Believers expected religious motives for writing autobiography, and Brown makes an effort to supply them, but at times he seems to have added religious references almost mechanically. In the paragraph quoted above, Brown tacks the passage of scripture onto an introduction dominated by a series of assertive first-person pronouns. From the opening pages of his narrative, Brown inadvertently reveals a strong personality which never completely submitted to the Shaker mold.

The first half of the autobiography follows the predictable stages of religious development found in most Shaker testimonies and life histories. Brown was born in 1824 in County Tyrone, Ireland. He limits the discussion of his family to the religious backgrounds of his relatives. After his mother's death in 1826, Brown's grandmother, who was not religious, and an aunt, a pious Methodist, care for him. Even as a child he is confused by the number of religious

4. Good intentions were not an orthodox standard by which Believers were judged. Rather, to paraphrase a Shaker commonplace, the tree is known only by its fruit.

5. In addition to "A Biographic Sketch," the following manuscripts by John Brown are in the Western Reserve Historical Society collection: "*Notes by the Way* . . . ," Lebanon, N.Y., 1871, VII:B–127; "Autobiographical Letters," Lebanon, N.Y., 1871–1874, IV:B–18; "An Address to Elder Daniel Boler, on His 70th Anniversary, May 2nd, 1874," VII:A–6; and "On Wearing the Beard," Lebanon, N.Y., 1873, VII:A–6. Additionally, Brown transcribed the autobiography of Nathan Williams and made one copy of the autobiography of Richard Pelham. Several tune books in his hand are also preserved.

sects and the rivalries among them. He is a serious child, and thinks a great deal about religion. "I felt when quite young an earnest, & deep anxiety to know the true and living way of God, and to this end would attend various religious assemblies" (5). Like most others who later join Believers, Brown experiences a period of isolation in his youth in which he searches for the true Church. Again in the typical pattern, an "audible voice" assures Brown that some day he will find the people of God. "Alone, surrounded by trees, I kneeled down secretly to pray, that I might have the true church made known to me . . . and . . . I felt responded to as satisfactorily, as tho' an audible voice had said, 'You shall know it & have a privilege in it'" (7).

At the age of fourteen, Brown is baptized into the Presbyterian order, the church of his father, but from the beginning he has doubts that it was the true Church. The doctrines of election and foreordination trouble him, and the conduct of a minister who promises to take the newly baptized Brown home with him but then fails to do so disillusions Brown. "This act done much towards weaning me from my birthright religion" (11). Brown selects this seemingly insignificant event, probably remembered years later only because of the disappointment he felt as a young adolescent, to stay in keeping with the basic pattern in spiritual autobiography. Brown becomes more certain that he has yet to find true religion, for, despite his membership in the Presbyterian Church, he "acquired evil habits" (14). Among the Shakers, lack of protection from sin was a sure sign of false religion.

After coming to Believers, Brown understands that the "audible voice" which he heard in his youth was not meant to lead him to the Presbyterians but to the Shakers. "The spirit that responded to that prayer was Elder John Hocknell, one of the first witnesses of Christ's Second Appearing, who came from England to America" (35). In a letter to Elder Harvey Eades, dated 10 November 1872, Brown gives the following description of this event and how Believers interpreted it: "When about 15 yrs of age, or in the year 1839, I resided in the home of my nativity, on the Eastern Continent, in the Northern province of Hibernia; I then prayed fervently to the Lord to know His will concerning me, and was answered in the affirmative, by the Spirit of Elder John Hocknell, one of the first founders of this Chh. from England. So saith our Spirit seers — the truth of which I have no reason to doubt. Yea I was led out like Abraham of old to a strange land, called to forsake all earthly kin, and to make sacrifices unto the Lord my God."[6]

The Shakers viewed Brown's immigration to America as an example of the workings of Divine Providence. The spirit of John Hocknell, they felt, was instrumental in leading Brown out of the wilderness (Ireland) and to the New Zion at Lebanon. Brown, on the other hand, describes his immigration in purely secular terms. "Between the age of 16 & 17 years, I began to feel inclined to leave my native land; I heard much about Australia, & finally proposed going there. . . . The matter was agitated amongst my relations, who finally advised me if I wanted to leave Ireland, to go to America, as I had some kindred, & acquaintances, in New York" (16). Although Brown within the larger structure of the autobiography interprets his journey as a step in God's plan for his life, religious motivation does not play a role in the youth's desire to leave Ireland. Rather, his natural restlessness and desire for adventure lead him to America. "I had no distinct object in coming to America, and while on the voyage I had something to buoy up my spirit, by the external excitement; & having but little care beyond that of pleasing the animal senses" (22).

Accompanied by his father, Alexander, Brown sails from Liverpool on 19 June 1841 and arrives in New York on 5 August 1841. John Brown was seventeen years old and "a Stranger in a new country" (24). The promises of the new land soon prove ephemeral. Brown had thought that important acquaintances could help him get a start in his new home, but he is disappointed. He seeks out the British consul, a friend of a distant relative, who reprimands Brown for failing to remove his hat.[7] He applies for a painting apprenticeship, but the employer tells him they do not take any Irish. Seeking "any port in a storm," Brown takes a job as a bar-

6. "Autobiographical Letters," 75.

7. Although not a common motif in Shaker narrative, the refusal to remove a hat is frequently found in Quaker journals, where it signifies contempt for civil authority. See Luella Wright, *The Literary Life of the Early Friends, 1650–1725* (New York: Columbia Univ. Press, 1932), 178.

tender even though he is a committed member of a temperance society and the job requires him to work on the Sabbath (27).

Looking back, after many years as a Believer, John Brown interprets these disappointments as necessary to prepare him to accept a Shaker life. "My rebuff by the British consul, my interview with the painter, and to see the demoralizing effects of alcohol, and the selfishness extant among all classes of society; these things combined, seemed to wean me from the pursuits of this sinful world" (31). Brown sees in his life a growing willingness to give up the needs of infancy, to be nourished by spiritual rather than earthly sustenance. The image of "weaning" is particularly appropriate, for Brown must give up the emotional as well as physical dependency on earthly kin and must substitute a spiritual family for his earthly relations.

When recounting the failure of the New World to meet his expectations, Brown for the first time in the narrative expresses nostalgia for his native country. "To me there is no name so sweet as Ireland. And if I then had wings to bear me aloft, and the speed of the lightnings flash, how quick I would have retraced my journey across the foaming deep, to joyfully greet the early associates of my despised native land" (26). Not only does Brown long to return to Ireland, but he also fears that he may never be accepted as an American, that he may always remain an outsider. "Ah! Woe is me, an Irishman in America. An Odium in Yankeedum," he laments (26).

Brown's father seems to have felt a similar desire to return to the old country. Unable to secure employment of any kind, Alexander Brown leaves New York. "After about two months of wandering up and down like Noah's dove, and finding no resting place, he took his leave of me under the profession of setting sail the next day for Hibernia's shores" (29). Brown hears nothing from his father for four months. Then he receives a letter in which Alexander Brown announces that he has joined the Shakers at Lebanon. Eager to be reunited with his father and having no idea of who the Shakers are, John Brown leaves the city and makes his way to Lebanon. Brown gives no hint of a religious motive for his journey to Believers. Rather, Brown's trek is that of a lonely, frightened youth seeking a home.

Although he confesses his sins to Elder Frederick Evans, the young Brown still doubts the need for confession, which to a former Orangeman smacks of "popery" (37). In a dream, though, Brown receives the assurance that these are indeed the people of God. He sees himself welcomed by the "Holy Savior in coming to his pure Ch.h.[Church]. . . . This felt like the richest, and most precious notice I ever received. His demeanor was sublimely grand in the extreme, and his spirit penetrating; the impressions melted every feeling of opposition, and I felt to bow my spirit in true subjection" (39). Such dreams appear frequently in Shaker conversion experiences, so frequently that they may have been expected, but John Brown's vision is pointedly abstract. He seems to be describing an emotional acceptance of Shakerism more than a concrete vision. The dream nevertheless serves two important functions in Brown's spiritual autobiography. First, it gives credence to Brown's contention that the course of his life was providentially determined and that joining Believers at Lebanon was the culmination of a spiritual pilgrimage. Second, the dream validates to the community John Brown's desire for membership and justifies his continuing life as a Believer to those who through the years seem to have felt some doubt about Brown's suitability for Shaker life.

In describing this period of his life, Brown skillfully manipulates his diction to indicate a double perspective, that of the young man before joining Believers, who interprets his experience in worldly language, and that of the mature Shaker, who discerns the religious meaning of his past and writes about it in the language of Believers. For example, after receiving his father's letter, the young Brown thinks that the "fates" have laid out his future (31). And when he first arrives at Mount Lebanon, he feels he has been left with the North Family to "work out my destiny" (33). But Brown as the author of "A Biographic Sketch," who has been a faithful Shaker for many years, does not speak of fate or destiny. Rather, he interprets these events within a religious framework: "The Event had declared itself to my understanding to be a spiritual manifestation, and the answer & fulfillment of my prayer" (33). He says that he has intended to present "a few outlines of the workings of the spirit, which led me to the fold of Christ in Zion" (33).

Brown's ability to switch from a secular to a religious mode of language is strikingly revealed in the following letter to Amelia [Calver?], written in about the same period as the autobiography. Brown's impatience with religious rhetoric and even his tendency to ridicule it comes through clearly.

> Our Sister M.M.G. says she wants to read my letter in The Lyceum. Well now that is a poser—am I qualified to come before that August body? What shall I write about, or say to interest the people? Amelia, if I only had a transcript of that Abracadabra. Well if you must have an offering to make for me in that assembly of Saints, I will present you with sentiments impressed on my mind in the form of a prayer as follows. . . .
>
> Beloved Gospel Friends—my soul aspires after a pure clean, righteous life, a life in which there is no shame; a life in which the Angels in Heaven & all the Consecrated in Zion upon earth are my companions. Heaven & Bliss immortal is what I seek: Where is it to be found: The response comes home in sweet silent accents—in the cross—in duty—in my self denying home, where sensual pleasures are crucified, to give place for a higher life in all the Divine attributes, more glorious than mortal tongue or pen can portray.

After much more in this vein, Brown again addresses the sisters: "What do you think of it, not to write to you until requested, and then direct my letter to somebody else? Aint it somewhat like going thro' Nebuchadnezzars furnace seven times heated? Don't you see I'm growing a little weary?"[8] In the same letter, Brown defends not having written sooner. "I couldn't gather the proper e'magnetic forces, or in Shaker parlance,—'I hadn't a gift.' Will that do?" Brown thus displays an unusual self-consciousness in his use of Shaker religious rhetoric.

Brown clearly realized that Believers expected a standardized vocabulary in testimony and autobiography. To Shakers, the use of conventional language was an indication that the writer's thoughts, feelings, and spiritual life fit an expected pattern, that neither in life nor language had he or she veered from the straight and narrow path. Brown, in the first part of his narrative, strives to convince his Shaker brothers and sisters that his life conforms to the standard model. Thus he adopts the rhetoric of the Shaker testi-

---

8. "Autobiographical Letters," 155.

monies to describe his life after becoming a Believer. The change in Brown's diction is so obvious and sudden that occasionally the two modes of experience and language clash. For example, Brown gives his impression of his first Shaker meeting in a phrase found time and again in Shaker descriptions of the effect of the Spirit on the participants: "Electric shocks played thro' my body" (36). He concludes his comments, however, with the mild, noncommittal statement, "The meeting impressed me pleasantly" (36). Here, as at other points in the autobiography, the Shaker religious rhetoric seems superimposed upon the experience of the seventeen-year-old John Brown.

Brown's accounts of his spiritual experiences after joining Believers are frequently clichéd, abstract, and lacking in both intensity and concreteness. His character, he says, has been elevated; he has found "consolation and peace"; he has discovered "how mortifying is the cross." On the Holy Mount he "tasted of the true wine of the kingdom which made me stagger and reel" (45-46).[9] In contrast, Brown's descriptions of everyday activities are fresh and detailed. He has an excellent ear for language and reports bits of dialogue verbatim. Through Brown readers hear the voices and idioms of nineteenth-century America. For example, soon after he comes among Believers, Brown is set to digging post holes. He is not accustomed to manual labor, and one of his companions remarks, "You're lazy aint you?" (42). Another time, a brother asks him, "What did you go to Ireland to be born for?" (17).

Brown is at his best when he speaks in his light, self-mocking, secular voice. Brown knew that his audience would deem such a tone inappropriate for spiritual autobiography. He did, however, leave some writings in this vein, among them an interesting account of a trip to New York in "Notes by the Way." The exuberant tone is set when Brown describes his motives for wishing to visit the city: "I wanted to see my youthful acquaintances, & expound unto them the way of life—I wanted to advise my brother as to his proper bearing towards his children here—I wanted a bathing

9. Brown in this line alludes to the hymn "Spiritual Wine" by Issachar Bates. See Patterson, *Shaker Spiritual,* 169.

sponge and I wanted a releasement to have a ramble and see the sights in 'Gotham'" (13). Throughout the narrative of his trip, Brown's religious objectives are undercut by his frank curiosity to see "the world." When describing events that, Brown knows, Believers would have viewed as spiritual signs, he is light, at times even humorous. When he visits the ironworks at Hudson, a workman throws dirty water on Brown. Wondering what he had done to merit this spiritual manifestation, he declares that the Spirit should speak more plainly if it wishes to prevent John Brown from wandering into forbidden paths. During the remainder of his journey, Brown follows his own "lead," giving delightful descriptions of Central Park, Coney Island, New York jails, and even a cemetery. Brown also encounters several prostitutes in the New York City jail and gives a dissertation on a Shaker's proper attitude toward them:

> Public print reports that in the City of N. York alone, there is 20,000 professed prostitutes, 10,000 who practice, but dont profess; and I suppose libertines in proportion. The self righteous pharisee will say to this class, "Stand off I am holier than thou." Here is a work of reform, a missionary field at home, without going to the Indies. . . . But in seeing these poor creatures in prison, especially the females, I was led to reflect on a circumstance which may not be out of place to introduce here. Some years ago I went out to cut cicuta, at the mountain house above the springs, I rode up part of the way with D^n Bates; he said, "You won't want to go into that house," from this remark I concluded it was a place of ill fame. The cicuta was close to the house so I considered it proper to get liberty, I went in, & one of the female inmates interrogated me—"Are you not afraid to come in here?" I replied, "I am not, I come to you in a friendly spirit, and our faith and manner of life is such, as to give us confidence to meet everyone in a Christ like spirit. . . ." I had no finger of scorn to point at those erring sisters in nature, and truly I felt as tho' the angels blest me for witnessing to the way of life & salvation: And the mental response was from their spirits— "God bless you, go on & prosper, & rejoice in the God of purity, which giveth true liberty. We would we were as you are, but O! the sacrifice, the mortification we can't endure, we're bound by sin, and cannot abreak the spell."
>
> The reproving Angel had no dirty water to shower on to me,

as in Hudson at the ironworks: but otherwise blessing, for having spoken a word of comfort, to "the despised of the earth." [10]

Even though he attempts to put his visit to the prostitutes within a religious framework, Brown cannot hide his irrepressible curiosity about the ways of "the world" and its people. Descriptions of such experiences, however, would clearly be out of place in a narrative recounting religious experience. Brown thus omits any account of this journey, or of the prostitutes living above Lebanon, from his autobiography.

The most poignant and moving episode that Brown relates in "A Biographic Sketch" is his father's departure from Lebanon and subsequent death. After several years among Believers, Alexander Brown announces his decision to leave the Shaker community because, he says, he refuses to "bow to man or woman, Angel or idol" (53). His son, however, attributes his father's apostasy to his addiction to alcohol. Brown says of his father, "The waves of nature borne him down the tide of woe, and hurried him on to desolation. . . . Habits contracted by many years bowing at the Shrine of Alcohol, were not so easily to be dispensed with, and altho' in many respects I esteemed him as a model of kindness & goodness, yet herein he became a prey to the adversary, and his days were cut short in righteousness" (53).

A year later Alexander Brown visits Lebanon. As he still opposes Believers, John Brown tells his father that he does not want to see him again. Some time later, as he is walking down the road, John Brown sees his father but passes him by without speaking. "He wended his way out of sight or knowledge of his destination: soon after, two men from West Stockbridge came to inform me of a man . . . whom they had found dead in the water under a Rail Road bridge" (56). Brown identifies the body as that of his father, but he refuses to help with arranging a funeral or paying its expenses, justifying his behavior on religious grounds. He seems to view this experience as a test of his own willingness to break all ties with the world and separate himself, once and for all, from his natural relations. His father's ignominious death is punishment for apostasy and weakness, and Brown hopes that his father may

10. "Notes by the Way," 30–31.

yet be a faithful Shaker in the spirit world. "Altho' his sudden exit from time in this unpleasant manner may serve to shock the sensitive mind; yet I have viewed this circumstance as a Merciful visitation of Providence to turn his wayward feet into paths of holiness & peace" (57).

John Brown seems to deliberately ignore the possibility of his own responsibility for his father's death. "A Biographic Sketch" leaves unanswered the question of whether Alexander Brown drowned accidentally or committed suicide after being rejected by his son. The religious framework of the narrative, however, allows John Brown to accept the death of his father as another example of providential action. Brown writes, "More than 18 years has elapsed since the occurrence I have narrated, and I feel at peace in having done the will of Heaven, and even the spirit of my earthly parent responds in thanks, & blesses me for obedience, & subjection to this gospel principle" (58).

Only in the Appendix to "A Biographic Sketch" and in his other writings does John Brown suggest that he still finds it difficult to live separated from natural relations as demanded by the Shakers, and that he feels guilt and regret over his relationship with his father. In "Notes by the Way," after telling that part of a letter he wrote to his brother in New York had been censored by the Elders, Brown comments: "Have I shown too much freedom? I have endeavored to do as I would be done by. In the course of my gospel experience I have been very reserved & aloof towards natural kin, necessarily so to get a gospel planting. But as Isaac was offered up as a living sacrifice to the Lord, and then returned to him again; So will our natural relation (after we are thoroughly cut off and dead to that order) be gathered and stand related to us in the gospel. As Mother Ann said, 'Mankind will be redeemed in generations'" (192). In "A Biographic Sketch" Brown several times compares himself to Abraham. Like Abraham, Brown left his native land and, following God's command, settled in a new land. More significantly, Brown sees himself as an Abraham who was called to sacrifice not his son, but his father, for the Shaker life demanded the sacrifice of the natural relation. But unlike Abraham, whose sacrificing hand was stayed by God, Brown was not prevented from completing the sacrifice of his closest kin. Still, he feels that he has met God's test and has proved his faith under the most trying of demands. Brown views the death of his father as a spiritual turning point in his own life; from this time on, his only ties are the spiritual ones to members of the Society of Believers.

Throughout most of the first section of "A Biographic Sketch" Brown consistently maintains the point of view of the mature Believer discerning the workings of Providence in his past experience. Not content to limit his narrative to incidents that fit this perspective, Brown seems dissatisfied with a conventional rendering of Shaker experience. Indeed, less than halfway through the account Brown seems to lose patience with his task. He remarks that he has not entered into the "specialities" of his experience "inasmuch as the general history of Believers are similar, it might not be interesting" (70). Brown, however, in an assertion of his own individuality, prefers to describe the personal difficulties and doubts he experienced while a member of the Shaker community. Therefore, although he is aware that he has reached the end of an ordinary Shaker autobiography, Brown continues writing. At first he records journal entries, and then, retracing his steps, he offers an alternate version of his life story.

The conclusion of a typical Shaker autobiography would attempt to show how the author, laboring with both hands and spirit, has succeeded in overcoming sin and temptation and has reaped the rewards of faithfulness. Brown, in contrast, expresses dissatisfaction with his present spiritual condition. "Disappointments are the lot of mortals in this sublunary sphere," writes Brown, "and so I have found it in travelling home to God: I looked for a swifter change from the earthly into the Divine, & heavenly character" (63). After brief references to his subsequent trials among the Shakers, the difficulty of subduing his carnal nature (a topic discussed with greater candor than in other Shaker autobiographies), and the prejudice he has experienced because he came from Ireland, Brown begins randomly to relate memorable events in his life as a Believer. He tells of making two "seed" journeys and of a visit to Watervliet. He records a significant dream of preaching to his Methodist aunt who has opposed Believers. She appears a second time and listens to him reluctantly. The third time she appears, she becomes an advocate of the Gospel. Soon after the dream, Brown learns that his aunt has died in an insane asylum in Toronto. He feels assured by the dream that she has become a Shaker in the spirit world. On another occasion, Brown receives "a spiritual manifestation of practical utility" (93): an aching tooth is healed. Another time, he is pleased to report, he overcame the temptation to listen to the reading of a letter that Elder Frederick Evans had withheld from him.

Once Brown begins to write randomly, forsaking the structure of the spiritual autobiography which had held his thoughts and pen in check, he records many diverse bits of information, selected not merely to reveal his spiritual progress or to show providential design, but simply to convey interesting events or to explore his own emotions. The experience among Believers most difficult for Brown to accept seems to be his move from the North Family in 1861, after having lived there for nineteen years, to the Church Family: "About a quarter of a century ago, I felt a longing desire to come to the Chh. and I thot' sometimes, O if I only could be good enough to be allowed a privilege there, how I should appreciate it: And when the time arrived for my removal, I was somewhat pleased with it, the animation and novelty of the change bore me along for some years with a good degree of vivacity. But the novelty has passed, the excitement ended, and what appears to the natural senses now is, merely a dull round of monotonous labor and toil, so that I am thrown onto my spiritual resources for true enjoyment" (117–18). Brown openly admits, and an unusual admission for a Believer it is, that he is bored with his life. "But, O for a change — some excitement to stimulate, & break the monotony" (117). His "spiritual resources" do not seem adequate to satisfy him. Perhaps more significantly, Brown feels unappreciated and unaccepted in his new home. He says he "loves to be free, loves meetings" (87), but in the Church Family he is reprimanded for speaking too often in meetings. He is further "mortified" when he insists on drying sage in his own way and consequently destroys $50 worth of the herb.[11] He also has difficulties getting along with some members

11. A "daybook" kept at Watervliet records the following for 9 January 1868: "More trouble about the pressing at the Herb house, John Brown has [fouled] up as others have done — & backs out of service there — For about two years there has been frequent changes there, because of the foolish fickleness of our young men." On Sunday, 12 January 1868, it is noted:

of his new family. He says that 1869 was a particularly bad year: "Dissatisfaction has been manifested towards me by an associate at the table, which finally resulted in his stabbing me slightly in the arm with a table fork" (149). At the next meal, Brown leaves a vacant chair between himself and his assailant, but Elder Daniel Crossman reprimands him. Brown thinks he deserves an apology, but the Elder refuses to support him. When Brown lists his New Year's resolutions and his successes and failures in keeping them, he consistently has the most trouble with his resolutions to "contend with no one" and "avoid taking or giving offence" (154). Brown also seems resentful that although he had used all but $9.57 of an inheritance to buy land for the North Family, when he left for the Church Family he was not permitted to take along tools that he had purchased with the remaining sum (145).

Brown's attachment to the North Family seems to have been very strong; he remembers with great love Abel Knight, who was there when Brown first joined Believers. The move to the Church Family left him feeling uprooted and out of place in the only home he had known in the New World. The Church Family also seems to have had some difficulty making a place for the contentious, outgoing, and volatile Brown. Perhaps Brown's feelings of not really being a part of his new Shaker family contributed to nostalgic reminiscences of Ireland and the natural relationships he had long ago given up. Brown's love of his native land, usually suppressed during the first part of "A Biographic Sketch," rises to a crescendo in the later sections, which contain some of the most explicit statements of personal feelings and unhappiness to be found in Shaker autobiography: "I sometimes feel lonesome, uncared for, unnoticed, nobody wants my society, my company is rejected because I came from Ireland, a poor despised & oppressed country, and this wakes up a longing desire to return to my fatherland, where a social warmth of spirit is experienced" (119).

Brown seems to fear that he is nearing the end of his natural life, and he is troubled by the prospect that the remainder of his life may be identical to the twenty-five years preceding it. Although

---

"Change in Herb Shop—John Brown leaves the press." Watervliet, N.Y., MS, OClWHi, V:B-333.

he knows that his bones will probably be buried in the north or-
chard with those of other Believers, he nourishes the hope that
somehow his life might end differently. In particular, Brown dares
to hope that he may once again visit Ireland and, perhaps, be buried
there (122). Brown, it seems, is not able to conclude his autobiography because he is dissatisfied with the ending of his life. He seeks,
in the few years left him, to change that conclusion.

Although openly admitting his personal reasons for wishing to
return to Ireland, Brown realizes that without a religious justification the Society would never sanction such a voyage. Therefore,
Brown attempts to convince the Ministry that the time is ripe for
an opening of Shakerism in Ireland, and that the Ministry should
send him as the first missionary. He reports that on 21 April 1867
he received an inspired communication from the "Spirit of El. Rufus Bishop," who calls Brown "The Beloved Apostle John" and instructs him to "go" as a "light" to his brothers in Ireland. Evidently,
a medium named Abigail Crossman received this message and
passed it on to Elder Daniel Crossman, who gave it to John Brown.
Although Brown does not include the message in "A Biographic
Sketch," he preserves a copy of it in "Notes by the Way" (107):

> John? Called from distant Lands to be
>   A Light to go before
> Thy Brethren, yet in darkness found
>   On Egypt's dismal shore:
> I saw thee when the gospel sound
>   First reach'd thy hungry soul,
> Midst Friends & kindred, call'd to leave
>   Thy native land and soil.
> At first, thy manly heart recoil'd
>   Not ready quite to pay
> The price in full! And all demands
>   Of conscience to obey
> But soon I saw thy spirit bow,
>   Saying: "Thy will," not mine
> Thou God of Love! Henceforth my soul
>   Forevermore is thine!
> Thus, is the promise, thine to share
>   Beloved Apostle John,

> Devoted heart, and hands to God
>   Eternal life will win,
>   Thy Friend & Brother
>   Rufus —
> (Abigail C. Med.) Received from E. Daniel
>   Crossman Sabbath day April 21, 1867

While Brown in his autobiography interprets the message as sanctioning his desire to return to Ireland, another interpretation is clearly possible. The communication seems to praise Brown for having *left* Ireland, and may have been intended to encourage him to give up past ties to country and kin and to subject his own will to that of God and the Elders. The message indicates that others within the community of Believers were aware of Brown's desire to return to Ireland, and, rather than encouraging such an aspiration, were hoping to help Brown resign himself to the Shaker life.

Although it seems clear that in this communication John Brown has been called *away* from Ireland to Believers in America, Brown in "A Biographic Sketch" chooses another interpretation, that he is called to "go" as a "light," or travel as a missionary, to his native land. Unable to obtain the support of the Ministry for this venture, Brown attempts to test the will of Providence. He writes letters to Ireland, telling himself that if he receives a response it will show that he should leave for Ireland, but, rather poignantly, Brown gets no answers to his letters.

Brown's "Autobiographical Letters," especially his correspondence with William Reynolds of Pleasant Hill, Kentucky, contains further information about Brown's efforts to return to Ireland. Reynolds visited Mount Lebanon, and Brown was thrilled to meet a man who was also born in Ireland. Brown hopes that in Reynolds he will find an influential Shaker who will sympathize with his desire to spread Shaker doctrines in Ireland. Brown retains copies of the letters he sent to Reynolds and other letters disapproved by the Ministry, which he never actually mailed. In a letter condemned by the Ministry, dated February 1873, Brown's attitude alternates between submission to the dictates of the Society and almost open rebellion against them. He declares that Shakers are becoming selfish, that they are shirking their duty to evangelize, and consequently are declining in membership. Brown says that he wants to go to Ireland not for pleasure, but "simply as a duty to my God & my nation. . . . I simply wish it understood, that I shall do my duty to the best of my ability, whether that is taking care of the cows 366 days in the year, or any other care or pursuit among Believers" (46). After over thirty years in the United States and in the Society of Believers, John Brown still considers Ireland to be his "nation." He further charges that "there seems a waning & dying out amongst us from the lack of a proper development of our individuality" (48). He implies that, in order to survive, the Society must be willing to evangelize and must allow its members more freedom to express their individual personalities.

In "A Biographic Sketch," when John Brown begins to discuss his desire to return to Ireland, he realizes that his autobiography has reflected his conflicting attitudes toward the Society. Neither his spiritual pilgrimage nor his book has progressed to its expected end:

> My success & strength hitherto has been in keeping open with my Lead, and one of my main trials this year has been a slackness in this. Thinking how little victory I had gained over my evil nature apparently, I would feel it is no use in going to the Elders, all this mortification don't amount to anything, I'm the same creature still: I have reported my shortcomings enough: I have suffered enough: now I'll stop, keep still, and go on and do what seems right, and not be always keeping myself under a harrow, and troubling the Elders.
>
> And I have been tempted to destroy this book, as tho' my writing was merely for selfglorification & fame: I am not certain as I am free from this, however, I shall leave it; but if it is unworthy to be kept as a Memento, my successors are at liberty to extinguish it: It may live or die as wisdom may dictate. (120)

For nearly thirty pages, Brown has alternated between journal entries and a random record of his thoughts and feelings. But he still feels that he has omitted material that should be recorded; so, beginning on page 125, Brown adds an "Appendix" to "A Biographic Sketch." In it he begins his autobiography over again, but this time, instead of writing about his spiritual history, Brown records nostalgic and painful memories of his childhood and youth which he could not fit into a religious autobiography.

Brown begins the "Appendix" with the death of his mother: "The funeral of my Mother, putting her coffin into the hearse, was the first thing that made an impression on my memory. I was then 2 yrs, 4 mo. & 20 days old" (125). Brown's father had inherited property but had lost it all because of his drinking. After his mother's death, John and his sister Eliza were sent to live with their grandmother, a widow accused of poisoning her husband because of jealousy. Like his father, his grandmother is addicted to alcohol, and under its influence her behavior is sometimes violent: "She would lock Eliza & I up in the house, & when she was gone to buy groceries etc. we would go out thro' the window to play with the other children, but be sure & go in ere she returned. I was her favorite. She would frequently beat my sister, when under the influence of liquor, finally she used her up for this life: the last beating she gave her, Eliza bled at the nose, was soon unable to walk, went to bed, & deceased in about a week. It was reported she died in consequence of bathing in the river, but I knew better. I was then about 7, & my sister 10 years of age" (129–30).

After Eliza's death, Brown's grandmother takes an oath on the Bible to give up drinking. In light of this story, Brown's harsh reaction to his father is perhaps more understandable. It seems likely that John Brown abhorred the effects of alcoholism more than apostasy, and throughout "A Biographic Sketch" Brown takes a strong stand against any form of alcohol.[12]

Neither the death of Brown's mother nor that of his sister was an event in which he was able to discern the workings of Providence. Although of great personal moment to Brown, the deaths played no role in bringing him into the fold of Believers. Conse-

12. There is a striking difference in Brown's reactions to the apostasy of his father and the apostasy of his nephew, Stewart Brown, who left Lebanon in 1867. In "Notes by the Way," 184, Brown includes a copy of a letter from Stewart defending his action. In the "Autobiographical Letters" Brown preserves a copy of a letter to his nephew, dated 1 September 1874. He writes: "Our positions in life have been reversed. I began with Methodist and culminate in Shakerism, & You began with Shakerism, & developed in Methodism; I have only to say let us catch our birds and compare their beauty. I have no stones to throw." When Stewart writes to say that he is getting married, rather than condemning him, his Uncle John wishes him happiness. Although clearly disappointed that none of his relatives remained among Believers, Brown has greatly mellowed in his attitude toward apostasy since the time his father left the Shakers. Brown's strong reaction against his father was likely tied to his feeling of having been deserted by him.

quently, Brown omitted these events from the first section of the book, the spiritual autobiography proper.

Brown proceeds with fond memories of his boyhood occupations. He attended school for nine years. He loved horseracing, cock-fighting, playing ball and marbles, and spinning tops. He enjoyed hearing law cases disputed, watching soldiers and bands, attending wakes, and visiting markets, fairs, and parties. In describing these amusements, Brown makes no effort to fit them into the former portrait of himself as the serious, religious youth led into sin by worldly companions. Instead, he expresses a deep, homesick long-ing for a boyhood forever past and a native country he may never see again. The past was not exemplary, but neither was it dull. John Brown thoroughly enjoyed the ways of the world.

The language used in the "Appendix" is simple and effective; it is not marred by the false rhetoric of religious or literary sources. Brown describes the celebration of the Battle of Boyne in which he joined the Orangemen. He remembers the excitement of elect-ing Lords to Parliament. He thinks fondly of his great-grandfather, and his heart is warmed by thoughts of Ireland and the people he left behind: "I love my native country with a never ending love, yet I feel sorry to think of it and the reminiscence of early years" (132).

But suddenly John Brown seems to remember that he is writing Shaker autobiography and such recollections and sentiments will not do: "Well, I think I've said enough about my nation, worldly history, and my fleshly selfish degenerate relation. I am sick & weary of the subject, disgusted with the thots & reflections of my life when without God, and without hope in the world: there is nothing in it that I desire to hold in remembrance: and why I have written this garbled narrative, is simply to show what I am thankful for, & the great salvation I found" (138).

So Brown switches to remembrances of his life since joining Be-lievers. This, he seems to think, should be a safe part of his past to explore. But his unhappiness and dissatisfaction again break through. He lists his failings for each week, revealing what he per-ceives as a lack of spiritual progress. Once he kicked a bucket out of his way. Another time he argued with a brother over mathemati-cal sums. On another occasion, he "failed . . . by cherishing in a slight degree a lascivious spirit in my thots" (155). And once, he says, "I spoke of the sayings of my father unnecessarily" (155). He soon stops recording his failures, explaining: "There is nobody I have so much trouble with as myself. There is nobody I am afraid of so much as myself. There is nobody I hate to sit in judgment over more than myself. I hate to meet myself fair & square with the truth. That's why I ceased recording failures of my 15 purposes for 1870. . . . I am inclined to be cowardly" (161).

Abruptly, Brown turns to a discussion of the failures he perceives within the Society. He thinks that the Church cannot remain as it was in the days of the founders and that the senses should be cultivated rather than suppressed. A single rule, he says, is not appropriate for everyone. And men should be judged by their motives, as well as by their actions. "Because it was found essential to reject the pleasures of the senses in many respects in order to lay the foundation of our heavenly institution, is it always going to be so? I think not" (166). In the next paragraph, though, Brown reverts to a more acceptable position: Believers must sacrifice the carnal life; right and wrong are determined only by the Elders, and not by individuals. "Those who indulge a fleshly sense under gospel privileges, make themselves recipients of evil spirits, & become as a cage of unclean birds" (167).

Brown realizes that his autobiography has failed to present a model for other Believers to follow: "I may have told some good things about myself, but as an offset, I have told some bad, so that I cannot be judged as being very partial to dear self, in telling a one-sided story, and showing only the bright side of the picture. I have been strongly tempted to write my autobiography over again, and write only that which I think would please, and of course strive to set myself forward in the best style, but if I undertook & succeeded, that would not represent me just as I am: therefore I shan't do it" (168–69).

After another defense of his beloved Ireland, some copied letters, and an account of a visit to Groveland, New York, Brown closes his autobiography with two prayers and a concluding address to the reader: "Dear Reader have charity, I know full well of imperfections both in my character and writings, but as I am only just getting out of the mud and slime of a wicked filthy selfish sinful nature, you cannot, ought not to expect perfection" (206).

In his final sentence Brown recommends to all, "both aged & youth, the cross borne by our Lord Jesus, & Blessed Mother Ann."

The first half of Brown's narrative presents a typical, if mediocre, rendering of Shaker experience. Yet with the "Appendix," Brown has added an introspective dimension which was totally lacking in the first half. Considered in light of the "Appendix," the earlier section is like a dialogue that Brown was carrying on with himself, antiphonally raising questions about the meaning of his past and providing appropriate responses. In the first section of his narrative, Brown presents one set of answers, for which he hoped to receive the approval of other Believers. In the "Appendix," Brown delivers a different set of answers which, while not likely to please his fellow Shakers, certainly render his narrative more interesting to the modern reader. By dividing his narrative into two texts, one an external portrait of himself, the other an exploration of the internal man, Brown presents a bifurcated self, two versions of one personality, each with its own past. The two characters in Brown's autobiography are never completely estranged from one another, yet they are never totally reconciled either.

In his addition to the autobiography, Brown nakedly exposes his personal conflicts, but he does not find an acceptable resolution. He records opposing points of view side by side, without any strong attempt at fusion or synthesis. It is as if Brown realized that to explore further the relationship between his individualistic feelings and the stringent life demanded by Believers would lead to questioning whether he was equipped, by personality and temperament, to lead the Shaker life. This question Brown refuses to confront directly, since abandoning the religious perspective he has adopted would mean confronting a life with no clearly discernible pattern or purpose.

Brown's autobiography strikingly reveals the difficulty of establishing firm standards of success or failure in spiritual autobiography. The Shaker audience would certainly have judged Brown's narrative a failure. That "A Biographic Sketch" is, so far as we know, extant only in Brown's own hand, and was not copied by Shaker scribes, may be an indication that other Believers did not regard it highly. Brown's narrative does not succeed as testimony to the Shaker life, since, rather than confirming the rewards accorded to Believers, it reveals that Brown has not reaped these rewards in his own experience.

To the modern critical reader of spiritual autobiography, however, Brown's narrative holds a great deal of interest. Such readers may discern another latent pattern in Brown's autobiography, which was not consistent with the expected paradigm of religious development. The informing theme of "A Biographic Sketch" is one of loss, of attachment inevitably followed by deprivation: the loss of a mother, a sister, a father, an aunt, and, finally, a niece and nephew who, having been raised by the Shakers at Lebanon, became apostates.[13] In such a context, the disillusionment which followed Brown's removal from his North Family home, the only home he had known in the New World, is more understandable. The satisfaction which Brown gained from his Shaker life was based on the belief that he had found a new family, one with ties based on spiritual rather than carnal relationships. When this belief was undermined by the difficulties he experienced in the Church Family, Brown once again felt as if he had been deprived of affection and familial bonds. Although this theme reappears throughout both sections of Brown's narrative, it could not be fully developed within the framework of spiritual autobiography. To record a lack never fulfilled, a longing never satisfied, would scarcely be appropriate in a portrait of the Shaker life.

It is much more difficult to evaluate whether Brown accomplished his own purposes in writing an autobiography than to postulate that his Shaker audience would have read his narrative with disapproval. Brown's goals, as stated in his introduction, are contradictory. He asserts that he wants to prove "that 'Now is come Salvation. . . .'" In the "Appendix," Brown explicitly acknowledges that he has failed in this aim, and he expresses his own dismay at his inability to write an exemplary religious narrative. At the same time, Brown's introduction reveals his strong desire to be remembered as an individual. "I want to live, — live forever," he pleads. Brown, it seems, would rather be remembered, with all his faults and weaknesses, than be forgotten. And in this aim Brown suc-

13. The membership roles from Lebanon, III:B–14B, record the following: "Stewart Brown, born March 8, 1842, Tyrone, Ireland   Off Mch. 19, 1867" and "Leticia, or Lucy Brown born, Jan. 15, 1857, N.Y. city Off."

ceeds. Through his dual perspective on himself and on Shakerism, Brown creates a convincing image of his own personality and distinguishes himself from the more ordinary and less memorable, even if more devout, Believer.

What finally emerges from John Brown's autobiography is a picture of a warm-hearted, impulsive, intelligent man, who has trouble curbing his tongue, his temper, and his "flesh"; a man who was never quite able either to subdue his enjoyment of the pleasures of the world or to squeeze his own individuality into the structured and limited forms offered by the Shakers. Neither his flesh nor his intellect could be totally content with the life of a Believer; yet John Brown never seems to have considered any alternative but living out his life as a Shaker. Lebanon was his home in a land still strange to an Irishman after thirty years in Zion. His dream of dying a Shaker in Ireland was never fulfilled, for Brown gave up his earthly life in Lebanon in 1875, only four years after writing "A Biographic Sketch."

John Brown's self-portrait emerges as one of the most individually distinct and most appealing to be found in Shaker narrative. The modern reader is carried along by the sense of self-discovery in Brown's "Sketch," by seeing how Brown is learning about himself and his past through the act of writing. Yet, in order to have written a unified autobiography, John Brown would have had to develop a new perspective from which to make sense of the totality of his life, a perspective which would have related his beginnings as a rather worldly Irishman with his condition at the close of the narrative. Had Brown succeeded in returning to Ireland in order to spread the Gospel to his native land, that event might have balanced his earlier doubt and dissatisfaction and might have served to link all phases of his life. As it was, Brown never fulfilled his expectations, leaving a narrative that concludes with the desire for unattainable goals. In real life, John Brown seems to have struggled against the boundaries of the Shaker life; in a like manner, his autobiography fights against the form of the Shaker spiritual narrative.

CHAPTER VIII

LIFE
AS VISION:
THE
"AUTOBIOGRAPHY"
OF MOTHER
REBECCA JACKSON

Now it came to pass . . . as I was among the captives by the river of Chebar, that the heavens were opened, and I saw visions of God.

EZEKIEL 1:1

Written before the Civil War by a free black woman, the autobiography of Rebecca Jackson is not only a narrative of considerable historical interest but an outstanding example of black autobiography and Shaker narrative art.[1] Rich in its use of religious language and metaphor, Jackson's "Autobiography" is a highly lyrical expression of the visionary imagination.

Rebecca Jackson, a black woman who lived with the Shakers at Watervliet during the 1840s and early 1850s, was a charismatic leader whose strong character and vigorous imagination attracted followers and aroused opposition wherever she went. Although she sought the sanction and blessing of the Shaker Ministry for her missionary work in "the world," Mother Rebecca, as she was known to her followers, was not content to remain for long under the direction of the Shaker hierarchy. Her belief that she had received a direct command from God was too strong for her to be contented with the opportunities offered by the Shaker religious organization.

Because she portrays her personal experience both in the language of early nineteenth-century black Protestantism and mid-nineteenth-century Shakerism, the sources of Rebecca Jackson's religious idiom are complex.[2] She was illiterate until past her thirty-fifth birthday,

1. Jean M. Humez, ed., *Gifts of Power: The Writings of Rebecca Jackson, Black Visionary, Shaker Eldress* (Amherst: Univ. of Massachusetts Press, 1981), presents in one convenient volume all the known writings of Rebecca Jackson. Unless otherwise indicated, references to Jackson's autobiography will refer to Humez's edition, and page numbers will be included in the text.

2. See Humez's fine introduction to Jackson's writings for the complex religious and

when a spirit taught her how to read. Thus, Jackson had minimal contact with written religious literature, limiting her reading to the Bible, particularly the major Prophets and Revelation, and to a few Shaker publications. The testimony, preaching, and songs she heard during the first three decades of the nineteenth century shaped Jackson's religious language and increased her appreciation of the persuasive power of imagery, metaphor, rhythm, and meter.

Rebecca Jackson began to compose an autobiography sometime after her first extended visit to the Shakers at Watervliet in 1843.[3] Written in phonetic spelling, unpunctuated, and unparagraphed, Jackson's narrative offers a unique opportunity to study the religious language of an antebellum black folk preacher.[4] Notable for its rich and complex use of metaphorical language, the autobiography of Rebecca Jackson also represents the ultimate formulation of tendencies found in many Shaker autobiographies: the concentration upon subjective religious experience, the fading away of interest in external events or circumstances, and the exultation in the workings of the Divine upon the soul of an individual.

The autobiographical manuscript which has survived in Jackson's own hand recounts the years between her conversion in July 1830 and her acceptance of the tenets of Shakerism in the spring of 1843. The narrative opens with an unusual and dramatic sequence in which Jackson describes her initial conversion. The power and beauty of Jackson's language in this passage can affect readers almost a century and a half later. (In order to give some idea of

historical milieu of Rebecca Jackson's life. In particular, Humez explores Jackson's participation in and conflict with the African Methodist Episcopal Church and her association with holiness groups. She also discusses Jackson's life in the context of the racial tensions in Philadelphia in the 1830s, the excitement generated by the abolitionist and feminist movements, and the struggle of black women to be accepted as religious leaders.

3. See Humez, 63–68, on the problem of the relationship among various manuscripts, their collation, and dating. Humez believes that "the autobiography probably relies on earlier material that does not survive and may have been composed as a sustained narrative between 1843 and 1845," 68.

4. Rebecca Jackson, [untitled autobiography], Watervliet, N.Y., n.d., MS, Berkshire Athenaeum Library, Pittsfield, Mass. References to this text will be cited as MPB. Two copies of Jackson's autobiography are extant and include additional material based on papers and manuscripts which have not survived. The one copied by Hollister is in OClWHi VI: B-39. Another copy, apparently based on Hollister's edition, is in the Library of Congress Shaker Collection.

Jackson's pronunciation and the rhythmical effect of her words, I have broken the opening lines of the Berkshire Athenaeum manuscript into phrases matching the sense of the lines and the logical breaks in the narrative, but have retained Jackson's original syntax, spelling, and capitalization.)

> Sen In the yeare of 1830 July
> I Was Wakend by thunder and Lighting At the brak of day
> and the beed Wich Had bin my resting plac
> in time of thunder for five yeares Was now Taking away
> A bout five yeares A go I Was A fected by thunder
> and alwayes after in time of thunder and Lighting
> I Woud hav to go to beed Becos it mad me So sick
> now my only plac of reast is taking A Way
> and I roes up and Wolket the floore beak and fouth
> Ringing my handes and criing under great feare
> I heared It sayed to me
> this day thy Soul is requiered Of thee
> and all my Sines from my Childhood
> rushed In to my mind like A over Sweling tiid
> and I expeced every clap of thunder
> to lanch my Soul at the Bare of God
> With all my Sines that I had ever dun
> I hav now languigs to Describe my feeling
> the Fuest thought I had Was to neel down at A chare
> That Stoud at the head of the garret Stares
> it was Sergested to me
> the fuest clap Will brak your Neck down the Stares Well
> then I thought I Would go down in to my Brothers room
> And git in to beed With my Brothers children
> I thought that Would be immodest
> and it Wod Not Save me
> for thee Lord could kill me in Beteene the children
> and Save them A live
> I then thought to A tempt to prauy for God
> To forgiv me all my sines
> jest as I was agoing to die
> I thought it Would be A insult
> to such A merciful God
> and all this tim it Was athundering and Lighting
> as if the heavenes and earth Ware a coming to gather

So it Semed to me at that time
and I feelt it Was jest
That I Should be Damed for Sining
agancest A Just And Holy God
I then feelt A love minggeld With Sorrow
To Ward A insuled God
how I had Sin Agane all my Dayes
While this thought With many more
roull A cross my trobeled brest
thay covered me With Shame feare and confution
to think of living All my dayes in Sin
and then diing and being driven from the presences
of A morcyful And holy God
it Was more then I could beare
I then thought I might as Well go to hall of of[f] my Neese
A criing for morcy as enny Ware elses
So down I neeld at the head of the garret Stares
Wich Was the fuest imprestion
and down I neeld and I Crid
and prayed to God With all my might and Stranth
the more I prayed the Wos I feelt
My Sines lik A montten
reched to the Skies
Black as Sakcloth of heare
and the heavenes Was As breas agance my prarers
and every thing above My head Was of one Solled blakness
and the fearful Foreboding of my Suddent destructon
cosed me to cri out In the bitterness of my Soul
Lord I never Will Rise from my nees
till thou for Christes Sak Sake [*sic*] has morcy on my poor
    Sinking Soul
or Sendes Me to hell
for I feelt as tho my Soul
had com in to the Chamer of Death
and in this moment of Dispar
the Clood busted
the heavenes Was clare
and the monten Was gon
my Spirit Was light
my heart Was field With Love to God and all mankind
And lighting Which Was A moment ago

the messinger of the Death
Was now The mesenger of peace Joy and consalation
and I Roues from my nees
ren down Sares
opened Door to let the lighting in the houes
For it Was like Shetes of Glory to my Soul   (MPB, 1–3)

Recurring images of storms, thunder, and lightning contribute
to the strength and unity of this passage. Jackson draws upon biblical imagery, particularly those parts of the Old Testament where
God manifests His power through storms, clouds, winds, thunder,
and lightning. In her usage, the external storm parallels an internal spiritual condition, the need for God's salvation. The storm
also symbolizes God's power over man. It terrifies the sinful and
unconverted Rebecca Jackson because it reveals God's terrible judgment. Those who are saved, however, ought to welcome God's
manifestations rather than fear them. Consequently, after her conversion, Jackson opens the doors of the house to let the lightning
in, welcoming God's spirit into her soul. While thunder represents
God's judgment, lightning signifies His grace.

Such imagery is unusual in Shaker testimony, autobiography,
or song, but it frequently appears in black conversion narratives
and black spirituals. Jarena Lee, a black African Methodist Episcopal preacher from Philadelphia and a contemporary of Rebecca
Jackson, uses similar language, though less powerfully presented,
when describing her sanctification: "That very instant, as if lightning had darted through me, I sprang to my feet, and cried, 'The
Lord has sanctified my soul!' . . . The first I knew of myself after
that, I was standing in the yard with my hands spread out, and
looking with my face toward heaven."[5] Many lines from the most
familiar spirituals, including "Steal Away to Jesus," contain language similar to that employed by Rebecca Jackson: "My Lord
calls me, / He calls me by thunder, / The trumpet sounds within
my soul. / I aint got long to stay here." And one of the best known
Judgment Day songs contains the verse: "Didn't you hear that thun-

5. Jarena Lee, *The Life and Religious Experience of Jarena Lee, A Coloured Lady, Giving an
Account of her Call to Preach the Gospel* (Philadelphia, 1836), rpt. in *Early Negro Writing 1760–
1837*, ed. Dorothy Porter (Boston: Beacon, 1971), 502.

der roll? / Yes I heard the thunder roll! / Didn't you see the lightnin' flashin'? / Yes I see the lightnin' flash!"[6]

In Rebecca Jackson's autobiography, the storm often recalls the partnership between the God of Sinai and Moses, for Jackson covenants to obey God's spirit, to follow the divine inner voice, instead of submitting to the expectations of mankind. Jackson also associates the storm with being "called out of Egypt." This phrase is particularly evocative, for it calls to mind both Shaker and non-Shaker associations. To blacks before the Civil War, the South was an Egypt from which they sought to escape, like the Israelites, rejecting the bondage of slavery. In religious literature, Egypt suggested the spiritual state of bondage to sin and the need for freedom through religious salvation. Rebecca Jackson's conversion was also the beginning of a pilgrimage to the Shakers, and, in retrospect, Jackson interprets being called out of Egypt as her call to separate herself from the world. Shakers often used similar metaphors when depicting their spiritual progress. They, too, flee Egypt, sojourn in the wilderness, and finally find a home in the promised land.

Rebecca Jackson's opening conversion narrative employs a series of similes derived from Isaiah, Revelation, and Deuteronomy, to express her feelings of separation from God and her realization of the immensity of her sins. Her sins weigh her down like mountains which must be lifted; they are black like the sackcloths of hair which block God's purifying light; the heavens are like brass, looming over the head of the accursed.[7] With her conversion, the weight of the mountains lightens, blackness dissipates, and brass shatters, permitting Jackson to come near to God.

The imagery in Jackson's opening lines, besides resembling that found in other black evangelical literature, depicts a type of conversion that is compatible with Methodist theology. She experiences

---

6. Harold Courlander, *Negro Folk Music U.S.A.* (New York: Columbia Univ. Press, 1963), 42, 69.

7. Jackson's conversion narrative is rich in biblical allusions. Her reference to sackcloth refers to Isa. 50:3, "I clothe the heavens with blackness, and I make sackcloth their covering," and Rev. 6:12, "And I beheld when he had opened the sixth seal, and, lo, there was a great earthquake; and the sun became black as sackcloth of hair, and the moon became as blood." Jackson's allusion to brass heavens comes from Deut. 28:23, where Moses reveals the curses which come upon those who do not obey the commandments of the Lord: "And thy heaven that is over thy head shall be brass, and the earth that is under thee shall be iron."

the conviction of sin; she repents; she finds salvation through grace. Her conversion implies a belief in justification by faith rather than works, a belief that God's grace alone is sufficient to save the most burdened of sinners. Such a conversion, unlike one to Shakerism, does not entail the acceptance of particular religious teachings or doctrines. Instead, it emphasizes the emotional experience, the liberating and joyful effects of the conversion upon the saved.

The power of the opening lines, however, does not depend simply on Jackson's skillful use of recurrent images. The passage derives its strength from Jackson's acute sense of rhythm and meter and gains beauty through the poetic devices appropriated from folk sermons.[8] Jackson employs the techniques of folk preaching—rhythm, meter, repetition of words, alliteration, and even rhyme—to reach an emotional and rhetorical climax, which coincides with the central point of the passage, the moment when God saves her soul.

Many lines in this passage display the familiar iambic rhythm of English poetry and rhythmical prose. Initially the pace is leisurely, the rhythm less obvious. At the beginning, long lines of fourteen and fifteen beats describe the storm. As the narrative moves from the external description of the storm to Jackson's description of her internal spiritual condition, the lines become shorter: "This day thy Soul is requiered Of thee." Such lines often fall into the pattern of iambic pentameter. The passage gradually gathers intensity. Lines of transition, representing Jackson's new understanding of her spiritual state, tend to become short and almost formulaic: "I heared It sayed to me," and "it was Sergested to me." As Rebecca Jackson moves toward the moment of her deepest despair, the lines become increasingly shorter, the pace faster, the suspense greater. These lines, many of them five, six, or seven syllables, transmit a sense of urgency. In these lines, too, the stress and accent shift, emphasizing the change that is taking place in Rebecca Jackson. Regular iambics become less frequent, and the lines often show syncopated rhythms. At the moment of deepest despair, Jackson beseeches God in long lines of strongly accented one-syllable words:

8. Bruce Rosenberg, *The Art of the American Folk Preacher* (New York: Oxford Univ. Press, 1970), 35–43.

"and the fearful Foreboding of my Suddent destruction / cosed me to cri out In the bitterness of my Soul / Lord I never Will Rise from my nees / till thou for Christes Sak . . . has morcy on my por Sinking Soul / or Sendes Me to hell."

This pattern of accents becomes even more pronounced as God transforms Rebecca Jackson's despair into an ecstasy of salvation: "And in this moment of Dispar / the Clood busted / the heavenes Was clare / and the monten Was gon / my Spirit Was light / my heart Was field With Love to God and all mankind." Through her skillful use of rhythm and meter, Jackson creates a rhetorical tension which parallels the anxiety in the soul of the unconverted. After this climactic moment, the pace of the narrative again slackens, the lines lengthen, and iambic pentameter once again predominates. In the lines immediately following those quoted, the conversion narrative merges into autobiography and Rebecca Jackson lapses into a prose undistinguished in either rhythm or imagery.

In addition to using rhythm and meter in her conversion narrative, Rebecca Jackson employs a number of other devices characteristic of folk preaching. End rhymes occur: day/away, me/thee, chare/stares, A live/die, beare/Stares, heare/prayers, Dispar/clar.[9] Repetition and alliteration are used, usually not at the beginning of phrases but within them. Over a third of the lines in this passage contain a phrase beginning with "my": my resting place, my sins, my mind, my soul, my days, my knees, my spirit. Accentuating the repetition of "my" is Jackson's tendency to follow the pronoun by sibilants. Thus Jackson links lines in this passage by the repetition of sound combinations. Finally, a number of phrases in the conversion narrative are almost formulaic, and are similar to those that appear in twentieth-century chanted sermons.[10] In particular, one meets with recurrent "all my days" and "all my sins," and with epithets for God: "A mercyful God," "A just and holy God," "an insulted God," and "A Mercyful and holy God."

In the conversion sequence that opens her autobiography, Rebecca Jackson carefully controls her religious language through expert use of biblical imagery and the folk preacher's rhetorical de-

---

9. Even more rhymes might have been present, depending upon oral pronunciation.
10. Rosenberg, 46–58.

vices. Its exceptional poetic qualities suggest that Jackson may have delivered versions of her conversion as testimonies and sermons during the 1830s and 1840s. Thus, years after the event, her inner ear guiding her pen, Mother Rebecca wrote a conversion narrative that retains the theology and the language of black evangelical Protestantism. Her experience among the Shakers seems hardly to have affected the quality of her recollection of this personal religious drama.

Shaker theology and Shaker language, however, do affect the autobiographical account that follows the conversion section. Jackson often reshapes her remembrances of experiences that occurred long before her first contact with the Shakers to accord with the perspective of Believers. Especially when she recounts her visions, Jackson's language continues to be exceptionally vivid; but when describing her pre-Shaker life, Jackson rarely pens a passage as sustained in rhythm or as lyrical in concept as the opening lines of her autobiography. The central metaphors and themes of Jackson's writing are, to be sure, in keeping with vision or dream narratives. Unlike the usual Shaker author, who records one or perhaps two crucial visions experienced during a spiritual crisis, Jackson proceeds from one illuminating experience to another, focusing on the internal rather than external events of her life.

Few women who were married before becoming Shakers wrote autobiographical narratives, and none of them details as fully as Jackson the struggles of a married woman to establish her independence and to lead a "virgin life." God first reveals the necessity of sexual renunciation to Jackson at the time of her sanctification in 1831.[11] After praying "and crying to God with all my might, soul, body, and strength, until my body became faint and weak," Jackson feels her "burden" rolling off: "I felt as light as air. I sprang upon my feet, shouting and leaping the high praises of God. . . .

---

11. For those members of Protestant holiness circles who believed they might attain perfection, sanctification was a moment when the converted moved beyond "justification," the moment when sins were forgiven, and obtained the power to lead a sinless life. Belief in sanctification was not compatible with Shaker theology, which maintained that perfection did not come suddenly and completely but was attained slowly through discipline and self-denial. Nevertheless, Jackson portrays her sanctification as a major step in her journey toward Shakerism.

I never had felt so happy in all my life. I then saw for the first time what the sin of the fall of man was, and I thought if I had all the earth, I would give it, to be a single woman. How to return home to my husband again I knowed not. These were my new thoughts, for it had never entered into my mind that was the sin" (76–77). Thus, like Ann Lee before her, Jackson personally receives God's revelation that sex is the original sin, and she concludes that she can never achieve holiness and perfection while intimate with her husband, Samuel. Jackson may well describe her sanctification in the language of evangelical Protestantism, but her conviction of the sinfulness of cohabitation separates her from most members of the Methodist and holiness movements. Her staunch advocacy of sexual purity is opposed by many, including her husband, not unexpectedly, and her brother, Joseph Cox.

Returning home after her sanctification, Jackson is not able to convince Samuel that sexual indulgence resulted in man's fall: "That was my great trouble. I used to cry to the Lord day and night to know what I should do, and it would be answered me, 'Be faithful and you shall live to see the day that you shall live as you desire'" (79–80). Jackson struggles with Samuel also about her need to follow God's directives and never submit to an earthly man. It isn't until 1836, however, after Jackson first attends a Shaker meeting, that she absolutely denies Samuel the right to exercise control over her body or her activities. In a section Jackson titles "My Release from Bondage," she relates: "I was commanded to tell Samuel I had served him many years, and had tried to please him, but I could not. 'And now from this day and forever, I shall never strive again. But I shall serve God with all my heart, soul, mind, and strength and devote my body to the Lord and Him only'" (147). Jackson is convinced that her "very life was at stake. . . . From that time, Samuel sought my life day and night. And if I had not had the gift of foresight given to me at the beginning, I must have fell in death by his hands. So by obedience to the light that was revealed in my soul, and also to my heavenly lead, I always was able to know what he was agoing to do before he did himself. For the God that I served was the master of his God" (145). It is impossible to tell whether Samuel was seeking his wife's physical life or, as seems more likely, was demanding a resumption of carnal relations, for Rebecca Jackson, by 1836, equated sexual intercourse with death. Sexual relations, she believed, would do violence to her spirit in the same way as murder would destroy her body. The special powers which she has received from God protect Jackson in her struggle with Samuel. She portrays this struggle as a battle between two opposing gods. Her god demands sexual purity; his demands sexual fulfillment. Rebecca's god proves more powerful, and Samuel finally confesses that "he was a wicked man, and asked me to forgive him, and said, 'Now, Rebecca, you may sleep at your own house, I will trouble you no more. Go forth and do the will of God'" (145–46).

In her narrative Jackson develops the theme of the quest for sexual purity by identifying sexuality with slavery. To Jackson, bondage may refer to the enslavement of black to white or the enslavement of woman to man. In the latter case, bondage to the life of the body hinders the life of the spirit. Especially in her visions, therefore, Jackson views men as threatening and violent; they are both tempters and enslavers, and often murderers as well.

Just as Ann Lee, after receiving her revelation on original sin, experiences visions of mystical marriage to Christ, so does Rebecca Jackson speak of a spiritual marriage after she repudiates her earthly one. At the moment when Jackson feels she has gained victory over Samuel and has been "released from bondage" to him, she sees

> a white ball, the color of a white cloud with the sun reflecting in it, which made it the color of gold. . . . It came from the right side of the Father and from the left side of the Son. . . . This ball seemed to proceed out of them both. And when I repeated that word [Thy Kingdom come], it began to roll from them to me. . . . And it came to me, entered into my heart.
>
> And as soon as it entered it became a man, and my heart became an arch, and a chair in it. He had a mantle on him. He raised himself up three times, wrapping his mantle, it caused black specks to rise up out of my heart and pass away into nothing. They were like the cinder of a burnt paper, about the size of mustard seed. And when it was all out, he wrapped his mantle close around him and sat down on this chair. And when he sat down, my heart and soul, spirit, and all that I possessed, sank into a sea of humility, and my soul was filled with the love of God. I was like one buried in a sea

of love, peace, quietness, joy, and thankfulness. I was indeed separated from all my kindred. (148–49)

The theme of a mystical marriage to Christ appears in other Shaker narratives, but Jackson portrays this experience in non-Shaker language.[12] Thus, while Shakers often received spiritual gifts of "gold balls" during the Era of Manifestations, Jackson's use of the ball image is uniquely her own. The ball that rolls from Christ into her heart is "a white cloud with the sun reflecting in it." Once more, Jackson depends on natural images from the Bible's prophetic books to describe experiences understood by other Shakers.

Like Mother Ann, Jackson believes that the spirit of God is within her, that she is His specially chosen instrument, and that she must speak and act only at His command. God, Jackson is convinced, has "called" her "out of the world" to bring His word to those in bondage to sin. Thus a major theme in her autobiography, rarely paralleled in Shaker literature, is Jackson's unassailable conviction that God prepared her for an extraordinary mission. In "The Dream of the Cakes," Jackson sees herself sitting "on a low stool before the griddle." She greases it and three times places a tablespoon of batter onto it. Each time "a beautiful people" eat her cakes: "They were all white. I did not see them before I saw them eating my cake." As the number of people increases, the size of her cake also enlarges, so that it is enough for all. Wondering why the people desire her cakes so, Jackson tastes a piece and finds it very sweet (99). This may reflect Jackson's uneasiness about preaching mainly to white congregations, offering her spiritual nourishment to whites rather than to blacks,[13] but it also expresses Jackson's sense of her spiritual mission in a metaphor well-known in Shaker literature. When Shaker writers like James Wilson use nourishment as a metaphor, however, they commonly see themselves craving the sus-

---

12. Jackson returns to this theme in other sections of her narrative. On one occasion she relates a "vision of the bride and groom" (169–70), and on another she dreams of a mystical marriage: "I dreamed I saw the God of all the earth. . . . And while He spoke to me a stream proceeded from His bowels. It was white like the light. It formed itself into two streams. One poured into Mary's [Mary S. Lloyd, known to Jackson in Albany] heart, the other into mine" (172).

13. Humez, 99, n 39.

tenance granted by Mother Ann and the Community of Believers. Jackson reverses this convention. Instead of seeking nourishment herself, she feeds those who hunger. Thus, in her visions Jackson often assumes a role usually reserved for Mother Ann.

In a vision of the "Bread of Life," Jackson expresses even more pointedly her belief that she has been chosen by God to nourish the world. She enters a house where she sees a large loaf of home-made white bread and a "large white man." "This man looked upon me with a grave countenance. While I was permitted to behold him, I received this knowledge: that bread was for me to give to the people, this man owned the house, the people, the bread, and all." Jackson interprets her dream to mean that God has given her His "holy word," which is the "Bread of Life" (176–77). In this dream, as well as others, Jackson envisions God as a white man, and it is curious that even the "bread" which God commands her to dis-tribute to the people of the world is white.

In order to go forward in God's work, Jackson must be confident that He will protect her from the destruction which menaces her on every side. Early in the autobiography, Jackson receives such assurance when a mob threatens worshippers in a camp meeting. Fearing that their tents will be set on fire during the night, the camp's leaders order everyone to remain quiet and avoid praying aloud. Jackson, however, cannot comply: "I felt that I dared not lay down without lifting up my voice aloud to God in prayer. My very soul burnt within me. And to do this, I found it would break the rule which the heads of the camp had made. However, I thought it was better to obey Him who ruled Heaven, earth, and Hell than feeble man, who I then saw was nothing, nor their God. For I saw their God was their flesh and it had crumbled into nothing" (113). Accomplishing God's will, Jackson leads her "little family" in prayer. When she awakes in the morning, she discovers that a candle, left burning in the night, had set two bonnets on fire and burned the table until "it was a vapor. . . . The ashes of the things which was burnt lay all on the edge of the table, as though an arm held them there." Although a sheet over the door of the tent hung beside the table and the floor was covered with straw, "there was no mark of fire on the sheet, no smoke, no ashes on the straws, only on the table" (114). Jackson views this remarkable deliverance as a sign that God will protect her from danger if she always follows her inner light instead of the orders of men.

One of the dominant themes of Jackson's visions is the threat of unpredictable violence and the need to escape or to find protection.[14] After her conversion and sanctification, Rebecca Jackson receives a number of remarkable visions, displaying conventional motifs of Shaker narrative, which show how she may be obedient to God and thus assure herself of His protection. In "My Holy Leader, A Woman," Jackson sees a woman "dressed in light drab. Her bonnet was close to her face. Her arms hung down at her side. She walked straight forward. She neither looked nor turned to the right hand nor left. . . . And it was spoken in my heart, 'This is the way I want you to walk and to dress and when you are as you ought to be, you will look like this woman and be like her'" (93). God sends Jackson this Shaker guide, her "holy lead," who incorporates the spirit of Mother Ann and teaches her the way to holiness. After her first visit to Watervliet in 1836, Mother Rebecca recognizes the woman who has been leading her: "The Shakers was dressed like the woman I followed three years who showed me how to walk through the world without looking right or left. She walked straightforward, and so did the Shakers. I had never seen anybody before that looked like her, and I never saw any people before that I loved as I loved this people" (145).

In the conventional manner, Jackson also receives visions that encourage her to keep searching for "God's true people on earth." Troubled by her call to lead a celibate life and wondering why no other people in the world seem to have received a similar revelation, Jackson sees "in the distance flocks of kids, white as snow, on beautiful green grass. They laid close to the ground. Their forefeet were crossed and their chin rested on their forefeet. They were many miles apart. They all looked like one kid yet I seen them distinct. And when I saw them, it was said to me, 'These are my people. These live the life that I have called you to live. And if you are faithful, I will bring you to see them'" (137).[15]

14. Ibid., 49.

15. Humez remarks that "this is an uncharacteristically 'allegorical' vision" since "the flocks of kids clearly represent the nineteen different Shaker communities" (137). While such straightforward allegory rarely occurs in Jackson's work, it is typical of many visions

Although many Shaker writers describe their need for protection, this theme takes on a particular urgency in Jackson's narrative. While other Shakers seek protection from sin and from their own natures, Jackson calls on God to protect her from violence, much of which is racial and sexual. Other Believers find security within the enclosure of the community. Stone walls surround the garden of the New Creation and fences protect the clean white houses of the Saints. Jackson, however, rarely expresses confidence in the protection offered by the community. When houses appear in her visions, they are often prisons instead of havens. Only direct access to God's power protects Jackson. Thus, even when Jackson employs conventional images and metaphors from Shaker literature, she often molds them to convey her personal fears. Consequently, the metaphors gain an intensity not often found in the writings of other Shakers. When Shaker writers dream of dangerous experiences — crossing ravines on bridges full of holes, traveling through the wilderness, confronting wild beasts — the reader is constantly aware that the meaning is spiritual, that the dreamers' fears are of religious damnation or spiritual failure. While Jackson does interpret her visions of danger through a "spiritual eye," there is the threat of actual physical violence.

In "A Dream in the Garden," Jackson finds herself in an arbor, surrounded by blackberry bushes, as if in an enclosed room with a door in the north end. "The blackberries were ripe, long and beautiful. I began to pick, and then I thought I had always heard that there was snakes in them. I looked, and just when I was agoing to pick, there was one just ready to jump at me. And when I looked the bushes was full all around me and over my head. Every one had their mouth open, their stings out, and they were ready to spring upon me." Realizing that only God can save her, Jackson cries out to Him for deliverance. On her way to the house, she must pass through a shed where "they were akilling a dog. As I passed the blood spun on my white apron. I shook my apron and all the blood was off and my apron was as clean as if it had not been on" (94). In this vivid vision, rather than writing of the "gar-

---

in Shaker literature. This vision clearly recalls Father James's vision of the Shakers as a flock of sheep.

ment spotted by the flesh," that cliche of Shaker parlance, Jackson
envisions her white apron splattered by the blood of a dog, an unclean animal. The image of blood powerfully suggests the uncleanliness of female sexuality. When Jackson renounces her carnal nature,
her apron is again clean and white. Although the dream occurs
early in her religious development, Jackson appends a purely Shaker
interpretation. The garden, which suggests Eden, is her fallen nature
which she must purify, and the blackberries represent "the fruit
on which her carnal propensities subsisted," recalling James Wilson's admonition to Believers to avoid "feeding the flesh." The garden in Jackson's vision is not the restored Eden that appears in
some Shaker literature but refers to the fallen paradise in which
Jackson's carnal nature imprisons her. Unlike Eve in the Garden
of Eden who succumbed to the temptation of the serpent, Mother
Rebecca, by abandoning the life of the flesh, has not only overcome sin but has also been released from bondage to man. As she
later tells us, Jackson believes that Eve was punished for her sin
not by the pain of childbirth but by becoming man's "servant, and
he was to rule over her untill the day of her redemption" (279).

In her visions Jackson weaves allusions to biblical passages, motifs from Shaker literature, and the language of early nineteenth-
century evangelism into a highly personal narrative that has an
emotional intensity absent from the often predictable visions of
other Shakers. "A Dream of Slaughter" presents motifs which appear in many of Jackson's visions: violence of men against women,
fears of imprisonment, the frantic need for escape, a fascination
with avenues to freedom (doors, rivers, gates, windows, or roads),
and salvation through obeying an inner voice. In this dream, Jackson discovers herself imprisoned in a house. As she looks out of
an east window, she sees a man approaching. Finding no escape,
Jackson sits down "on a chair by the west window with my face
to the north. He came up and came right to me. He took a lance
and laid my nose open and then he cut my head on the right side,
from the back to the front above my nose, and pulled the skin down.
The skin and blood covered me like a veil from my head to my
lap. All my body was covered with blood. Then he took a long
knife and cut my chest open in the form of the cross and took
all my bowels out and laid them on the floor by my right side" (94–

95). A voice tells her to sit still, as if she is dead, for the man "has no mercy." When the man and a companion return, the voice commands them "not to touch me again. . . . And they both fled from before me by the power of that voice. And then I found what it was that keep me alive. He had not as yet taken out my heart, but my entrails were laying all this time by my right side of the door." This dream, vividly communicating Jackson's feelings of helplessness and fear as she attempts to follow her vocation, is inspired by Isaiah 53:7, "He was oppressed, and he was afflicted, yet he opened not his mouth: he is brought as a lamb to the slaughter, and as a sheep before her shearers is dumb, so he openeth not his mouth." Interpreted by many Christians as an allusion to the sacrificial death of Christ on the cross, this passage helps Jackson justify silence in the face of persecution. This vision may well present Jackson as Christ, the sacrificial victim, but it also shows that she must sacrifice her reproductive life (her "bowels") for the gospel.

In another long and complex dream, Mother Rebecca has been washing quilts. She is in a square room surrounded by water. Her situation is dangerous, but she sings and continues washing. When she comes out of the room, Jackson sees a road running north and south and a steeple with a "little white cord."[16] She grabs hold of the cord and leaps to the top of the steeple, where she is "above all earthly things." Her tub and quilts have disappeared, and Jackson turns down the road to the south. She sees three pictures

> all of one size and of one appearance, very majestic, long, and beautiful, of the male order. . . . Each one was on a black cloud. And there was three heavy claps of thunder. Each clap came out of each cloud. I found I had traveled a long distance — no house nor shelter near, as far as my eyes could see, and I saw a heavy thunderstorm rising. I wondered what I should do. It was said, 'turn back.' I turned, and when I turned in the same road that I came — for I never turned out the road in all my journey . . . , I saw a beautiful white cottage into which I was told to enter, which I did. And when I found myself

---

16. This peculiar detail also appears in other visions of the Era of Manifestations. See, for example, "2nd Book: A Collection of Sacred Writings Given by Inspiration at the Second Family of New Lebanon Commencing Dec. 1840," MS, Sabbathday Lake, Me., 202. Other seemingly obscure references in Jackson's visions, the appearance of eagles, for example, are also found in Shaker visions of this period.

in so beautiful a house, sheltered from the storm, I was filled with joy and rejoicing. And it was said to me, 'This is yours.'" (101)

Although Jackson has succeeded in finding protection by following the voice which speaks to her soul, a "sister" plants doubts in her mind. [17] Says the sister, "'Why, how can you live here? Nobody lives here.' 'Why, this is my cottage, and I am as happy as a lord.' 'Why, the sun never rises here.' 'The sun never rises here?'" Looking to the west, Jackson sees a "fourth picture, like the three I saw in the south — same size, same height in the heavens — and it faced the east and it was on a black cloud. And as I kept repeating, 'The sun never rises here? No? Why, yonder she is arising — arising now!' 'Well, she has only rose to you,'" responds the sister (102).

Rebecca Jackson does not interpret this dream. Hollister, her copyist, understands it as a vision of the Civil War, but it is not necessary to see the dream as foretelling historical events since it expresses the recurrent concerns of Jackson's life. The dream contains many of the familiar leitmotifs of her narrative: the desire to wash herself and others clean, her flight above the earth into a spiritual realm, the storm and thunder, the sense of being on a pilgrimage, the desire to keep straight on the path which God has ordained for her, the search for protection and shelter, and the movement from one dangerous situation (the room surrounded by water) to another (the storm). The function of the white cottage is like that in other Shaker visions: it is God-given protection which shelters the seeker from the storm raging in the outside world. Although the sister tempts Jackson, she discovers that the sun at the cottage does, in fact, rise in the west. Jackson refers to the sun in the feminine ("Why, yonder she is arising — arising now!"), and her vision probably alludes to the passage from Revelation which Shakers interpreted as a reference to Ann Lee: "And there appeared a great wonder in heaven; a woman clothed with the sun." Other Shaker visions support such an interpretation. Calvin Green, for example, once envisioned a "road appearing endless towards the

17. Humez, 100, n 40, says that this "sister belonging to the Covenant group who was also present in 'The Dream of the Cakes' is revealed in this dream to be hostile. Later we learn that her initials are A.B. and that she is jealous of RJ's growing influence in the Covenant Meeting."

East & West" signifying "that it is the gospel path that commenced by the rising of the Divine Sun in Christs second appearing agreeable to his parable in Matt 24 27 It will shine further & further towards the West."[18] While Christ, the first "son" of God appeared in the east, Mother Ann, the second appearance in the female, appeared in the west. Thus, this vision emerges from Jackson's commitment to Shakerism and is testimony to her confidence in the white cottage and her faith in Mother Ann's gospel.

When recounting visions that occurred before joining the Shakers, Jackson often mingles Shaker language and theology with that of non-Shakers. In the pages that close the Berkshire Athenaeum manuscript, however, the Shaker perspective completely controls Jackson's vocabulary, imagery, theology, and even the structure of her narrative. Portions of this passage are strongly rhythmical, suggesting that, like the opening conversion vision, they may have been shaped by oral presentation.[19]

In December 1842 and January 1843, Mother Rebecca paid her first extended visit to the Shakers at Watervliet, New York. After returning to Albany on 21 January 1843, Jackson felt that God wants her to testify to the truth of the Shaker gospel. Some of Jackson's followers resisted her testimony, and Mother Rebecca herself seemed to struggle against Shaker theology. The final eighteen pages of her narrative recall this inner struggle and record its resolution in a series of dreams, visions, and "operations of the spirit." These visions are rich in the imagery and symbolism common to many Shaker personal narratives.

While Jackson is in Albany, high winds intermittently buffet the house where she stays. She records on 13 March 1843 that

> I layed down and Sleep
> When I Wok the Wind Was blowing as if it Woud Lift The
>   House in to the are
> and I Was A frad of the Souffering of my Body under the
>   rouning of the house
> and in this feling I prayed To thee Lord to give me Strangth

---

18. Green, "Parentage of the New Creation," MS, OClWHi, VII:B–66C.

19. As in the opening conversion vision, I have once again broken the MPB MS into sensible lines, but have retained Jackson's original spelling. I have done the same with the concluding section of "The Resarection" presented later in this chapter.

and in a fuw menets I Was brought in to the Shower of floweres
and as I looket throu I Seen the blessed Santes com throu
the floweres
and I Was in the house that I Was in the dram the night
before   (MPB, 139)

Like the thunder and lightning in the conversion narrative, the
wind in this passage is a sign of God's presence. Earlier, however,
the thunder and lightning had a wide range of meanings; here,
Jackson uses the wind as a precise symbol to represent the purification process that a convert to Shakerism must undergo. The old
life, the life controlled by the physical senses, must be destroyed
before the spirit can be reborn.

During her visit to the Shakers, Mother Rebecca began to confess her sins, but she never completed "the work of confession."
While Shakers most often represent the process of confession as
a cleansing fire which transforms the old life into a new substance,
Rebecca Jackson reinterprets the image of the storm to express
her new religious understanding. Mother Rebecca's description of
the house where she resides also shows her increasing tendency
to employ symbolic, almost allegorical, religious language. In the
opening conversion, Jackson hides from the storm in the garret
of the house. When God saves her soul, she opens the door to embrace the lightning. The house retains its mundane function, and
it is not used as a symbol. In the latter sections of her narrative,
however, Jackson most often uses the house to represent her physical body, the "life of the flesh," the body being the *house* of the spirit.
In the passage quoted above, Jackson writes, "I Was A frad of the
Souffering of my Body under the rouning of the house." Symbolically, she is afraid of the physical suffering that the "self-denying
way" might impose. Her vision reveals that another house, a house
of the spirit, will await her when she completes the process of purification. In the vision, she finds herself removed from the house
in the storm and brought into another house, a world of saints
and flowers.

The concluding section of the Berkshire Athenaeum manuscript,
entitled "The Resarection," describes the final stage in Rebecca Jackson's spiritual development, her conversion to Shakerism, and her
acceptance of its theology.

The Resarection

April the 1 1843 Sating by A tabel
the Wind blwing in A terrable Maner
I feelt A frade and thought it Was not Saft to Be in the house
yet I felt not to dou enny thing With out knowing
Wather it Was the Will of thee Lord
For me to go out or to Staye In the house
I feelt desierous to pray
I ast thee Lord if I mit
And what I mit pray for
he tould me to pray to his father
to Rase me up in the resarection of his Son
So down I neeld in prare
ernisly intreting the Almighty to resarect my Soul
In To his deare Son
And While I Was Weeping and praying
in the Grat agney of my Soul
prostterated befor God
the father Spok to me and Sayed
What is the matter
What aleth thee
What are you criing A bout
hav I not Sent my Son to you
What more dou you Whont
What is the resarection
but your rising out of your natuer
into the natuer of your lord
And Savour Jeues Christ
rising out of your feeling
in to your Savours feelinges Wich are heavenly
pray to die to Thy hearing
then thou Will rise in the heareing of thy Savour
and then thou Will heare his vois
and know it from All outheres
and you will be able to allwayes obay
pray to die to your Seeing
and to rise in the Seeing of thy Savour
and then thou Will See the differenc
betweene Gods holy Will
and thy carnel Will

pray to die to thy Smele
and then thou Will rise in the Smeling
Of thy blessed Savour
and then thou Will Smels
the ouder of Holyness
and the Sweetness of his kingdom
and then thou will Desier
to be fead at his tabel in his kingdom
Wich is With in thee
And not at thy tabel of carnel desier
pray to die to thy taest
and to Rise to the taest of thy Savour
Wich is to dou all His Will in All thing
Wich is the foued of thy Soul
as it Was the foued of his Soul
to dou His fathers Will
When he Was on earth
as he sayed
it is my met and drank to Dou my Fathers Will
and in that he was alwayes reddy to Suffer
for that Was His fathers Will
he com in to the Wourld to Suffer
that We might be Saved
and that is What I hav could thee for
and in thy taest thou never can dou it
thy Taest is to dou thy owne Will
his taest is to dou my Will
tharfor thou muest Die
that thou may live
becoues he lives
pray to die to thy understaning
That thou may rieas in the understaning of thy blessed Savour
And then thou Will understan all his Will consening thee
as He understoud all my Will When he Was in the Wourld
      consening Him
the Wourld knowed him not
as it knowes thee not
but if thou art Faithful
the Wourld Shal know thee in tim of trobbeel
pray to die To thy Speach
that thou may rieas in the Speach of thy blessed Savour

then thou Will Spack of him and of his kingdom
and of ites richouesness and holyness
and all ites glory to all that I Send Thee
and then thou Will not Speak of thy Self
Thou has bin wary anchsues
to Seave the Souls I Sent thee tou
but they Woud not heare Thee
now thou has donn that—
and I hav A nother Work for thee To do
thee muest Stand for the gospel of thy blessed Savour
that Has bin troudoon underfoot lo thes 1843 ful yeares
I haf chousen Thee as one of my Witness
and that is the resen I could thee out of Egypt
by thunder and lighting and in Philadelphia that Wicked citty
Ware thou had no one to Speak tou that knowed me or my Son
Yea I lead thee by A way thou now not of
yet thou beloved me and Followed on untill I hav Sent thee
    my Son
and he Will go With thee The Wilderness throu
and brang thee out With Shoutinges of Joy
and thee Will be glad that thou ever knowed me thee Lord
    thy God
and this is the resen Wi I give thee power over the Cloudes
    So often
and now I Speak to Thee by the Windes
O be faithful my Child
this is the resarection
Thou art in it now
be Shoure that thou rieseth to the glory of Thy God
and that is in obedence to thy Savour in all thinges
Thou muest love and obay him in all thinges
and the Wind Was a blowing all this tim
as if it Woud blow everything to peces   (MPB, 144–46.)

The first lines of this passage suggest Jackson's description of her first conversion: the wind blows outside; she feels afraid and uncertain about God's will for her life; she weeps and prays "in the Grat agney of my Soul." From this point on, however, both the religious language and the structure of the passage stand in contrast to the initial conversion narrative. Absent from the later passage are many of the poetic devices so important in the earlier narrative. Little or no rhyme is evident. Alliteration is less frequent. Rhythm and meter, although important, do not build to an emotional climax released in an ecstasy of salvation. Yet this passage, just as remarkable for its power and beauty, illustrates the influence of Shaker theology upon Mother Rebecca's religious language.

In describing her first conversion, Mother Rebecca emphasized her fears of hell and damnation, her conviction of sin, and her separation from God. Her subsequent feelings of joy and liberation assured her that God had saved her soul. In contrast, the final section of Jackson's autobiography does not emphasize an emotional experience. Instead, it focuses on Jackson's need to understand the tenets of Shakerism. Following a pattern more common in Shaker than evangelical Protestant literature, Jackson has God speak to her in his own voice:

> What is the matter
> What aleth thee
> What are you criing A bout
> hav I not Sent my Son to you
> What more dou you Whont

God does not so much assure Jackson of her salvation as He explicates the Shaker interpretation of the resurrection. He tells her that the resurrection is not an event occurring after death but one which, for the Believer, can begin in this life. "What is the resarection but your rising out of your natuer into the natuer of your lord and Savour Jeues Christ," He asks.

God then speaks to Mother Rebecca at great length, revealing to her the difference between the physical man and the spiritual man, between the unresurrected and those who live "in the resurrection." The dichotomy between carnal and spiritual man is the principle around which Jackson structures this passage. God instructs her through a series of antithetical parallel constructions, each focusing upon a different sense. First, he exhorts, "Pray to die to Thy hearing then thou Will rise to the hearing of thy Savour." The hearing of the physical man, bound to the world of the senses, contrasts with the hearing of the man reborn in the spirit, who hears with a spiritual ear. Jackson develops this antithesis for each of six senses: hearing, seeing, smelling, tasting, understanding, and speaking. Instead of seeing with her physical eyes, she must see God's will with her spirit eye. Instead of smelling the odors of this world, she must smell the sweetness of God's kingdom. Instead of tasting the food of carnal man, she must be nourished by obedience to God's will. Instead of heeding her own understanding, she must submit herself to the "understanding of the Blessed Savour." Instead of speaking with her own voice, she must speak only as the mouthpiece of God.

No longer does Jackson perceive her mission as feeding the people of the world her "sweet cake," for in this passage, God instructs her to nourish her own soul by doing His will. Jackson thus seems to be reinterpreting her vocation. Instead of going into the world to convert the sinful and bring salvation to those in bondage, Jackson now believes she must separate herself from the world by joining the Shaker community. Although she had always attempted to follow the divine inner voice in her preaching, God now demands a total renunciation of her own speech. For more than a dozen years Jackson had traveled and preached the word of God; now she finds that God requires that this itinerant evangelism come to an end. Thus, God's instructions help Jackson to reinterpret her original conversion and her subsequent ministry in light of Shakerism. She understands that God called her "out of Egypt by thounder and lighting and in Philadelphia that Wicked citty" so that she might eventually become a witness to the Shaker gospel. Jackson now believes that her lack of success as an itinerant minister was due to her incomplete understanding of God's will for her life. In essence, the passage depicts Rebecca Jackson's struggle to submit her own will to the will of God and, implicitly, the Shaker Ministry.

Rebecca Jackson once again skillfully manipulates line length and meter to create a beautiful example of Shaker religious language. As God begins to instruct her, He speaks in loose, accentual verse, most lines containing three or four accented syllables. The metrical construction of the series of parallel phrases is particularly effective, for Jackson counterposes trochees and anapests in a rhythmical syncopation that highlights the contrast between the physical and spiritual natures. Note the metrical structure of the following lines:

> pray tō dįe tō thy taést
> and tō Rise tō the taést ōf thy Savoūr
> Wich įs tō doū all His Wīll in All thing
> Wich įs the foued ōf thy Sóul
> ās it Wās the foued ōf his Sóul
> tō dóu His fáthērs Wíll

Although each of these lines contains three accented syllables, Jackson varies the placement of the accent in order to emphasize the theological meaning of the passage. Each of the lines, in the complete passage, beginning with "pray to die" opens with two trochees and follows with an iambic foot. Trochaic meter is often termed a "falling" rhythm. In contrast, the lines beginning "and to rise" display a "rising" rhythm of anapests or iambics. In the middle line of the above excerpt, "Wich is to dou all his will in All thing," the stress falls upon the "all," re-emphasizing that Mother Rebecca must totally submit her own will to the will of God. The latter lines of the above passage all begin with unaccented syllables, a pattern more common in English prosody. Rebecca Jackson sustains this complex metrical pattern in a lengthy passage of over fifty lines.

Twice, in short dramatic lines, God summarizes his message to Mother Rebecca. About midway through this section, He says

> tharfor thou muest Die
> that thou may live
> becoues he lives

The shift in rhythm in the first line, which opens with a trochee, once again directs the reader's attention to the theological importance of this statement. These lines state the central paradox of Christianity as reinterpreted by the Shakers. Their message is not simply that Christ died so that Rebecca Jackson might live but that she herself must die, symbolically, in order to live. The death that God requires is the death of her sensual nature.

Jackson's skillful use of meter to emphasize important points of theology is also evident in God's final exhortation:

> O be faithful my Child
> this is the resarection
> Thou art in it now

Here Mother Rebecca learns that she need not wait until the millennium for the resurrection; she is living in it already. This understanding constitutes a second conversion, an assurance of salvation through an understanding that it has already been received.

In the final two lines of "The Resarection," Rebecca Jackson brings the action of her narrative back to the real-life setting in Albany, New York:

> and the Wind Was a blowing all this tim
> as if it Woud blow everything to peces

At this point in the manuscript, Jackson draws a line to separate this section from the final lines of her autobiography. The closing passage presents a symbolic conclusion to the struggle with Shakerism which Jackson portrayed in the previous section.

> April the 8
> I found my Strangth A leving me
> I Sat down on A char
> I found myself A going under A strong opperation of the power
>   Of God
> Wich I never had befor
> my boweles my head my eyes my eares my nous
> face mouth nack brast heart back armes lages And knees
> my handes becom nom having the feeling of deadness
> I found I Was coming to the chamberes of death
> I Saw a vision Wich I had 10 yeares A go
> and in it I now Saw my all Was at Stak
> and my Salvation Was at hand
> and it depened on my Suffering With him
> that I might rise With him over all My enemyes Which Ware
>   all in me
> and Whan they are all dead I Shall ries in Christ Jeues thee
>   Lord
> and then I Shal no longer live to the soues of my corrupt natuer
> but to the will[20]

In this passage, Rebecca Jackson symbolically represents the death of her natural, carnal life. All her sense of her physical body leaves

---

20. The Berkshire Athenaeum MS breaks off at this point, 146.

her, so that she is numb to the sensations of this world. The struggles previously interpreted as external battles against God's enemies she now understands as internal warfare. The enemy is not
outside Rebecca Jackson but within her. Her enemies are her own
senses and the persistence of her own will. She understands that
when these are dead, "then I Shal no longer live to the soues of
my corrupt natuer but to the will [of Christ in all things]."[21] This
passage, then, seems to represent Jackson's final submission to the
will of God, and to Shakerism.

Although the Berkshire Athenaeum manuscript breaks off at
this point, Jackson's other writings reveal that her conviction that
God's will and Shakerism are synonymous does not persist. Although Jackson joined the community at Watervliet in 1847, she
remained there only four years. The conflict between her understanding of her vocation, her belief that she must always follow
God's voice within her, and the Shaker Ministry's strict control
over the physical movements and proselytizing activities of Believers seems finally to have led Rebecca Jackson back into the world.
Although convinced that the Shakers were God's true people, Jackson nevertheless found it difficult to remain among them. She could
not finally believe that God had called her "out of Egypt" into the
isolated, white, Shaker community. Instead, Jackson continued to
believe that God intended her for special work in the world, directed primarily at her black brothers and sisters. The Shakers,
Jackson discovered, were not sufficiently concerned about the plight
of blacks. "After I came to Watervliet . . . and saw how Believers
seemed to be gathered to themselves, in praying for themselves
and not for the world, which lay in midnight darkness, I wondered
how the world was to be saved, if Shakers are the only people of
God on earth, and they seemed to be busy in their own concerns"
(220). Jackson also expresses grave doubts about the ability of the
Shakers to protect her from evil in the world. On 13 July 1848,
about a year after joining Believers, she dreams: "I was going south
to feed the people. And I was in a room on an elevation at the
north side, with my face to the south." A lion springs on Jackson;
he has her hands in his mouth. She prays, and the lion falls back.

21. Humez completes the line from Hollister's copy of Jackson's autobiography.

When she calls to the Shakers to shoot the lion, she discovers that they have no guns. "'Well,' said I, 'He will return.' I then flew south" (213). Only direct appeal to God saves Jackson; the Shaker pacifists have no power over the beast that threatens to devour her. Such visions seem to encourage Jackson to continue to seek protection directly from God, rather than rely on the Shaker community for her safety.

Even as a member of the community at Watervliet, Jackson continued to have dreams of violent portent. Shortly before she left the Shakers for the first time, Jackson dreamed that she and Rebecca Perot were in a garden and "a sister was with us." The dream seems to be set in the Shaker community. Suddenly the "sister" disappears, and Jackson realizes that "the people designed to kill us. I wanted Rebecca to make haste, and we would fly to Philadelphia, but she hindered me a long time. At last we went. And as we went, we met the people. The men had killed all the women and children, and were dragging them like dogs through the street. I flew westward above them all untill we came to a street that ran north and south. Rebecca went south, and I kept on west" (223). Jackson seeks shelter in a building, but the men pursue her. Three times she flies away, but each time men follow her and lock her in. Finally, a young boy leads her out into a room containing a bulldog and a lion. In order to escape, Rebecca Jackson must pass between them. She prays, and escapes unharmed.

Accompanied by her beloved companion, Rebecca Perot, Jackson left Watervliet in 1851 and returned to Philadelphia "to labor with & for her people."[22] In a letter to Sister Susan Smith of 12 November 1854, Rebecca Jackson explains why she left Believers. Although she departed from Zion in great sorrow, Jackson believed that she had work to do in the world. She had been unable to obtain the blessing of the Elders for this work, and, "being always led by an invisible lead, I could not submit to anything outward, that was contrary to the inward, and this being hid from my outward lead, they could not give me a gift to come away, though

22. Hollister, "Reminiscences," 188–219, gives a number of details about Jackson's life which he learned on a visit to the Philadelphia community.

I begged hard for it" (250). In 1857 Jackson returned to Watervliet, where she spent a year. In the fall of 1858 Jackson received the blessing of the Shaker ministry to return to Philadelphia and continue her vocation as the leader of a small group of Believers, mostly black women. Jackson spent her remaining years as "Eldress" of a community that carried on Shaker customs and beliefs although it was never an independent Shaker society.

Rebecca Jackson's autobiography is unique among Shaker narratives in many of its themes and concerns. The differences may be attributed in part to the circumstances of Mother Rebecca's life, for the narrative conveys the experiences, hopes, and fears of a black woman living in the United States before the abolition of slavery. The Shaker testimony, which had such a great influence on most Shaker first-person narratives, seems to have had little effect on Rebecca Jackson's "Autobiography." Jackson creates a spiritual autobiography that does not end with conversion, as do many Shaker narratives, but begins with her initial experience of salvation during the thunderstorm. Revelation has only then begun to influence the life of Mother Rebecca, and it continues to determine the pattern of her experience. Because Rebecca Jackson's autobiography depends so little on historical remembrance, it need not adhere to the particularities of time and space. Unlike other Shaker examples which, whether organized around a journey or particular themes, preserve a linear structure in order to present a pattern of progress and development, Rebecca Jackson's narrative is shaped purely through the recurring images and metaphors of her dreams and visions. While dreams are a common feature of other Shaker autobiographies, they usually function to reinforce the reader's perception of the linear, forward movement of the author's life.

In such narratives, a vision often signals a turning point in spiritual development or a culmination of the search for God. But in the "Autobiography" of Rebecca Jackson, dreams and visions are not merely structural devices; they are the entire substance of the narrative. In real life, Jackson never travelled South; she never experienced the fears and horrors of physical bondage. By moving beyond a retelling of the events in her life and by sharing her

visionary experiences, Rebecca Jackson imparts a deeper understanding of her motivations, her emotions, and her personal destiny than could be conveyed through a more conventional spiritual
autobiography.

CHAPTER IX

FISHERS
OF MEN:
THE
"BIOGRAPHIC
MEMOIR"
OF CALVIN GREEN

You see the ways the fisherman doth take
To catch the fish, what engines doth he make?
Behold! how he engageth all his wits
Also his snares, lines, angles, hooks and nets.
Yet fish there be, that neither hook, nor line,
Nor share, nor net, nor engine can make thine;
They must be groped for, and be tickled too,
Or they will not be catched, what e'er you do.

Pilgrim's Progress

Calvin Green enjoyed thinking of himself as a "fisher of men" who lured "gospel fish" into the net of Shakerism.[1] During his long life (1780–1869), Green traveled through New England, New York, and Pennsylvania, searching for "good gospel fishing places" and offering potential converts the "bait" of Mother Ann's message.[2] Just as Christ had left his apostles in the world to do God's work, so Mother Ann, Calvin Green believed, had left it to the first generation of Believers to continue her work in the world. In his mid-eighties when he wrote his memoir, Green was perhaps the last surviving Shaker to have known Mother Ann personally. His life story to a great extent parallels that of an entire generation of Believers who had individually experienced the shaking power of Mother Ann's personality and had built the United Society in America.

Green's "Biographic Memoir," written between 1861 and 1866, records the early state of Shaker society, the beginning of Shaker missionary activities, and the publication of major documents of Shaker theology.[3] Green is considered to be "one of the most im-

1. Green, of course, is appropriating a New Testament phrase. See Matt. 4:19 and Mark 1:17. Although Bunyan uses similar metaphors, there is no evidence that Green was familiar with *Pilgrim's Progress*.

2. Green frequently uses such metaphors to describe his missionary activities between 1807 and 1832.

3. Calvin Green, "Biographic—Memoir," Lebanon, N.Y., 1861, MS OClWHi, VI:B–28. Page numbers given with extracts refer to this work unless otherwise indicated. This manuscript is Green's original, in his own hand. The OClWHi collection also contains two copies of the "Biographic Memoir" made by Alonzo Hollister, and the Library at Sab-

portant figures in the development of Believers' life and thought during the first half of the nineteenth century," and his "Biographic Memoir" has been important in preserving Shaker history: "This magnificent inside view of Shaker history by one intimately involved in its making is without doubt not only the most valuable, but also the most ambitious accomplishment of any Believer in the field of autobiography."[4] Green's lengthy autobiography is often almost picaresque as it follows the many adventures of a itinerant Shaker minister. Green did not intend his narrative to be merely a history of the Shakers, however. He cherished the hope that his life story would increase younger members' appreciation of their Shaker heritage and would strengthen their commitment to the Shaker way. Within the Society of Believers it was the most frequently copied and widely read of all Shaker autobiographies.

Green dedicates his memoir to "the children of the new creation of God" who are "the genuine Lovers & followers of the Holy Lamb & Heavenly Bride—The Lord Jesus & Blessed Mother Ann" (440). These children to whom he dedicated both his life and his autobiography are, Green writes, his "only relation." The dedication underscores the importance of the spiritual family both in Shaker theology and in Green's own understanding of his life. In portraying Mother Ann as the Bride of Christ, Green revives a notion common among the first Shakers, who sometimes thought of Mother Ann and Christ as spiritual lovers who produced children of "the new creation."[5] Green, however, regards himself not only as a child of the Heavenly Parents but as a spiritual father as well.

Green, then, offers his autobiography as the spiritual inheritance from a father to his children.[6] More specifically, he addresses the

---

bathday Lake, Me., contains a copy made by Otis Sawyer. The memoir has yet to be published, but a critical edition of Green's autobiography will be essential to a definitive history of Shakerism.

4. Theodore E. Johnson, Foreword, "Biographical Account of the Life, Character, & Ministry of Father Joseph Meacham . . . by Calvin Green, 1827," ed. Theodore E. Johnson, *Shaker Quarterly* 10 (Spring 1970):20.

5. Swain points out that references to Mother as the Bride of Christ were not found in Believers' later publications. Green is expressing a notion more congenial to Shakers living in the early part of the century than in the 1860s, when he wrote his memoir.

6. Shea notes that Puritan autobiographers often addressed their narratives to their children, and he discusses the problem and implications arising from speaking to this intended audience (III–51).

FIGURE 6: Shaker Meeting Room, Lebanon, New York. (Courtesy of the Western Reserve Historical Society.)

volume to Calvin Green Reed, his namesake and a successor in the leadership of the Lebanon Society. Reed, Green implies, is a much beloved son who fills the place in the Society vacated by his father. On a broader level, Green regards all Shakers, both present and future members of the Society, as his children. He thus bequeaths his "Biographic Memoir" to those of the next generation who, rather than building up the Society as Green did during his lifetime, must sustain it in the future.

In developing his life story from birth and childhood to maturity, Green traces a progression from spiritual dependency to assumption of spiritual leadership. His narrative does not detail individual spiritual progress in quite the same way as do other Shaker autobiographies. Having always lived within the protection of the Society, Green never faces the temptations of the outside world. He presumably never commits those sins, sexual or otherwise, which produced so much guilt among other seekers of the true religion; he never searches the world, testing the available religions and discovering their inadequacy; and he never undergoes a conversion experience. The "Biographic Memoir" relates Green's assumption of the "mantle" of leadership among the Shakers. When Green is tested, he is not tested for his worthiness to become a Believer but for his worthiness to lead others, to serve as a spiritual father to the community.

As a Shaker leader, Green presents his life as paradigmatic of the life of the Society. His introduction states the dual aim of his narrative, to give an "account of the various scenes of my life" and to describe the "events which have taken place in the progress of Believers; with which I have been contemporary" (2). The major stages of the development of the Shaker community, in Green's view, parallel the stages of his personal progress. More than anything else, the relationship Green perceives between his personal spiritual history and the history of Shakerism is what gives structure to his exceedingly rich and complex personal narrative.

Green finds it significant that he was born in 1780, the very same year "that the gospel opened in this favored region — which the providence of God and the outpourings of his spirit had prepared. I was born just four months & twenty two days after the first Public Discourse opening the Testimony of our gospel was delivered by

Elder James Whittaker, at Watervliet—At that period the general opening began in America" (3-4). Green's own birth, then, coincided with the birth of the United Society of Believers on American soil.

Green was proud to be one of a very few to have been "born a Shaker." His father, Joseph, was a shoemaker. His parents never married: "The religious Revival which preceded the opening of the Gospel, of which they were both powerfully awakened subjects and subsequently their embracing the gospel, I understand prevented them from assuming one name" (3). His mother, Thankful Barce, four and a half months pregnant, joined Mother Ann at Watervliet in 1779. Mother Ann, "knowing her state," promised the young woman that "if she would obey the gospel—give up the world and the flesh entirely, she would suffer none of the usual troubles & pains of childbirth." Barce, a schoolteacher from a good family, was likely troubled by the growing evidence of her sin and the uncertainty of her future. She therefore embraced Mother's gospel, vowing to renounce the flesh forever. When Green's birth took place, Barce "was under the operations of heavenly power, singing & talking in other tongues when the child was born." Barce was convinced that Mother's word to her had been fulfilled. Green writes, "The Little one was born under operations, of shaking power . . . I was Born a shaker—Have lived a shaker—and am sure I shall die a shaker, and live an immortal shaker" (3-4).

Green's birth seemed to foretell a great future. Not only did it verify the promises of Mother Ann to her early followers, but it also suggested to Green a parallel to the birth of Christ. Although Green admits that the "supernatural agency . . . in the savir's birth was far superior," he nevertheless discerned divine intention at work in his own birth. Most often, however, Green perceives himself as a "type" of Christ's early followers. "When I was a Babe," writes Green, "our Blessed Mother Ann, took me from my mother's arms into her own, and blessed me. . . . This to my view heavenly notice has ever felt to me, as the real Christ taking in his holy and lovely arms and 'Blessing the little child'" (18). Mother Ann is the Second Appearance of Christ. To be noticed by her, in Green's narrative, is to be noticed by Christ.

Green compares his childhood with the early moments of the

Society when it struggled to establish itself and find the proper "order" by which to grow and prosper. Thus he inserts much important information about the conditions under which the first "gathering" of Believers occurred. Until the age of eight, Green lived with his mother or with other Shaker "out families" in the vicinity of Lebanon. Like William Leonard, Green found that his biological family was unable to provide adequate care. His own deprived early experience, Green believes, demonstrated both the superiority of the spiritual family over natural parent-child relationships and the need for Shakers to be gathered into well-ordered communities.

> Whilst under the charge of my Mother & living with her, I never suffered for food or raiment; but as she had to get her own support & mine in great measure by the labor of her hands, she had to work wherever her trades were the most needed. . . . I had to live in a large part of the scattered families of Shakers at New Lebanon and Hancock—Thus having to live in many places as it were among strangers, I could not always be with her nor under her protecting care I had to experience many trying scenes incident to such a state —and had full opportunity to see the vastly superior state which Believers afterwards attained in all respects. (6)

In 1788 Green joined his father, Joseph, who soon thereafter united with the Church Family at Lebanon. Because the Family had made no provision for the care of children, it sent eight-year-old Green to the brickyard, later the location of the East Family, to be a chore boy. The winters were cold and food was scarce. His supervisors had little sympathy for children, and Green says they left him "under hard masters" (7).

In this period, during the first gathering of Believers, conditions were difficult for all members of the Society. Provisions were inadequate; Believers had hardly any bread or milk. They lived mostly on "meat, such fish as we could get, porrige, salt meat broth, & potatoes" (9). Green continues:

> In short we labored hard, lived poor what we should now call very poor, had crowded & poor accommodations—They tryed to do as well by the children as their means & knowledge would permit, but I was hungry all the time, for the children in general partook of

the same zeal to support the cause as the grown members, & worked hard, but were not overfed. Our clothing was very inferior but for this I cared little. Up to this period it was found that the children had rather more than their proportion of the hardship . . . sufferings & privations which the shakers had to experience — until order was established & spiritual wisdom was gained & relation was gained, & by hard labor they acquired a competence of temporal subsistence and convenience —. (9)

By means of such descriptions, Green delineates his own place within the history of the Society. He demonstrates that as a child he suffered as much, if not more, than the founding members. Green's purpose in detailing the hardships suffered by the first Believers is also didactic. By comparing the former conditions with the present, prosperous state of the Society, Green hoped that young Believers would be grateful for the struggles of their forefathers and would commit themselves to preserving their predecessors' accomplishments.

In March 1790 Green received "a privilege" to join the Church Family. "I was then in my tenth year, was small of my age very poor, from I think hard fare & being ambitious, overworked, I grew slow & was so poor that this summer I weighed only 40 pounds, and my wrists was scasly larger than my thumb now is" (9). During the ten years after Mother first opened the gospel in America, both Green and the Society were tested. God sent a drought just as Believers began to gather, and He permitted one of the first dwelling houses to burn; but by attending faithfully to their labors and not becoming discouraged, both Green and the early Society began to grow and prosper. Green would certainly have been happy to place himself among those early heroes of Shakerism: "They lived heroically, and gloriously did they conquer themselves and the difficulties of that day and time, laying broad and deep the foundations of the house of the Spirit's building, where their latest successors find rescue, blessing, home and salvation. Well may we bless those heroic souls, who, from 1787 through the early years of the nineteenth century, toiled and struggled and conquered the world within and without and left so glorious an inheritance."[7]

7. White and Taylor, 79.

The second period of testing for Green and for the Church was not brought on by material deprivations but by spiritual defections. During the 1790s numerous apostasies shook the Society and tested Green's commitment to Shakerism. It was only after the youth order dissolved in the spring of 1796 and after those who had stood firm became a part of the First Family that Green felt his real spiritual growth beginning. "Apostasy had ceased and all the rising generation who stood the test of the aforesaid trying ordeal, proved faithful to the cause, and leading characters in the future work of God, & I believe not one of them finally fell to the world" (29).

Green's physical growth kept pace with his spiritual progress, for during one year alone he grew six inches in height. The physical and spiritual growth of the individual, Calvin Green, becomes in the "Biographic Memoir" an emblem for the progress of the Society, both materially and spiritually.

For a year Green went through "heavy labor," and spiritual manifestations provide verification of his progress. He confessed his sins and, shortly after, received a "spiritual baptism": "When about 19 years of age, before meeting I had labored for the power of the spirit and as I pitched a song for laboring I heard a pouring over my head as if a large vesel of water was pouring down and instantly a power fell upon me with great force & run all over & thro my whole system. . . . I consider [it] to be a real baptism of the holy spirit to infuse into my soul the life powers of the gospel and after to such a young man as I then was just entering upon the stage of manhood—" (30).

As confirmation of his growing faith, Green received in vision a second "baptism" which expanded his understanding of Shakerism and refocused his arrogant intellect: "I had an extreme aspiration for knowledge & a very independent mind—and on this round my crosses & trials have been extremely severe, Here has been my greatest struggles & most trying crosses, to give up my own life in this way was harder than all the rest" (20). This vision, which occurred around the turn of the century, puts Shakerism into the wider context of the history of God's revelation to man throughout the ages:

> The everlasting work of the eternal elements thro' Christ appeared to me like a boundless ocean of the waters of life. . . . I saw that

this endless fountain centered in the gospel which produced the Church of genuine Shakerism. This ocean rolled forward in waves, one wave after another. . . . Each wave brot forth an increas to those who were in it, one after another without end (those just entering the work must come into the first wave, if it be a thousand years hence, for the first wave will always remain first to the end of time) —and saw that these living waters would yet flow to all the world . . . visible & invisible. I also saw that each rolling wave as it unrolled dissolved a portion of the life & elements of the natural inferior order, which is comprehended by the term natural state. Therefore I clearly saw that in no other way than by rejecting the lusts & propensities of the elementary life of this natural world — and thereby really progressing in these unrolling waves of spiritual increase, into higher degrees, could any soul ever gain a heavenly state. . . . I had previously been enlightened & confirmed in my faith by spiritual operations, as a child & as a youth. . . . But at this time I felt my soul as a man baptised into the elements of Eternal Life, into which I am sure I have been travailing[8] & growing more & more to this Day. (36-37)

As the early "spiritual operation" confirmed Green's childhood faith, this vision "enlightened" his adult intellect. Although Green never lived outside the Shaker community, he seems to have been extraordinarily sensitive to the intellectual currents of his time. His vision of the progressive nature of religious revelation helped Green defend Shakerism as a rational religion based on a correct understanding of the Bible, history, and human nature. In all of Green's writings, the notion of historical and religious progress is paramount. Like his non-Shaker contemporaries, Green possessed great optimism that in the New World man would be regenerated and that a new era in human history had begun. During his long ministry, Green preached the doctrine that spiritual progress is both historical and individual.

In spite of this intellectual defense of Shakerism, Green believed that the orderly development of man's religious knowledge came not through any rational means but through God's supernatural revelation. He articulated the doctrine of the four dispensations,

8. Although the usage of "travel" developed from the earlier "travail" Green seems to use the terms interchangeably.

developed by Shaker theologians during the first decade of the nineteenth century to explain God's redemption of man through history.[9] Such theories were a staple feature of sectarian theology, but Shakers interpreted sacred history according to their belief in the necessity of sexual purity. In the first dispensation to Abraham, God required circumcision, a sign that he intended men to destroy the life of the flesh. In the second, Mosaic dispensation, God gave men laws indicating the need for purification from sexual pollution. Only with the coming of Jesus, however, in the third dispensation, did men have before them the example of a completely pure life, one lived entirely "out of the flesh." After the advent of Christ, his followers were unwilling to accept fully the new revelation of the necessity for celibacy. In the following centuries, his teachings were distorted, so that a fourth dispensation, the Second Appearing of Christ in Mother Ann, was required in order to reveal clearly the sexual root of all evil. Green's belief in "the history of redemption" helped him to understand his own life and shape his autobiography. He asserts that in each era God selected certain men and women, those who were in "the line of promise," as "chosen seed." Although these persons were conceived through sexual union and born in the normal manner, their births were "supernaturally directed," and Green felt that his own birth, like that of Christ, had occurred under divine auspices. In each generation, in each dispensation, these specially chosen men and women were God's instruments for religious progress.

Since Shakerism held out the possibility that all men and women might live perfect lives, modeled after Christ and Mother Ann, Shaker autobiographers like Green could compare themselves to the Holy Parents without appearing unduly presumptuous or self-righteous. Nevertheless, Green felt that he was destined for a special role, and he compares himself to prophets of other eras who spread the revelation of their dispensation. Like Samuel, who "began a new order in Israel," Green helped to begin a new order in America.[10] He compares his mother to the mother of Samuel, for both, Green says, were willing to break the ties of natural affec-

9. Marini discusses the development of the dispensational theory in detail (136–55).
10. *Testimony*, 4th ed., 486.

tion in order to prepare their sons for their spiritual missions. He also compares himself to Paul, the great prophet of the third dispensation chosen by God to spread the gospel of Christ to the world. Richard Bushnell, himself destined to become a leader of the Society and Green's companion on missionary journeys, recognized Green as a figure of Paul. Writes Green, "[W]hen [Bushnell] first saw me it struck his view that I looked just like good old St. Paul" (69).

Green clearly regarded himself as a prophet of the fourth dispensation who had been chosen to spread the gospel of Mother Ann to the world.[11] Even though Green felt himself lucky to have been born during the final dispensation, he believed that each individual must begin his spiritual travel in the state of natural man in which all, like Adam, are born. According to Green, the stages of the individual's spiritual development must recapitulate the historical progress of revelation. Thus the theory of the four dispensations of divine revelation provided Green with a model for the structure of his autobiography. As a newborn infant, he was in the natural state of man. In his youth, he zealously observed the laws of the Society. This period corresponded in some measure to the Mosaic dispensation. But he had not yet been "baptised in the spirit," an experience Green probably equated with the third dispensation, when the "new law" of Christ replaced the "old law" of the Mosaic dispensation. Green entered into this stage of spiritual development only after much spiritual labor and the confession of his sins. Still, Green required another baptism, which he believed occurred in the vision of "the boundless ocean." This vision satisfied Green's demand for a system of rational beliefs, and it confirmed once and for all his acceptance of the revelation of the fourth dispensation, that further spiritual progress was possible only by renouncing the life of the flesh. This final "conversion vision" occurred just as Green approached his twenty-first birthday, a time when he had to decide whether or not to accept the Shaker covenant for himself. The vision signifies Green's full acceptance of the Shaker way and the beginning of the vocation of his maturity.

The development of Green's life continued to coincide with the

---

11. Green also interprets both the Bible and events in his own life typologically, following a method of religious interpretation commonly used by the Puritans. See Sacvan Bercovitch, ed., *Typology and Early American Literature* (Boston: Univ. of Massachusetts Press, 1972).

development of the United Society. As Green reached adulthood, the Society had come "into order" and was ready to "open" its gospel to the world. Spiritual signs indicated that some "would be called into the work" (41) of spreading the message of Mother Ann and gathering converts into the Shaker communities. In 1805 the Ministry sent Benjamin Seth Youngs, John Meacham, son of Joseph, and Issachar Bates into Kentucky and Ohio, where the great frontier revivals of the Second Great Awakening were under way.

Since his youth, Calvin Green had been under "divine impressions" that some day he would be called to "travel much, to preach, and write to propagate the divine principles" and would "become an active agent to gather souls to the kingdom of Heaven" (43). After becoming part of the Church Family, however, Green learned that he must not articulate such aspirations but must "labor down into deep mortification that is subjection of spirit & self abasement" (43).

Nevertheless, in 1807 the Ministry recognized what Green had known all along, that he was suited to become one of the chief instruments to open the gospel in the eastern states. Mother Lucy announced the Ministry's decision to Green: "We feel a gift in union for you to go into the North family—to labor in the gathering order to find a gift as a preacher of the gospel and gather souls to it—I send you said she—as a mouth & messenger for the Church . . . go & be faithful, labor for the gift of God in that work—Were it necessary to alter your name I should call you Aaron, but it is not Calvin is a good name, Elder Calvin was an able preacher to open the testimony of the Gospel" (43).

Early in his narrative, Green relates that his mother named him after Calvin Harlow, the first Bishop of Hancock, who "was greatly gifted in public speaking to open clearly the testimony of the Gospel. . . . Some who have been acquainted," writes Green, "have remarked that they thot my gift in that line of opening the gospel, resembled his more than any other one. It has been stated that he was seen in vision and said his mantle of peculiar gifts rested upon me" (5). Such signs, Green implies, indicate divine sanction for his vocation as a gospel missionary.

During the early years of the opening of the gospel, Green assumed large responsibility for transmitting "a new order of light and understanding of the nature & power of Christ's second appearing" (57). The task of answering the "metaphysical questions" of potential converts fell chiefly to Green. The social order of the community had been established before the turn of the century, but it was during the first decade of the nineteenth century that Shaker theology developed. In these years, men like Calvin Green in the East and Benjamin Seth Youngs in the West contributed greatly to the development and articulation of the Shaker understanding of religious history.

Green's description of his years as a Shaker preacher is rich in anecdotes similar in theme to those of Methodist itinerant preachers: prayers are remarkably fulfilled; unusual conversions occur; and apostates and opponents of Shakerism are providentially judged, often by painful and untimely deaths.[12] Green, like the ministers of other denominations, seems to have collected religious lore to use in his preaching, to persuade his listeners and to enliven his message, and perhaps, like Peter Cartwright, even to catch the attention of unruly audiences. Deviating from most Shaker narratives, Green's "Biographic Memoir" even includes a few humorous stories.[13]

Green often uses such stories to testify to the "mantle" of leadership which he believed had descended upon him and to the divine power which flowed through his preaching. Once, after he preaches "powerfully" at Savoy, "it began to snow rapidly with wonderful large flakes & it thundered tremendously, the lightening gleaming through the snow." As the people returned home from the meeting, further signs gave sanction to Green's message. The air was "full of lights, these lit on and covered their horses & covered their own clothes & if they attempted to brush them off they would stick to their hands. Also these lights lit on the fences and stakes by the road side." In the meeting, a man had confronted Green with bibli-

12. Byrne, 103-56, 193-210.

13. Shakers were not noted for their humor. In Green's memoir the following story is told: "Caty Estes . . . wanted to be a Shakeress; but her husband Thomas . . . dreaded the cross; on Caty's telling him she wanted to unite with us, he answered, 'You may go to be a Shaker if you're a mind to, & I'll go among the Shakers & get me another wife.' This was before he had seen the sisters after he had seen us she says to him—'Do you want to get one of them women for a wife?' No says he—'I had as lief go to bed with a spirit as to one of them'" (105).

cal verses that, he contended, refuted Shakerism. When this man later approached the ball of light and pointed at it, "the ball hissed at him like a goose, he meant to show that he was not afraid, but this struck him with such awe that he durst not approach but draw back" (93).

On another occasion, a round glowing object appears in the assembly after Green preaches. Three times it darts down from a window. "The last gleam struck James Cornell & he immediately fell on his knees & attested that early in the morning that day he heard an audible voice declaring that this doctrine by the shakers was the true gospel" (96). Green includes such stories not merely because they are entertaining; for Green and his readers, these signs attest to the truth of the Shaker gospel and show that the Shaker ministry is under the guidance of Divine Providence. By using accounts of the experiences, testimonies, and even the dreams of others, Green validates the portrait of himself as a man singled out for special gifts and anointed for a divinely sanctioned mission. Yet when Green praises the success of his work or the effects of his sermons, he often appears self-righteous and self-congratulatory, as if he is taking credit that, as Green would be the first to admit, belongs to higher authority. Green uses anecdotes, then, to solve two vexing problems of autobiography: how to convincingly relate miraculous or magical events while retaining the trust of the reader, and how to portray himself as heroic while keeping the sympathy of an audience that appreciates humility.

Green structures his narrative around major turning points in his career and in the history of the Society. His original call to the ministry and the opening of the gospel to the world was one such turning point. The death of Mother Lucy in February in 1821 was a second. Green implies that with her death a new period of Shaker history, and thus his own personal history, began. Not only did Green feel great love for Mother Lucy, who, he reminds us, had been one of the earliest leaders to show great concern for the education and welfare of the children in the Society, but he also viewed her, as did other Shakers, as his spiritual mother. Her departure symbolized the passing of spiritual leadership from the first generation of converts to a younger generation of Believers, many of whom had not grown up in the Society. It is after Mother Lucy's death that Green began to assume a role beyond that of Shaker missionary as spiritual father to the community.[14]

In the North Family, or Gathering Order, where Green lived, Peter Pease, the first Elder, was both inexperienced and infirm. Much of the burden of leadership fell upon Green's shoulders. In 1826 Elder Peter was seriously injured in a fall from a wagon. Green, greatly troubled, and "being broke of rest & much fatiged on his account," retired to rest during the day. In vision he received an "impressive warning" of his future role within the Society. The door of the room opens and there appears "a well looking middle sized woman clad in a handsome green gown . . . having to appearance a little boy about a year old in her arms also clad in a green gown —As soon as she came near the pretty little Babe stretched out its arms with an extatic motion towards me, & she let it go out of her arms, then it sprang to me & clung round my neck & kissed my cheeks so earnest that it seemed as if it would off a piece" (312). Green believes that the woman was a messenger sent from Mother Ann to show him that the order, during Pease's illness and after his death, will cling to him and that an era of increase, symbolized by the color green, will follow. He readily associates the color of the woman and child's gowns with his own name and his role in increasing the membership of the Society. The female messenger dressed in green also suggests both Mother Ann and Mother Lucy, recently departed, turning over the young Society to Green's loving care. As they were mothers to the Society, so Green must be its father. Once again in this vision, Green sees himself as a father to Shaker children, here to the "Babe" in green. The physical affection expressed in several of Green's visions clearly demonstrates the familial bond that Green feels unites him with other Shakers.

In 1832 the Ministry instructed Green to leave the Gathering Family and return to the First Order. Green was not entirely happy

14. In the period from 1821 to 1831 Green also made several of the most significant missionary journeys of his career: his labors in western New York, which contributed to the founding of the Sodus Bay community, later Groveland, and his missionary expedition to the Philadelphia region. Instead of using his travel as an emblem of spiritual progress, Green in his descriptions of his journeys contrasts life in "the world" with life in the Shaker community. Traveling in western New York, Green everywhere sees "the sick, the lame, and the nasty," examples of "the fruits of the flesh" (143).

with this change because it signaled the end of his role as missionary to "the world." No longer the itinerant Shaker preacher, he
now was obliged to consolidate the gains in membership achieved
during the preceding decades and confirm these new converts in
the principles of Shakerism. Just before Green left the Gathering
Order, he once again received a vision of the boy in green. The
child, grown in size, is now about five-years-old. "He sprung round
so lively that, it made me think of a satyr—soon he saw me &,
sprang like a dart to me & climed up & clung round my neck &
kissed my cheeks several times as fervently as did the pretty Babe"
(314). Green believes that the child, or angelic guardian, is telling
him goodbye and giving him his blessing. The two visions of the
child in green symbolically sum up Green's experiences during the
twenty-five years he spent in the Gathering Order. They were years
of growth and increase in the Society, and Green had been instrumental in bringing the Society to its prosperous state. He left behind him not a full-grown man but a lively and healthy child in
need of instruction and training in order to reach his full potential.
Shakerism permitted Green the experience of fatherhood, but it
also required a willingness to forego personal attachments, even
those based on spiritual rather than blood relationships. Green's
vision reveals the difficulty of loosening such ties; the child still
clings to Green, and Green himself is reluctant to part from him.

Only in a third vision of the child does Green reconcile himself
to the new work which lies ahead. One morning when he awakes,
Green finds an infant in his bed:

> This at first startled me, for it looked like a real human child—I
> thot can it be that some female has come in & put this child in
> my bed to get rid of it—Then concluded that was impossible be-
> cause I was easy to wake, hence believed it must be a spirit: And
> turned over on my left elbow & looked it direct in the face—It was
> clad in a green gown with a beautiful white cap on its head—
> appeared to be about 2, or 3 months old. As I looked it in the face—
> it lying on its back, opened its beautiful eyes & looked me fair in
> the face—Its eyes were a pleasant deep blue—Every thing about
> it appeared to me as the most perfect picture of innocence of any
> thing I ever beheld—and I said in my mind—"pretty little innocent,"
> When it looked in my face, it made a pleasing motion such as Baby's

do when pleased & smiled — & instantly disappeared — & it seemed that I absorbed this little innocent, & it went all thro' my whole system, & produced a glow of the most Heavenly & innocent feelings that I ever experienced.

Green, who could not bear being parted from his child (the community), in this vision sees the child absorbed into himself. Green and the child become one; his own identity merges with that of the Society of Believers. Green's vision is one of mystical union, not like Mother Ann's union with Christ, but union with the Society. The child in green thus becomes a complex symbol in the "Biographic Memoir." At times, he signifies the Society itself which must be nourished in order to grow and which needs the paternal care of Calvin Green. At other times, he represents the innocence and simplicity needed by Green himself in order to accomplish these goals. Green also suggests that the child is his guiding spirit who will accompany him and direct him in his work. In the overall context of the "Biographic Memoir," the vision of the child also reflects Green's compelling desire to produce Shaker offspring. [15]

Before he moves to the First Order, Green receives another vision elucidating his mature understanding of his part in the Shaker mission and revealing him as a successor to the Christ spirit, in the male line, just as leaders like Mother Lucy were successors to the spirit of Mother Ann in the female line. Green relates that on a Saturday evening in May 1828, after he had retired to bed, he saw "a wonderful convulsion & shaking all over this land." A stream of light flowed due east from an opening in the center, revealing an assemblage of Believers. All the people of the world, "greatly alarmed and awakened," looked toward the Shakers as the source of "all these wonderful operations." A powerful voice was heard saying:

"Behold the savior cometh, go ye forth to meet him" . . . I looked earnestly to see the savior — soon I saw him sitting on a comely seat

15. Another vision, not recorded in the "Biographic Memoir," also reveals his deep concern with the question of how Shakers might engender spiritual offspring. Entitled "Parentage of the New Creation," Lebanon, N.Y., 1829 MS, OClWHi, VII:B–66C, the vision occurs in the summer of 1829, between the first vision of the babe in green (1826) and its second appearance in 1832.

with one standing on each side — imperceptably I found myself standing at his right hand, the one there before was gone — I saw the
savior as plain to my view as I ever see any person — He had a fair
& wonderful pleasant countenance — his eyes were deep blue but
rather tinged with gray, very pleasant but penetrating — His hair appeared clear, as near as I can describe about the color of a bright
chestnut fully ripe, was thin but perfectly covered his head, & on
his forehead, was cut in a perfect circle, from the top of his ears
about I thot five inches as neat as could be in a circle above his
eyebrows. . . .

He looked smillingly upon me & said "you did not think you was
so near me, when you looked so earnestly to see me" In spirit I
answered "I did not" . . . Soon after this, I saw him (scripture like,
"meek & lowly, & seated on an ass colt, leading his followers on
to the New Jerusalem — & the great multitude strewing their garments in the path. . . ."

I saw the Holy City seated on a hill which appeared to be level
with a gradual assent thereto. I did not then enter to behold its
order & glories, but viewed it a short distance. It appeared clean
with a pleasing white glow, such as earth does not afford. . . . But
the Believers generaly continued their rejoicing & worship & instruct-
ing inquirers, who still were around them. . . . For their work yet
was evidently . . . to remain with the people in the world, to gather
souls & help them on to follow the savior to the Heavenly Jerusalem.

Unlike the dreams of many Shaker autobiographers, Green's vision of the New Jerusalem does not reveal the way to personal salvation. Rather, it shows Green's place in God's plan for the redemption of the world. Green sees that the Shakers are "the medium
thro which all souls must pass to follow the savior." In the vision
the savior is a Shaker brother with piercing blue eyes and chestnut
hair cut in Shaker fashion. As Christ rides toward the Holy City
and his crucifixion a week later, Green and his Shaker comrades
assume the mantle to continue the Savior's work. In the New Testament, when the disciples ask to sit on Christ's right and left hand,
Christ answers, "It shall be given to them for whom it is prepared"
(Mark 10:37–40). Green sees that Christ has prepared a place for
him, not in the Heavenly City, but in the world. Even if Christ
himself is no longer in the world, Christ's spirit is alive, embodied
in the United Society of Believers, and Calvin Green is its leader,

sitting at the right hand of the Christ spirit. The work of establishing the Kingdom of God on earth continues.

Green interprets the vision both as expressing present reality as well as future events. Although he believes that "the great shaking [had] begun cotemporary with the second advent of Christ" in Mother Ann, he feels that "a new era of more powerful shaking & revolutionary convulsions [had] now begun, which would progressively increase till it would convulse, shake & break down every system & institution of mans invention, civil, political & ecclesiastical" (351). The vision in some measure predicts Green's labors during the coming decades for a spiritual regeneration that would touch those who had never known their spiritual parents; it also foretells the era of spiritual manifestations, as Green sees in retrospect. The Civil War, in progress as he writes, Green regards as evidence that God is progressively destroying manmade institutions in order to fulfill the promise of the millennium.

The landscape of Green's vision clearly reveals the analogy Shakers drew between the Community of Believers on earth and the spiritual New Jerusalem. Green sees the Heavenly City as an image of a Shaker village. The setting on a hill, to be climbed by all who wish to enter the city, reflects the belief that all must begin their spiritual travel in the low valley of humiliation and journey upward toward perfection. The Holy City is in "order," and clean and white. The Shaker community on earth, then, is a figure of the spiritual New Jerusalem.

As Green's vision foretold, the shaking power of Mother's Work was soon evident among Believers. Green himself received many spiritual gifts, including songs and tunes, during this period. He heard sounds of war before the Mexican conflict begins, and later he became the instrument for seventeen spirits, including Joel, Daniel, Seth, Elijah, and Zechariah.

He continued to experience visions that help him resolve personal conflicts. When the Ministry asks him to help prepare for publication the *Divine Book of Holy Wisdom,* by Paulina Bates, Green resisted. But a vision, soon after, changed his mind. After lying down to bed, Green sees "a bright light." He feels himself in a trance, and the light changes "into the appearance of a beautiful pleasing white cloud, which came to me & put her beautiful arms around my neck and kissed me—I felt greatly surprised & earnestly asked in mind 'what can this mean' My guardian answered this is Holy Wisdom—the angel answered 'she has come to anoint you to help prepare that book which must be prepared as her testimony'" (355).

From the 1830s through the 1850s, Green's activities centered on writing and editing the Society's publications. In the 1860s the Ministry once again called Green away from Lebanon. He traveled to Groveland, where he replaced Joseph Pelham as Elder in the Gathering Family. When his labor at Groveland was completed, the Society there prepared a goodbye dinner for Green: "I felt my work done here, except the work of properly ending—on my birth day at 83 years of age—At the First Family they got an excellent dinner for the aged Brethren & Sisters, at this I was invited & placed at the head of the table—several of whom had written essays expressing their love, thanks & blessing to me for my labors among them, & their determination to be faithful in the gospel" (429).

In a Sabbath meeting before he departed from Groveland, Green, in a sense, listened to his own eulogy. The members of the Society at Groveland praised Green as their spiritual father, who had been instrumental in the founding of their community and the establishment of Shakerism in America: "Eldress Polly Ann also in an affecting & eloquent speech, bore a strong testimony of my helpful labors & underrating [?] firmness in word & deed to the primitive principles of the Gospel—testified that I said that neither fear, favor nor affection, could ever cause me to deviate from the principles & orders of the genuine primitive gospel, & that my works had proved it to be truth" (430).

Green responded with a testimony of his own that sums up many of the concerns expressed throughout his life, the need for strong and able leadership in the Society and the necessity for all members to submit themselves to "a visible leading Head" (431). Green, no doubt, was urging the members to be as obedient and loyal to the succeeding Elder as they had been to him. He was also passing his mantle of leadership to the next generation. Green then gave the Society his thanks and farewell: "And now as I am about to part with you in body (tho not in spirit) I must bid you a sincere & affectionate—Farewell. With my kind love & everlasting blessing to all who are prepared to receive my fervent Gift, as all who mean to live obedient *are"* (432).

On his journey back to Lebanon, Green visited Watervliet and sadly notes the decline in membership. A few pages later, he remarks "for a long time I have been impressed that the state of Believers was such that nothing short of a pentecostal operation . . . would purge out that which was decayed & wrong . . . and prepare them to be the real agents of Divine power & Wisdom, to effect that renovating work among the human race for which God thro' Christ's second manifestation in the order of the Divine parentage had raised up" (438).

Green's "Biographic Memoir" thus ends on a note of sadness. The parallels between the development of the Society and Green's own life prove accurate to the end. As Green grew old and declined in health, so did the United Society. Calvin Green participated in the rise and growth of Shakerism, and he also lived to document its decline. At the close of his autobiography, Green is an elderly parent, fervently hoping and praying that his children will not squander the inheritance which he has worked so hard to gather.

Chapter X

CONCLUSION:
The Shaker
Literary
Imagination

During the nineteenth century, Shakers produced an exceedingly rich body of first-person narratives which demonstrate both the continuity and variety of spiritual autobiography in America. Like other sectarian Protestants, Believers in Christ's Second Appearing sought to discern the workings of Divine Providence in their lives. They, too, were convinced that God's will might be perceived through the events of history and of a single individual's life. While in some respects Shaker autobiography resembles the spiritual narratives of other Americans, it cannot be properly understood outside the context of the Shaker cultural and religious milieu. Shakers repeatedly shaped their autobiographies and testimonies to support a distinctive world view, asserting that their own experience proved a dual Godhead that is both masculine and feminine, the sinfulness of the sexual relation, the continuing unfolding of God's revelation, and the necessity of living within a highly structured community of saints. Shaker narrative differs from other American spiritual autobiography not only in the theology that it champions but in the language in which it is written.

As new members of the Society of Believers learned to obey rules of behavior and to participate in worship, song, and dance, they also learned a new religious vocabulary through which they interpreted both past and present experiences. When they joined Believers, novitiate Shakers confessed their sins, recounting their past lives and identifying the providential signs that had led them to the Society. Encouraged by the leaders of the Society, they adopted a distinctive religious language which served both a social and a religious function, for it marked the individual's union with the community. Just as Shaker dress set them apart from "the world," so Shaker parlance separated Believers from "the world's people."

Usually composed some years after the author joined the Shakers, testimony and autobiography demonstrated to the community that the author had shaped past experience to fit the Shaker mold. The corpus of Shaker autobiography suggests that writers did not primarily seek to imprint their individual personalities upon their narratives. The great majority of Believers wrote, not to present their pasts as different from those of other Shakers, but to demonstrate that their experiences and even their visions conformed to an expected pattern. Through writing testimony or autobiography, Shakers confirmed to themselves and to their readers that they had indeed traveled the "straight and narrow" path and that they had correctly interpreted the steps along the way. In telling the story of their lives, believing Shakers reaffirmed their commitment to the religious perspective of the community and proclaimed their union with fellow Believers.

Despite the centrality of Shaker religious language and theology in Shaker narrative, the experiences of Believers as settlers in the New World contributed to the major themes in their works. Immigration to the new land, clearing the wilderness, building communities, and participation in late eighteenth-century millennial expectations—all these left their mark on the content of Shaker literature. Consequently, Shaker personal literature displays a number of themes in common with more accessible and more familiar American literature. Shaker authors sometimes portrayed themselves as new Adams and Eves; they frequently juxtaposed the garden and the wilderness. They believed in the possibility of individual perfection, and felt confident that mankind continually progresses toward more advanced stages of religious development.

Nevertheless, many themes of Shaker narrative undeniably stand apart from the mainstream of American literature. Instead of being informed by an overriding "American myth," Shaker autobiography grew out of a much more specifically defined system of religious belief. When Shaker writers emphasized the necessary steps required to fulfill the purpose they saw in history, they focused on mortification of the self, acceptance of religious authority, celibacy, and communal ownership of property. Implicitly, therefore, Shaker authors expressed a radical criticism of the assumptions of the dominant culture. They rejected patriarchal religion and its embodiment in an all-masculine clergy, sexuality and social organization based on the biological family, the sanctity of private property, and participation in the democratic political process. Shaker literature often calls into question a number of highly cherished American values, while at the same time it espouses a set of radical ideals which many other nineteenth-century Americans considered unconventional, if not dangerous.

Consequently, an underlying theme in the Shaker personal narrative is the tension created by the conflict between the ideals of Shakerism and the values held by the dominant society. Since most Shaker authors were converts, they had at one time been a part of the outside world and had accepted its values as normative. Conversion to Shakerism necessarily required that they discard many previously held assumptions. Thus, in their narratives, Believers felt compelled to expose the inadequacies of life in "the world" and to assert the superiority of the Shaker way. Shaker autobiography aimed to explain and to justify the radical changes that have occurred in the authors' lives. This tension between two sets of values is apparent even in narratives of those who came to the Shakers as children and never experienced a conversion away from the values of the world. In these autobiographies, the writers usually present a crisis in which they compare the attractions of life outside the Shaker community to the satisfactions within it. Calvin Green contrasted the biological and the spiritual family, and he was convinced of the superiority of spiritual fatherhood. Harvey L. Eades, of South Union, Kentucky, who like Green was born a Shaker, was tempted by an uncle to go to college and become a "great man." Eades realized that he might exchange his Shaker "butcher's frock" for a "broadcloth coat," and that instead of "driving oxen in the mud" he might study languages and become a scholar. But Eades chose to be "little" rather than "big," to remain among God's people rather than seek recognition from "the world's people."

The expected structure of Shaker autobiographical narratives, therefore, was one of stark contrasts between the world abandoned by the author and the New Creation, the millennial community.

The basic literary problem of Shaker autobiography was how authors could link these contrasting parts of the narrative into a coherent whole. In order to connect their past and present experiences, Shaker authors most often selected metaphors that imply a dichotomy and suggest contrasting clusters of images. Pairs of images frequently appear in Shaker narratives: hungry/fed, naked/clothed, dirty/clean, polluted/pure, sick/well, fragmented/whole, anxious/peaceful, proud/humble, dangerous/safe, wilderness/garden, nature/community. Shaker writers drew many of these images from the natural life, and several sets of images might appear in any one narrative. To illustrate abstract concepts, the Shaker author chose specific symbols; a wild beast, for example, would indicate danger, whereas an enclosed place would represent safety. Such metaphors bridged the gap between past and present life, since they were understood on two levels, one physical and one spiritual. Shaker readers were constantly aware that thirst, for example, had two meanings, one relating to the physical body, one to the spiritual state. Most of the prominent metaphors of Shaker literature also appear in the Bible, and Shaker writers were keenly aware of the scriptural associations suggested by their choice of metaphors and images.

Metaphors alone did not provide sufficient structure for most Shaker narratives. The writer who wanted to reveal the transformation from one condition to another found in the vision a crucial device that could link past life and present experience, embody the central metaphors of the narrative, and symbolically, yet concretely, portray the metamorphosis that had occurred in the writer's life. In the vision, the autobiographer received instruction telling how he or she might move from one level of understanding to another, from "the world" to the community of Believers. The vision, however, was more than a convenient tool for Shaker writers. It also expressed a religious conviction: that even while living in the body Shakers had access to the spiritual world and could draw upon a supernatural realm of experience.

Unlike some other sectarian religious groups, Shakers did not demand a single, dramatic conversion experience as a demarcation between the state of salvation and the state of damnation. Instead, the theology of Believers emphasized the gradual change in the seeker's life. Therefore, Shaker literature contains another group of metaphors which, rather than expressing strong contrasts, describe progressive development. Shakers depicted spiritual growth as analogous to the growth of trees, flowers, and vines, or as the movement of ocean waves. A few metaphors prominent in Shaker literature express both the experience of radical change and the progressive growth of spiritual life. For example, Shaker writers used travel both to portray change from one world to another and to suggest the necessity of continual movement along the spiritual path. Shaker writers most often used metaphors emphasizing organic growth to describe their lives after becoming Believers, rather than to portray pre-Shaker experiences. Because so few Shaker autobiographers described their Shaker lives in detail, these metaphors are not as important in Shaker literature as in other products of Shaker religious imagination: song, poetry, and drawing.

Despite their dependence on the vocabulary and conventions of a highly unified culture, Shaker autobiographers nevertheless retained distinct narrative voices which express the uniqueness of the individual author's personal experience. In the most successful narratives, authors skillfully manipulated the conventions and traditions of Shaker literature to tell their own stories. They used theology, metaphors, the convention of the vision, and stories about the heroes and heroines of the Faith to present distinctive images of themselves. Such authors shaped the stories of their lives to meet the expectations of an audience familiar with various forms of the Shaker personal narrative. At the same time, they chose from Shaker religious language metaphors that expressed their personal concerns.

Shaker writers, therefore, carefully selected metaphors that joined together individual experience and the experience of the group. James Wilson belabored a pattern of hunger and nourishment in his past life and simultaneously reaffirmed the community's religious convictions. William Leonard presents his deprived childhood as support for the Shaker belief in the inadequacy of the biological family. The narratives that confirmed the pattern of a lack in the outside world that is fulfilled by Shakerism were the ones most appreciated by the Shaker audience.

Such predictability of form does not necessarily result in uninteresting or repetitive narratives. Skillful Shaker authors creatively shaped the events of their past so that their individual personalities clearly emerge from their narratives. Thus Jane Blanchard, exceedingly strict in observing the proper literary and theological boundaries, nevertheless created a beautiful example of Shaker narrative art. One of the most conventional narratives, Blanchard's autobiography is satisfying precisely because it so completely fulfills the requirements of Shaker testimonial literature. Shaker writers and their readers derived much satisfaction from observing how authors reworked the experiences of their lives to meet the narrative expectations of Shaker readers.

Shaker narratives of less predictable form frequently express unresolved conflicts. William Leonard's autobiography, for example, does not totally convince the reader of the superiority of the Shaker life; almost inadvertently, Leonard revealed the great sacrifice he has made in order to live as a Shaker. Even more strongly, John Brown's "Memoir" betrays the author's doubts about Shakerism. Looking back over his life, Brown discovered that he regrets the loss of familial ties and national identity. He craved the secular excitement, and perhaps the sensual pleasure, of life in the world.

Rebecca Jackson's autobiography is a particularly complex example of Shaker narrative, for it demonstrates how an exceptionally imaginative and creative writer could synthesize materials from Shaker culture and other religious traditions. Jackson structured her narrative according to two contrasting sets of values—those of the outer, ordinary world and those of inner, spiritual experience —but she discovered that the inner, spiritual world revealed to her in visions, dreams, and through her "inner voice" does not coincide perfectly with its embodiment in the Shaker community. Thus, even after becoming a Shaker, Jackson continued to experience the tension between two sets of values. Unlike the typical Shaker autobiography, Jackson's narrative expresses an ongoing conflict between God's will, expressed in direct revelation, and the will of men, including men and women of the Shaker community. A number of Shaker personal narratives suggest this tension between individual personality and the requirements of communal experience. Although few authors explored such tensions straightforwardly, they often employed visions and metaphors to hint at the difficulties of submitting mind and will, as well as hands and heart, to the Shaker way.

The dualistic structure of the Shaker personal narrative mirrors the ideals of Believers, who, renounced "the world, the flesh and the devil" and attempted to create another world in the American wilderness, a world that reflected a divine spiritual archetype. Caring little about recording the mundane details of their lives, Shaker authors used metaphors and visions to construct an image of the New Creation. The particular language and structure of Shaker literature reflect the specifics of belief, and recall George Santayana's explanation of what it means to have a religion: "Thus every living and healthy religion has a marked idiosyncrasy. Its power consists in its special and surprising message and in the bias which that revelation gives to life. The vistas it opens and the mysteries it propounds are another world to live in; and another world to live in — whether we expect ever to pass wholly over into it or not — is what we mean by having a religion."

BIBLIOGRAPHY

PRIMARY SOURCES

Aitken, Robert. "Shaker and Vegetarian: Autobiographical Sketch of Robert Aitken." *The Independent Vegetarian Advocate* 6 (Jan. 1891):21–23.

[Autobiographical Sketches of Enfield, Conn., Shakers.] MS, DLC, Shaker Collection, no. 2.

Avery, Giles B. *Autobiography by Elder Giles B. Avery, of Mount Lebanon, N.Y.* East Canterbury, N.H.: The United Society, 1891.

Barber, Miranda. [A volume of inspired writings, containing an illustrated 15-page key to the meanings of the signs that appear in the inspired drawings.] Lebanon, N.Y., 1854–1855. MS, OClWHi, VIII:C–1.

Bates, Issachar. "A Sketch of the Life and Experience of Issachar Bates." *Shaker Quarterly* 1 (Fall 1961):98–118, 145–63; 2 (Spring 1962), 18–35.

Bathrick, Eunice. "Autobiography." Harvard, Mass., n.d. MS, OClWHi, VI:A–5.

Bear, Elder Henry B. "Elder Henry B. Bear's Advent Experience." Whitewater, Ohio, n.d. MS, OClWHi, VI:B–37.

Beaver, Orrin M. [Untitled.] Watervliet, N.Y., n.d. MS, OClWHi, VI:A–11.

Bishop, James B. "The Infant Experience of James Bishop Together with Some Information from Other Authors, in Relation to Our Blessed Mother, Ann Lee." Lebanon, N.Y., 1835. MS, OClWHi, VI:A–6.

Blake, Rhoda. "Sketch of the Life & Experiences, Begun in 1864, Completed in 1892, As Copied and Amended by Alonzo G. Hollister, 1873–76." Lebanon, N.Y. MS, OClWHi, VI:B–23.

Blanchard, Jane E.S. "A Sketch of Her Experience Previous to 1868." New Enfield, N.H., n.d. MS, OClWHi, VI:B–37.

Blanchard, Jemima. [Untitled testimony.] Harvard, Mass., n.d., MS, OClWHi, VI:A–8.

Brewster, Eldress Dana. "Autobiography." MS, Sabbathday Lake, Me.

Briggs, Nicholas. "Forty Years a Shaker." *Granite Monthly* 53 (Jan. 1921):19–32; (Feb. 1921):56–65; (Mar. 1921):113–21; (Apr. 1921):463–74.

Brown, John M. "An Address to Elder Daniel Boler, on His 70th Anniversary, May 2nd 1874." Lebanon, N.Y., 1874. MS, OClWHi, VIII: A-6.

———. "Autobiographical Letters, etc. by an Hibernian; Culminating in Shakerism. Dedicated to the Elders of the Church, New Lebanon, Col. Co., N.Y." Lebanon, N.Y., 1871–1874. MS, OClWHi, IV:B-18.

———. "A Biographic Sketch & Religious Experience by John M. Brown, First Order, Chh. Mount Lebanon, N.Y." Lebanon, N.Y., 1866. MS, OClWHi, VI:B-35.

———. "Notes by the Way, Inspiration, Letters, etc., Being a Repository of Thots, Sentiments, and Gospel Feelings From Time to Time as Occasion Called Forth, Written for Edification & Commencing June AD. 1866." Lebanon, N.Y., 1871. MS, OClWHi, VII:B-127.

———. "On Wearing the Beard." Lebanon, N.Y., 1873. MS, OClWHi, VII:A-6.

Brown, Thomas. *An Account of the People Called Shakers: Their Faith, Doctrines, and Practice, Exemplified in the Life, Conversations, and Experience of the Author During the Time He Belonged to the Society.* Troy, N.Y.: Printed by Parker and Bliss, 1812; rpt. New York: AMS, 1972.

Buckingham, David. [Untitled testimony.] Watervliet, N.Y., 1843, MS, OClWHi, VI:A-11.

Bullard, Harriet. "Journal." Lebanon, N.Y., 1889. MS, OClWHi, V:B-172.

Carr, Mary Frances. *The Journey of Life.* Concord, N.H.: Rumford Printing Co., 1905.

Coolbroth, Eldress Harriet. "Sketch of the Life of Annie S. Colley." Canterbury, N.H., 1845. MS, Sabbathday Lake, Me.

Curtis, George Washington. "George Washington Curtis's Experience As Related by Him While on a Visit to Canterbury, July 10, 1868." MS, OClWHi, VI:B-4.

Doolittle, Mary Antoinette. *Autobiography of Mary Antoinette Doolittle Prior to Becoming a Member of the Shaker Community in the Year 1827.* Mt. Lebanon, N.Y.: The United Society, 1880.

Dyer, Mary Marshall. *A Brief Statement of the Sufferings of Mary Dyer, Occasioned by the Society Called Shakers.* Concord, N.H.: Printed by Joseph C. Spear, 1818.

Elkins, Hervey. *Fifteen Years in the Senior Order of Shakers: A Narrative of Facts Concerning that Singular People.* Hanover, N.H.: Dartmouth Press, 1853.

Evans, Frederick William. *Autobiography of a Shaker and Revelation of the Apocalypse.* New York: American News Co., 1888; rpt. AMS Press, 1973.

———. *Shakers: Compendium of the Origin, History, Principles, Rules & Regulations, Government, and Doctrines of the United Society of Believers in Christ's Second Appearing.* Albany, N.Y.: C. Van Benthuysen, 1867; rpt. New York: AMS Press, 1975.

———. *Shaker Communism; or, Tests of Divine Inspiration.* London: J. Burns, 1871.

———. *Tests of Divine Inspiration or the Rudimental Principles by Which True and False Revelation, in All Eras of the World Can Be Unerringly Discriminated.* New Lebanon, N.Y.: The United Society, 1853.

Ferris, David. *Memoirs of the Life of David Ferris, an Approved Minister of the Society of Friends.* Philadelphia: Merrihew & Thompson's Press, 1855.

"Fifteen Years a Shakeress." *Galaxy* (Jan.–April 1872):29–38, 191–201.

Green, Benjamin. *Biographical Account of the Life of Benjamin Green, in Which Are Set Forth His Pretensions to the Throne, Written by Himself.* Concord, N.H.: The Author, 1848.

———. *The True Believer's Vademecum or Shakerism Exposed: Together with an Account of the Life of the Author, from His Birth to the Period of His Joining & Leaving the Society of People Called Shakers.* Concord, N.H.: Printed for the Author, 1831.

Green, Calvin. "Biographic — Memoir — of the Life and Experience — of Calvin Green." Lebanon, N.Y., 1861–1869. MS, OClWHi, VI:B-28.

———. "Biographic Memoir of the Life, Character, and Important Events in the Ministration of Mother Lucy Wright." Lebanon, N.Y., 1861. MS, OClWHi, VI:B-27.

———. "Biographical Account of the Life, Character, and Ministry of Father Joseph Meacham." Ed. Theodore E. Johnson. *Shaker Quarterly* 10 (Spring, 1970):20–32, (Summer 1970):51–68, (Fall 1970):92–102.

———. Biography of Elder Henry Clough." Lebanon, N.Y., 1860. MS, OClWHi, VI:B-24-26.

———. "Journal of a Journey to Philadelphia and Its Vicinity— May, 1828, Kept by Calvin Green." Lebanon, N.Y., 1828. MS, OClWHi, V:B-98A.

———. "Parentage of the New Creation." Lebanon, N.Y., 1829. MS, OClWHi, VII:B-66C.

———. "A Treatise upon the Work of God in Different Ages." Lebanon, N.Y. MS, Sabbathday Lake, Me.

[Green, Calvin and Seth Y. Wells.] *A Summary View of the Millennial Church, or United Society of Believers (Commonly Called Shakers) Comprising the Rise, Progress, and Practical Order of the Society, Together with the General Principles of Their Faith and Testimony.* Albany: Published by order of the Ministry in Union with the Church, 1823; 2nd ed., 1848.

Grosvenor, Roxalana L. "Incidents Related by Some of the Ancient Believers of Their Own Experience & Intercourse with Mother and the Elders." Watervliet, N.Y. MS, OClWHi, VI:B-9.

———. "Sayings of Mother Ann and the First Elders, Gathered from Different Individuals, at Harvard and Shirley, Who Were Eye and Ear Witnesses: The Divine Word of God, Revealed Thro Them at Different Times and in Various Places, Collected Together by Roxalana L. Grosvenor." MS, Sabbathday Lake, Me.

Haskell, Betsy. [Untitled testimony.] Enfield, Conn., 1843. MS, OClWHi, VI:A-2.

Hicks, Elias. *Journal of the Life and Religious Labours of Elias Hicks.* New York: I.T. Hopper, 1832; rpt. New York: Arno Reprint, 1969.

Hollister, Alonzo Giles. "Autobiography of the Saints or Stray Leaves from the Book of Life." 2 vol. Lebanon, N.Y., 1886. MS, OClWHi, VI: B-37.

———. "Reminiscences, by a Soldier of the Cross." Lebanon, N.Y., [ca. 1908]. MS, OClWHi, X:B-31.

Hunt, Thomas. "Autobiography." MS, DLC, no. 186.

Jackson, Rebecca. "Diary." Watervliet, 1849–1861. MS, OClWHi, V:B-335. The diary consists mostly of dreams dictated by Rebecca Perot, i.e., Rebecca Jackson, Jr.

———. *Gifts of Power: The Writings of Rebecca Jackson, Black Visionary, Shaker Eldress.* Ed. and Introd. Jean McMahon Humez. Amherst: Univ. of Mass. Press, 1981.

———. [Untitled autobiography.] Watervliet, N.Y., n.d. MS, Berkshire Athenaeum, Pittsfield, Mass.

———. [Autobiography and testimony.] Watervliet, N.Y. Copied by Alonzo G. Hollister, 1877–1896. MS, OClWHi, VI:B-39.

Knight, Jane D. *Brief Narrative of Events Touching Various Reforms by Jane D. Knight Who Was Reared in the Society of Friends, and United with the Shakers at Mt. Lebanon, Columbia Co., N.Y. in the Year 1826, in the Twenty-Second Year of her Age.* Albany, N.Y.: Weed, Parsons and Co., 1880.

Lamson, David Rich. *Two Years Experience Among the Shakers: Being a Description of the Manners and Customs of that People, The Nature and Policy of Their Government, Their Marvellous Intercourse with the Spiritual World, The Objects and Uses of Confession, Their Inquisition, in Short, a Condensed View of Shakerism As It Is.* (1848; rpt. New York: AMS Press, 1971.

Lawrence, Garrett. "A Visionary Dream." Lebanon, N.Y., 1818, MS, OClWHi, VII:B-66C.

Leonard, William. "Autobiography." Harvard, Mass., n.d. MS, OClWHi, VI:B-5.

Libbey, William G. "Autobiography of a Quondam Sailor." *Shaker 8,* nos. 3-12, Feb. 1878, pp. 46-47; Apr. 1878, pp. 96-98; May 1878, pp. 120-22; June 1878, pp. 145-46; July 1878, pp. 169-71; Aug. 1878, pp. 197-98; Sept. 1878, pp. 227-29; Oct. 1878, pp. 251-53; Nov. 1878, pp. 279-81; Dec. 1878, pp. 309-11.

Liddil, Susan Cole. "Susanna the Shakeress." Union Village, Ohio, 1879. MS, DCL, no. 336a-336e.

"Lives of the Visionists of White Water." Whitewater, Ohio, 1841. MS, DLC, no. 251.

Lyon, John. "Incidents in the Early Life of Elder John Lyon." Enfield, N.H., 1861. MS, OClWHi, VI:A-3 and VI:B-36.

Lyon, Lydia. [Untitled autobiography.] Enfield, N.H., 1862. MS, OClWHi, VI:B-37.

Mace, Aurelia. "Sister Aurelia's Journal, 1896-1902." MS, Sabbathday Lake, Me.

Meacham, Joseph. "A Collection of the Writings of Father Joseph Meacham Concerning Church Order and Government; Evidently Intended for Waymarks, for All Who Are or Should Be Called in Spiritual or Temporal Care, in the Church." Ed. Rufus Bishop. Lebanon, N.Y., 1791-1796. MS, OClWHi, VII:B-59.

_____. *A Concise Statement of the Principles of the Only True Church.* Bennington, Vt.: Haswell and Russell, 1790.

Myrick, Elijah. "A Testimony and Declaration of the Late Wonderful and Divine Manifestations of the Goodness of God to His Chosen People." Harvard, Mass., 1843. MS, OClWHi, VI:A-5.

Offord, William. "An Autobiographical Sketch of a Shaker, Who Was Excommunicated from the Wesleyan Methodist Society, in England after Being Twenty-eight Years a Member, and Fifteen Years a Preacher." Lebanon, N.Y., 1870. MS, OClWHi, VI:B-38.

Pearson, Julia E. "Autobiography." Watervliet, N.Y., 1871. MS, OClWHi, VI:A-11.

Pelham, Joseph. "Brief Narrative of the Religious Experience of Joseph Pelham." Groveland, N.Y., 1863. MS, OClWHi, VI:B-2-4.

Pelham, Richard. "Sketch of the Life and Religious Experience of Richard W. Pelham." North Union, Ohio, 1862. MS, OClWHi, VI:B-45-48.

Perkins, Elder Abraham. *Autobiography of Elder Abraham Perkins and In Memoriam.* Concord, N.H.: Rumford Press, 1901.

Rankin, John, Sr. "Autobiography." South Union, Ky., 1845. MS, OClWHi, VI:B-37.

Rathbun, Reuben, *Reasons for Leaving the Shakers.* Pittsfield, Mass.: Chester Smith, 1800.

Rathbun, Valentine. *Some Brief Hints of a Religious Scheme, Taught and Propagated by a Number of Europeans, Living in a Place Called Nisquennia, in the State of New York.* Hartford, Conn., 1783.

"Remarks on the Necessity of Reforming the Morals & Improving the Religious Condition of Our Youth and Children." Lebanon, N.Y., 1830. MS, OClWHi, VII:B-66C.

Rowley, David. "Religious Experience." Lebanon, N.Y., 1854. MS, OClWHi, VI:B-23.

Rude, Hiram. "Autobiography." Lebanon, N.Y., n.d. MS, OClWHi, VI:A-6.

Sampson, Proctor. [Untitled autobiography]. Lebanon, N.Y., 1853. MS, OClWHi, VI:B-17.

"2nd Book: A Collection of Sacred Writings Given by Inspiration at the Second Family of New Lebanon Commencing Dec. 1840." MS, Sabbathday Lake, Me.

Second Family Daybook. Watervliet, N.Y., 1847–1865. MS, OClWHi, V:B-333.

Smith, Phoebe. [Untitled testimony.] Lebanon, N.Y., 1843. MS, OClWHi, VI:A-11.

South Family Daybook. Watervliet, N.Y., 1847–1868. MS, OClWHi, V:B-333.

Stewart, Philemon. *A Holy, Sacred and Divine Roll and Book.* Canterbury, N.H.: The United Society, 1843.

Stout, Hosea. *Autobiography.* Ed. Reed A. Stout. Salt Lake City: Utah Historical Society, 1962.

Webster, E.H. "Is Woman a Slave?" *Shaker and Shakeress* 3 (Feb. 1873):13–14.

[Wells, Seth Y., ed.] *Testimonies Concerning the Character and Ministry of Mother Ann Lee and the First Witnesses of the Gospel of Christ's Second Appearing; Given by Some of the Aged Brethren and Sisters of the United Society, Including a Few Sketches of Their Own Religious Experience: Approved by the Church.* Albany, N.Y.: Printed by Packard & Van Benthuysen, 1827.

_____. *Testimonies of the Life Character, Revelations and Doctrines of Our Ever Blessed Mother Ann Lee, and the Elders with Her; Through Whom the Word of Eternal Life was Opened in This Day of Christ's Second Appearing: Collected From Living Witnesses, By Order of the Ministry, in Union with the Church.* Hancock, Mass.: n.p., 1816.

_____. *Testimonies of the Life. . . .* 2nd ed. Albany, N.Y.: Weed, Parsons & Co., Printers, 1888.

Wells, Seth Y., comp. "Unpublisht Testimonies of Mother's First-Born Children in America." Lebanon, N.Y. MS, OClWHi, VI:B-42-3.

Wells, Seth Y., and Green, Calvin. "Rules for Editing Inspired Writings for Publication." Lebanon, N.Y., 1844. MS, OClWHi, VII:B-173.

White, Anna, and Leila Taylor. *Shakerism: Its Meaning and Message.* Columbus, Ohio: Press of F. J. Heer, 1905; rpt. New York: AMS Press, 1972.

Whitney, Abraham. [Untitled.] Shirley, Mass., 1832. MS, OClWHi, VI: A-8.

Whittaker, James. Letter to brothers in Hancock, Mass., 25 Feb. 1782. MS, OClWHi, VII:B-66C.

Wickersham, George. *How I Came to Be a Shaker.* East Canterbury, N.H.: n.p., 1891.

Williams, Nathan. "A Brief Sketch of His Life." Lebanon, N.Y., 1863. MS, OClWHi, VI:B-37. Manuscript transcribed by John M. Brown.

Wilson, James. "Autobiographic Memoir of James Wilson Senior. Written in Canaan—Upper Family, Between May 1867-1868." Lebanon, N.Y. MS, OClWHi, VI:B-34. The memoir is copied by Alonzo G. Hollister.

———. [Untitled autobiography.] Lebanon, N.Y., 1868, MS, DLC, No. 149.

———. [Untitled testimony.] Lebanon, N.Y., 1843. MS, OClWHi, VI: A-6.

Worster, Abijah. "Testimony & Autobiography." Harvard, Mass., 1826. MS, OClWHi, VI:A-5.

Wright, Mother Lucy. "Sayings." Lebanon, N.Y., 1821. MS, OClWHi, VIII:B-114.

[Youngs, Benjamin Seth.] *The Testimony of Christ's Second Appearing Containing a General Statement of All Things Pertaining to the Faith and Practices of the Church of God in the Latter-day; Published in Union by Order of the Ministry.* Lebanon, Ohio: Press of John McClean, [1808?]; 2nd ed., Albany, N.Y.: Printed by E. and E. Hosford, 1810; 3rd ed., Union Village, Ohio: B. Fisher and A. Burnett, Printers, 1823; 4th ed., Albany, N.Y.: The United Society, 1856.

Youngs, Isaac Newton. [Untitled autobiography.] Lebanon, N.Y., 1848. MS, OClWHi, VI:B-36.

SECONDARY SOURCES

Alho, Olli. *The Religion of the Slaves: A Study of the Religious Tradition and Behavior of Plantation Slaves in the United States 1830–1865.* Finnish Folklore Communications, No. 217, Helsinki, 1976.

Andrews, Edward Deming. *The Gift to Be Simple: Songs, Dances and Rituals of the American Shakers.* New York: Dover, 1940.

————. *The People Called Shakers: A Search for the Perfect Society.* New York: Dover, 1963.

Andrews, Edward Deming, and Faith Andrews. *Fruits of the Shaker Tree of Life: Memoirs of Fifty Years of Collecting and Research.* Stockbridge, Mass.: Berkshire Traveller Press, 1975.

————. *Visions of the Heavenly Sphere: A Study in Shaker Religious Art.* Charlottesville: Univ. of Virginia Press, 1969.

Bercovitch, Sacvan, ed. *The American Puritan Imagination.* London: Cambridge Univ. Press, 1974.

————. *Typology and Early American Literature.* Boston: Univ. of Massachusetts Press, 1972.

Bester, Arthur. *Backwoods Utopias.* Philadelphia: Univ. of Pennsylvania Press, 1950.

Blanshard, Brand. "Early Thought on the Inner Light." In *By-ways in Quaker History.* Ed. Howard Brinton. Wallingford, Pa.: Pendle Hill, 1944, pp. 153–78.

Brinton, Howard. "Dreams of the Quaker Journalists." In *By-ways in Quaker History.* Ed. Howard Brinton. Wallingford, Pa.: Pendle Hill, 1944, pp. 209–31.

Brown, Ira. "Watcher for the Second Coming: The Millennial Tradition in America." *Mississippi Valley Historical Review* 29 (1952):441–58.

Bunyan, John. *Grace Abounding to the Chief of Sinners.* Oxford: Clarendon Press, 1962.

————. *The Pilgrim's Progress.* Harmondsworth, England: Penguin, 1965.

Burridge, Kenelm. *New Heaven New Earth: A Study of Millenarian Activities.* Oxford: Basil Blackwell, 1969.

Buttrick, George Arthur, ed. *The Interpreter's Dictionary of the Bible.* 4 vols. New York: Abingdon, 1962. Suppl., 1976.

Byrne, Donald. *No Foot of Land: Folklore of American Methodist Itinerants.* Metuchen, N.J.: Scarecrow Press, 1975.

Campbell, D'Ann. "Women's Life in Utopia: The Shaker Experiment in Sexual Equality Reappraised—1810 to 1860." *New England Quarterly* 51, No. 1 (Mar. 1978):23–38.

Campion, Nardi Reeder. *Ann the Word: The Life of Mother Ann Lee, Founder of the Shakers.* Boston: Little, Brown, 1976.

Cohn, Norman. *The Pursuit of the Millennium.* New York: Oxford Univ. Press, 1970.

Collins, John J., ed. *Apocalypse: The Morphology of a Genre.* Semeia, 14. Missoula, Mont.: Scholar's Press, 1979.

Courlander, Harold. *Negro Folk Music U.S.A.* New York: Columbia Univ. Press, 1963.

Couser, G. Thomas. *American Autobiography: The Prophetic Mode.* Amherst: Univ. of Mass. Press, 1979.

Cox, James M. "Autobiography and America." *Virginia Quarterly Review* 47 (Spring 1971):252–77.

Desroche, Henri. *The American Shakers; From Neo-Christianity to Presocialism.* Trans. John K. Savacool. Amherst: Univ. of Mass. Press, 1971.

Douglas, Mary. *Natural Symbols.* Baltimore: Penguin, 1973.

Early Shaker Spirituals Sung by Sister Mildred Barker with other Members of The United Society of Shakers, Sabbathday Lake, Maine. Daniel W. Patterson, Notes. Rounder Records 0078.

Endy, Melvin B., Jr. *William Penn and Early Quakerism.* Princeton, N.J.: Princeton Univ. Press, 1973.

Festinger, Leon, Henry W. Reichen, and Stanley Schachter. *When Prophecy Fails.* Minneapolis: Univ. of Minnesota Press, 1956.

Finnegan, Ruth. *Oral Poetry: Its Nature, Significance, and Social Context.* Cam- I ✿ lge, England: Cambridge Univ. Press, 1977.

Fox, Frank. "Quaker, Shaker, Rabbi: Warder Cresson. The Story of a Philadelphia Mystic." *Pennsylvania Magazine of History and Biography* 95 (Apr. 1971):147–94.

Geertz, Clifford. "Religion as a Cultural Symbol." In *Reader in Comparative Religion.* Ed. William A. Lessa and Evan Z. Vogt. New York: Harper & Row, 1965, pp. 204–16.

A Guide to Shaker Museums, Bibliography, and Libraries. Old Chatham, N.Y.: Shaker Museum Foundation, Inc., revised biennially.

Guimond, James. "Nineteenth-century American Millennial Experiences." *Shaker Quarterly* 13 (Spring 1973):3–5, 39–55.

Hansen, Klaus J. *Mormonism and the American Experience.* Chicago: Univ. of Chicago Press, 1981.

Hayden, Delores. *Seven American Utopias: The Architecture of Communitarian Socialism, 1790–1975.* Cambridge, Mass.: MIT Press, 1976.

Hintz, Howard. *The Quaker Influence in American Literature.* New York: Fleming H. Revell, 1940.

Howarth, William L. "Some Principles of Autobiography." *New Literary History* 5 (1974):363–81.

Humez, Jean M., ed. *Gifts of Power: The Writings of Rebecca Jackson, Black Visionary, Shaker Eldress.* Amherst: Univ. of Massachusetts Press, 1981.

Jacobs, Louis. *Jewish Mystical Testimonies.* New York: Schocken, 1977.

James, William. *The Varieties of Religious Experience: A Study in Human Nature.* London, N.Y.: Longmans, Green, 1952.

Johnson, Theodore. "Biographical Account of the Life, Character, & Ministry of Father Joseph Meacham . . . by Calvin Green, 1827." Ed. and

Foreword Theodore E. Johnson. *Shaker Quarterly* 10 (Spring 1970):20–32; (Summer 1970):51–68; (Fall 1970):92–102.

Kaplan, Louis. *A Bibliography of American Autobiography.* Madison: Univ. of Wisconsin Press, 1961.

Kern, Louis J. *An Ordered Love: Sex Roles and Sexuality in Victorian Utopias — The Shakers, Mormons, and the Oneida Community.* Chapel Hill: Univ. of North Carolina Press, 1981.

King, Emma B., Library. *Catalogue of the Emma B. King Library of the Shaker Museum.* Old Chatham, N.Y., 1970.

Labov, William and Waletzky, Joshua. "Narrative Analysis: Oral Versions of Personal Experience." In *Essays on the Verbal and Visual Arts.* Ed. June Helm. Proc. of the 1966 Annual Spring Meeting, American Ethnological Society, 1967, pp. 12–44.

Lapsansky, Emma Jones. "'Since They Got Those Separate Churches': Afro-Americans and Racism in Jacksonian Philadelphia." *American Quarterly* 32 (Spring 1980):54–78.

Lerner, L.D. "Puritanism and the Spiritual Autobiography." *Hibbert Journal* 55 (1957):373–86.

Loomis, Roger Sherman. *The Development of Arthurian Romance.* New York: Norton, 1963.

Lynen, John. *The Design of the Present: Essays on Time and Form in American Literature.* New Haven, Conn.: Yale Univ. Press, 1969.

MacLean, John Patterson. *A Bibliography of Shaker Literature with an Introductory Study of the Writings and Publications Pertaining to Ohio Believers.* Columbus, Ohio: Fred J. Heer, 1905.

Marini, Stephen A. *Radical Sects of Revolutionary New England.* Cambridge, Mass.: Harvard Univ. Press, 1982.

Melcher, Marguerite. *The Shaker Adventure.* Cleveland, Ohio: Case Western Reserve Univ., 1968.

Minter, David. *The Interpreted Design as a Structural Principle in American Prose.* New Haven, Conn.: Yale Univ. Press, 1969.

Neal, Julia. *By Their Fruits.* Chapel Hill: Univ. of North Carolina Press, 1947.

Olney, James. "Autos*Bios*Graphein: The Study of Autobiographical Literature." *South Atlantic Quarterly* 77 (1978):173–223.

————. *Metaphors of Self.* Princeton, N.J.: Princeton Univ. Press, 1972.

————, ed. *Autobiography: Essays Theoretical and Critical.* Princeton, N.J.: Princeton Univ. Press, 1980.

Pascal, Roy. *Design and Truth in Autobiography.* Cambridge, Mass.: Harvard Univ. Press, 1960.

Patterson, Daniel W. "'Bearing for the Dead': A Shaker Belief and Its Impress on the Shaker Spiritual." *Shaker Quarterly* 8 (Winter 1968):116–28.

_____. *The Shaker Spiritual.* Princeton, N.J.: Princeton Univ. Press, 1979.

Piercy, Carolina. *The Valley of God's Pleasure: A Saga of the North Union Shaker Community.* New York: Stratford House, 1951.

Porter, Dorothy, ed. *Early Negro Writing 1760–1837.* Boston: Beacon, 1971.

Propp, Vladimir. *Morphology of the Folktale.* 2nd ed. Trans. Laurence Scott. Introd. Svatava Pirkova-Jakobson. Rev. and ed. with a Pref. by Louise A. Wagner. New Introd. Alan Dundes. Austin: Univ. of Texas Press, 1968.

Raboteau, Albert J. *Slave Religion: The "Invisible Institution" in the Antebellum South.* New York: Oxford Univ. Press, 1978.

Richmond, Mary L. Hurt. *Shaker Literature: A Bibliography Compiled and Annotated by Mary L. Richmond.* 2 vol. Hancock, Mass.: Shaker Community, 1977.

Rosenberg, Bruce. *The Art of the American Folk Preacher.* New York: Oxford Univ. Press, 1970.

Sandeen, Ernest R. *The Roots of Fundamentalism.* Chicago: Univ. of Chicago Press, 1970.

Sapir, Edward. "Language." *Encyclopedia of the Social Sciences.* New York: Macmillan, 1933, Vol. 9, pp. 155–169.

Sayre, Robert F. "Autobiographies and Images of Utopia." *Salmagundi* 19 (Spring 1972):18–37.

_____. *The Examined Self: Benjamin Franklin, Henry Adams, Henry James.* Princeton, N.J.: Princeton Univ. Press, 1964.

_____. "The Proper Study—Autobiographies in American Studies." *American Quarterly* 29 (1977):241–62.

Schwartz, Hillel. "The End of the Beginning: Millenarian Studies, 1969–1975." *Religious Studies Review* 2 (July 1976):1–15.

Semmel, Bernard. *The Methodist Revolution.* New York: Basic Books, 1973.

Sernett, Milton C. *Black Religion and American Evangelicalism: White Protestants, Plantation Missions, and the Flowering of Negro Christianity, 1787–1865.* Metuchen, N.J.: Scarecrow Press, 1975.

Sharrock, Roger. "Spiritual Autobiography in *Pilgrim's Progress*." *Review of English Studies* 24 (Apr. 1948):102–219.

Shea, Daniel B., Jr. *Spiritual Autobiography in Early America.* Princeton, N.J.: Princeton Univ. Press, 1968.

Shumaker, Wayne. *English Autobiography: Its Emergence, Materials, and Form.* Berkeley: Univ. of California Press, 1954.

Smith, David E. "The English Pilgrimage of Man: Metamorphosis of a Theme in American Literature." *Ball State Univ. Forum* 7 (Spring 1966):65–72.

_____. *John Bunyan in America*. Bloomington: Indiana Univ. Press, 1966.

_____. "Millenarian Scholarship in America." *American Quarterly* 17 (Fall 1965):535–49.

Smith, Sidonie. *Where I'm Bound: Patterns of Slavery and Freedom in Black American Autobiography*. Contributions in American Studies, No. 16. Westport, Conn.: Greenwood, 1974.

Smith, Timothy L. "Righteousness and Hope: Christian Holiness and the Millennial Vision in America, 1800–1900." *American Quarterly* 31, No. 1 (Spring 1979):21–45.

Stone, Albert E. "Autobiography and American Culture." *American Studies: An International Newsletter* 12 (Winter 1972):22–38.

_____. "Cato's Mirror: The Face of Violence in American Autobiography." In *Prospects: An Annual of American Cultural Studies*. Ed. Jack Salzman. New York: Burt Franklin, 1977, Vol. III. pp. 331–69.

_____. "The Sea and the Self: Travel as Experience and Metaphor in Early American Autobiography." *Genre* 7 (1974):279–306.

Swain, Thomas. "The Evolving Expressions of the Religious and Theological Experiences of a Community: A Comparative Study of the Shaker *Testimonies* from Oral Traditions to Written Forms as Preserved in Four Documents." *Shaker Quarterly* 12 (Spring 1972):3–31; (Summer 1972): 43–66.

Taylor, Dennis. "Some Strategies of Religious Autobiography." *Renascence* 27 (1974):40–44.

Titon, Jeff Todd. "The Life Story." *Journal of American Folklore* 93 (July–Sept. 1980):276–92.

Underhill, Evelyn. *Mysticism: A Study in the Nature and Development of Man's Spiritual Consciousness*. New York: World, 1955.

Watkins, O.C. *The Puritan Experience: Studies in Spiritual Autobiography*. London: Routledge and Kegan Paul, 1972.

Watkins, Owen. "Some Early Quaker Autobiographies." *Journal of the Friends Historical Society* 45 (1953):65–74.

Weiss, Virginia M. "Every Good and Simple Gift." *Shaker Quarterly* 13 (Fall 1973):79–94; (Winter 1973):132–42; 14 (Spring 1974):21–38.

_____. "A Travel into Warfare: A Consideration of the Figures of the Heavenly Journey and the Internal Combat with Evil in the Shaker Experience." *Shaker Quarterly* 11 (Summer 1971):47–80.

Western Reserve Historical Society. *A Guide to Shaker Manuscripts in the Library of the Western Reserve Historical Society*. Cleveland, Ohio: Western Reserve Historical Society, 1974.

Whitworth, John McKelvie. *God's Blueprints: A Sociological Study of Three Utopian Sects*. London: Routledge and Kegan Paul, 1975.

Williams, Richard E. *Called and Chosen: The Story of Mother Rebecca Jackson and the Philadelphia Shakers.* Metuchen, N.J.: Scarecrow Press, 1981.

————. "Mother Rebecca Jackson. One of the Black Shakers in Philadelphia." *Shaker Messenger* 9 (Spring 1979):3–5.

Woolman, John. *The Journal of John Woolman.* Ed. Amelia Mott Gummere. New York: Macmillan, 1922.

Wright, Luella. *The Literary Life of the Early Friends, 1650–1725.* New York: Columbia Univ. Press, 1932.

INDEX

Adams, George, 109
autobiography, Shaker, 14-20, 44-66, 67-68, 74-75, 82-83, 103-6, 133-35, 210-16; Bathrick, Eunice, 52; Bishop, James, 48-51; Blanchard, Jane, 107-15; Brown, John, 134-40, 144-57; Colley, Annie S., 24; Green, Calvin, 189-209; Hollister, Alonzo, 85-89; Jackson, Rebecca, 159-88; Leonard, William, 104-6, 116-32; Lyon, John, 59-63; Lyon, Lydia, 40; Rankin, John, 53-54; Rowley, David, 54-55; Williams, Nathan, 41-43, 56-59; Wilson, James, 74-82, 89-99
Avery, Giles B., 83

Babbit, Abigail, 5
Barce, Thankful, 45-46, 193
Bates, Issachar, 7, 8, 10, 14, 39, 142n, 200
Bates, Paulina, 207
Bathrick, Eunice, 52, 55
bearing for the dead, 26-27
Bishop, James, 48-51
Bishop, Rufus, 68
Blanchard, Jane, 104-15, 124, 215; "A Sketch of Her Experience," 107-15; vision, 108
Blanchard, Jemima, 67-68
Brown, Alexander, 138-39, 144-46, 152
Brown, John M., 133-57, 215; "Autobiographical Letters," 141, 150-51, 152n; "A Biographic Sketch," 134-40, 144-57; "Notes by the Way," 142-44, 145, 149
Brown, Lucy, 156n
Brown, Stewart, 152n, 156n
Buckingham, David, 55

Bunyan, John, 17-18, 52n, 116-17, 119-21, 124, 126; *Grace Abounding*, 52n, 116, 120-21; *Pilgrim's Progress*, 116-17, 119, 124, 126, 128, 189n
Bushnell, Richard: 81, 199

Calver, Amelia, 133, 141
Cartwright, Peter, 201
Chauncy, Elizabeth, 27
Chauncy, Israel, 26
circumcision as metaphor, 39-40
Clark, Zeruah, 25
Colley, Annie S., 24
community, Shaker, 10-11, 31, 38; depiction in narrative, 30-34, 40-43, 64-65, 79, 119, 129-131, 172, 206-7
confession, 4, 11, 39, 81, 128, 140, 177
conversion, descriptions of, 45-46, 52-53, 69, 71-80, 94-95, 140, 159-66, 177-85; influence on autobiography, 83, 212
Cooley, Ebenezer, 27
Cox, Joseph, 167
Crossman, Abigail, 149
Crossman, Daniel, 148, 149

dance as metaphor, 71-74, 79
dispensation theology, 197-98
Doolittle, Mary Antoinette, 104
Dunlavy, John, 84

Eades, Harvey L., 137, 212
Enfield, N.H., 110, 112-13
Era of Manifestations, 17-18, 28n, 111; spiritual gifts during, 69, 73, 207; testimonies during, 68-69; visions during, 174n
Evans, Frederick, 39, 140, 147

230